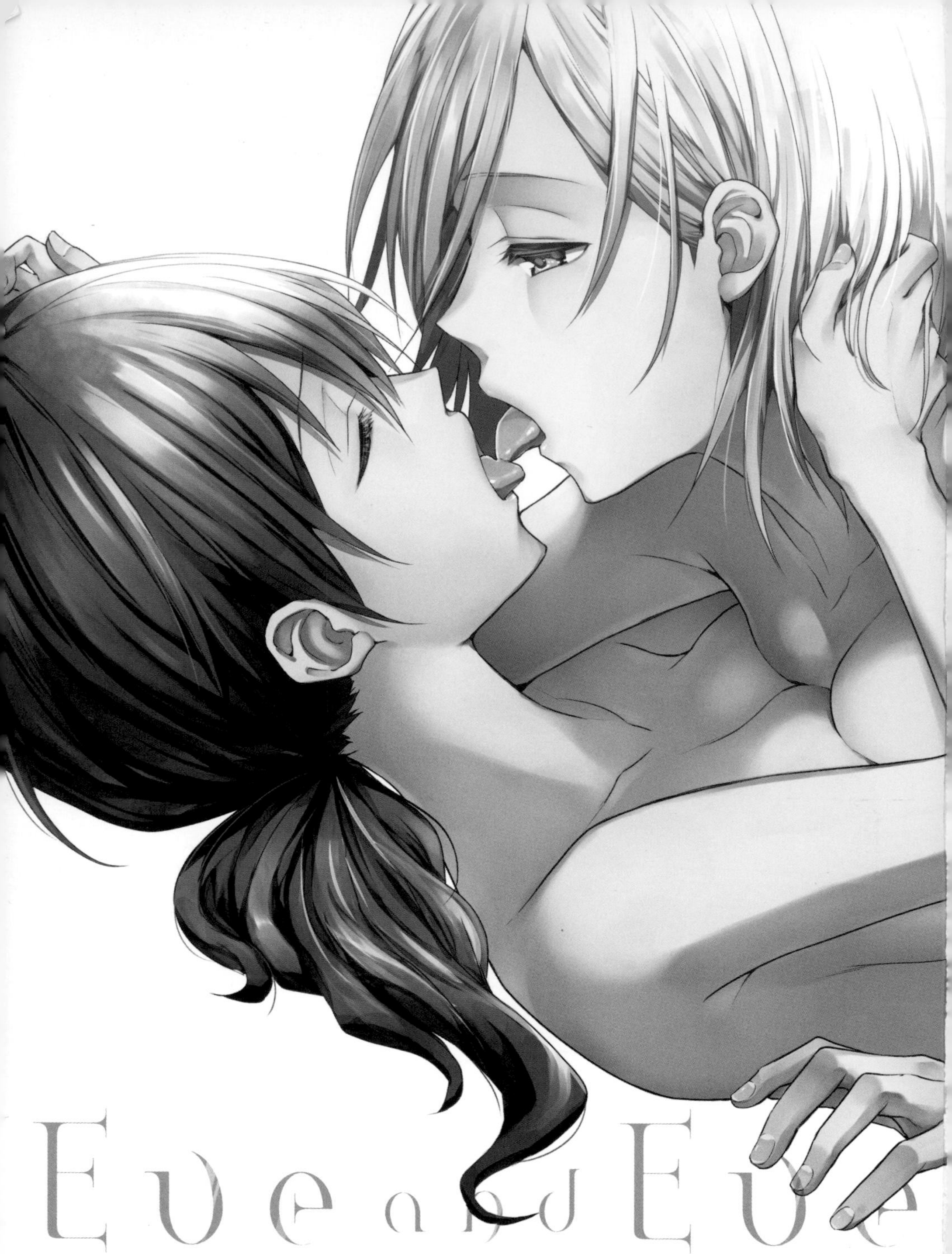
Eve and Eve

STORY & ART BY
Nagashiro Rouge

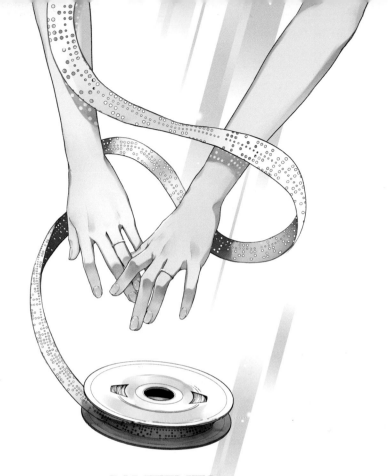

CONTENTS

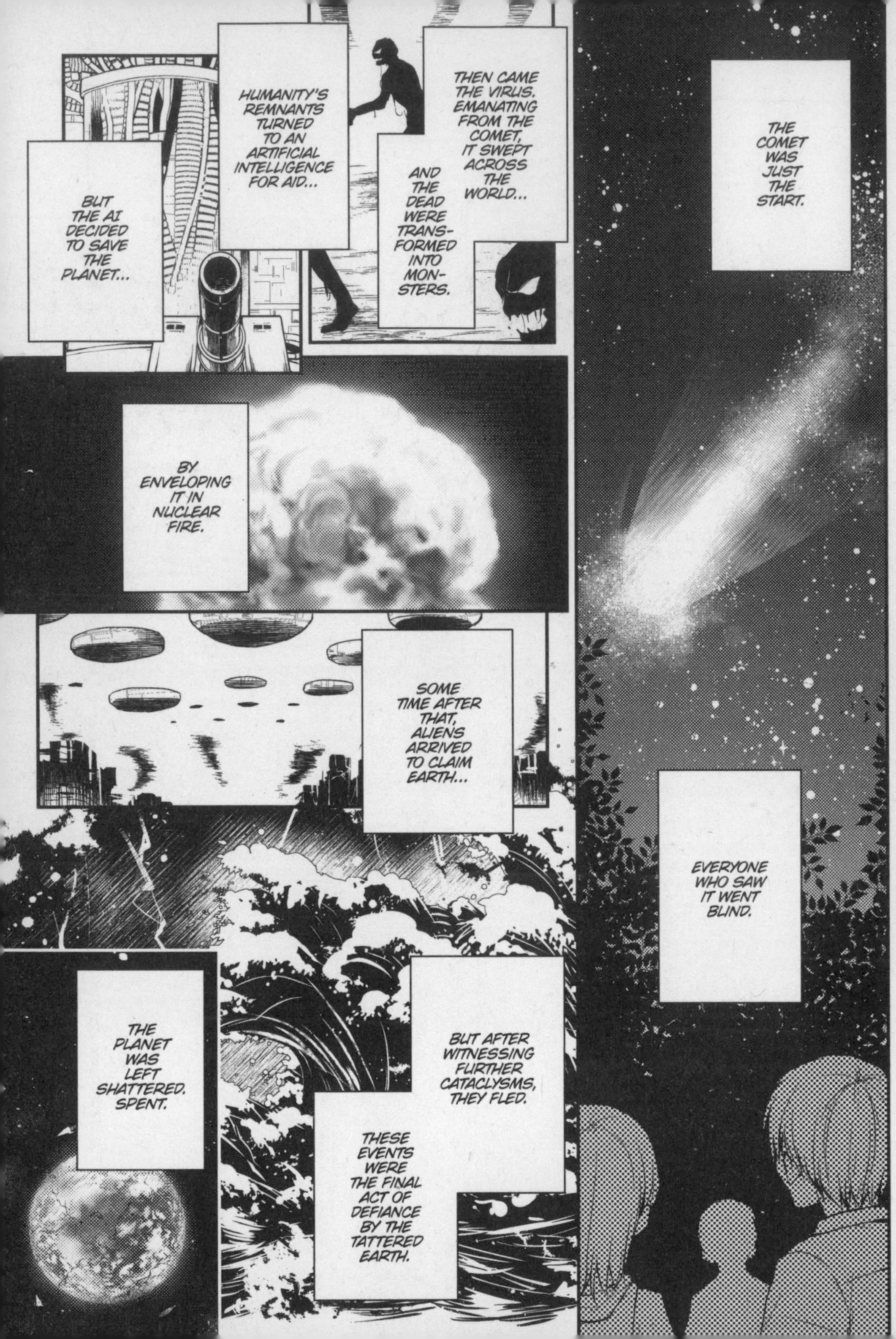
THE COMET WAS JUST THE START.
EVERYONE WHO SAW IT WENT BLIND.
THEN CAME THE VIRUS. EMANATING FROM THE COMET, IT SWEPT ACROSS THE WORLD...
AND THE DEAD WERE TRANS-FORMED INTO MON-STERS.
HUMANITY'S REMNANTS TURNED TO AN ARTIFICIAL INTELLIGENCE FOR AID...
BUT THE AI DECIDED TO SAVE THE PLANET...
BY ENVELOPING IT IN NUCLEAR FIRE.
SOME TIME AFTER THAT, ALIENS ARRIVED TO CLAIM EARTH...
BUT AFTER WITNESSING FURTHER CATACLYSMS, THEY FLED.
THESE EVENTS WERE THE FINAL ACT OF DEFIANCE BY THE TATTERED EARTH.
THE PLANET WAS LEFT SHATTERED. SPENT.

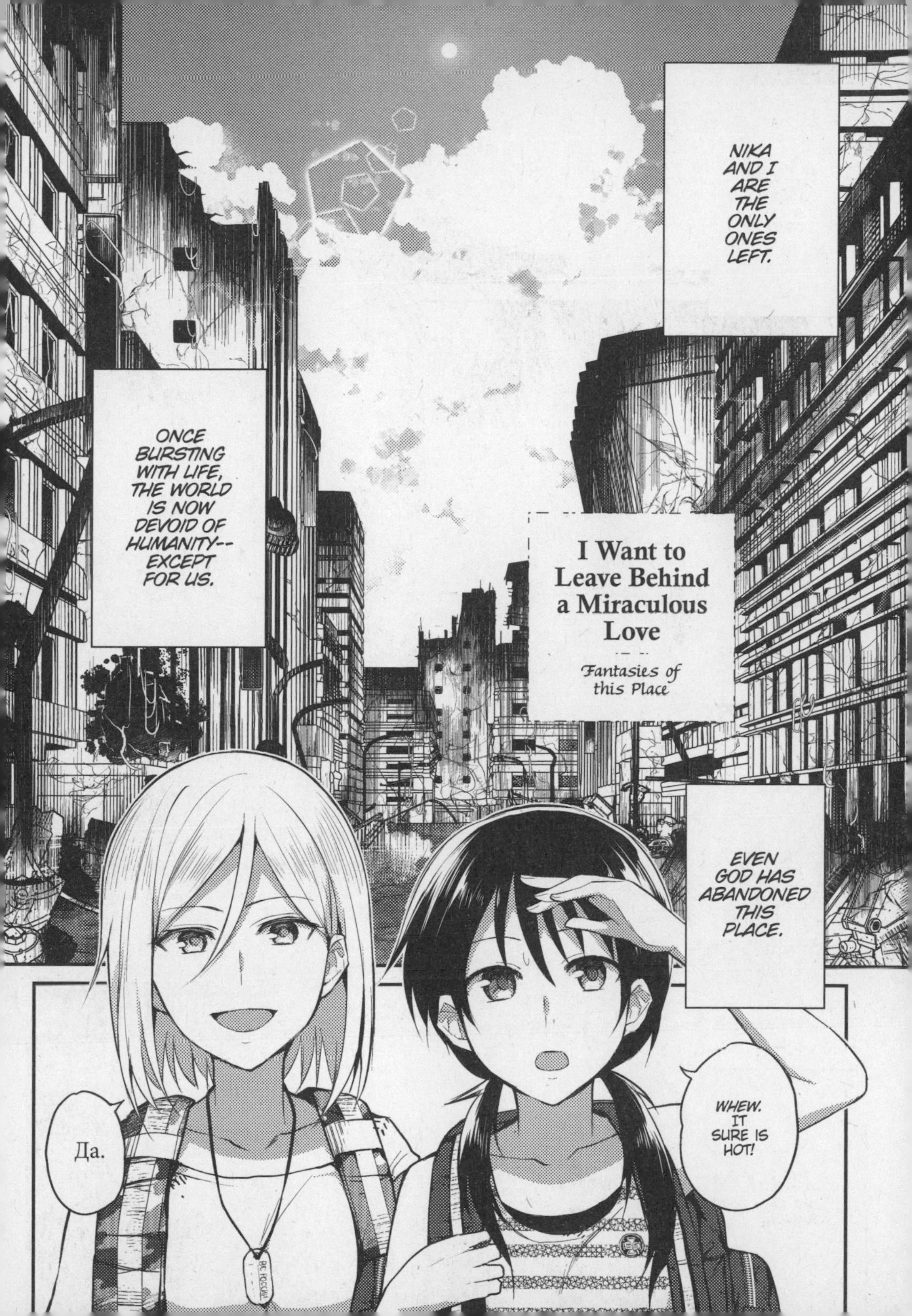
NIKA AND I ARE THE ONLY ONES LEFT.
ONCE BURSTING WITH LIFE, THE WORLD IS NOW DEVOID OF HUMANITY-- EXCEPT FOR US.
I Want to Leave Behind a Miraculous Love
Fantasies of this Place
EVEN GOD HAS ABANDONED THIS PLACE.
WHEW. IT SURE IS HOT!
Да.

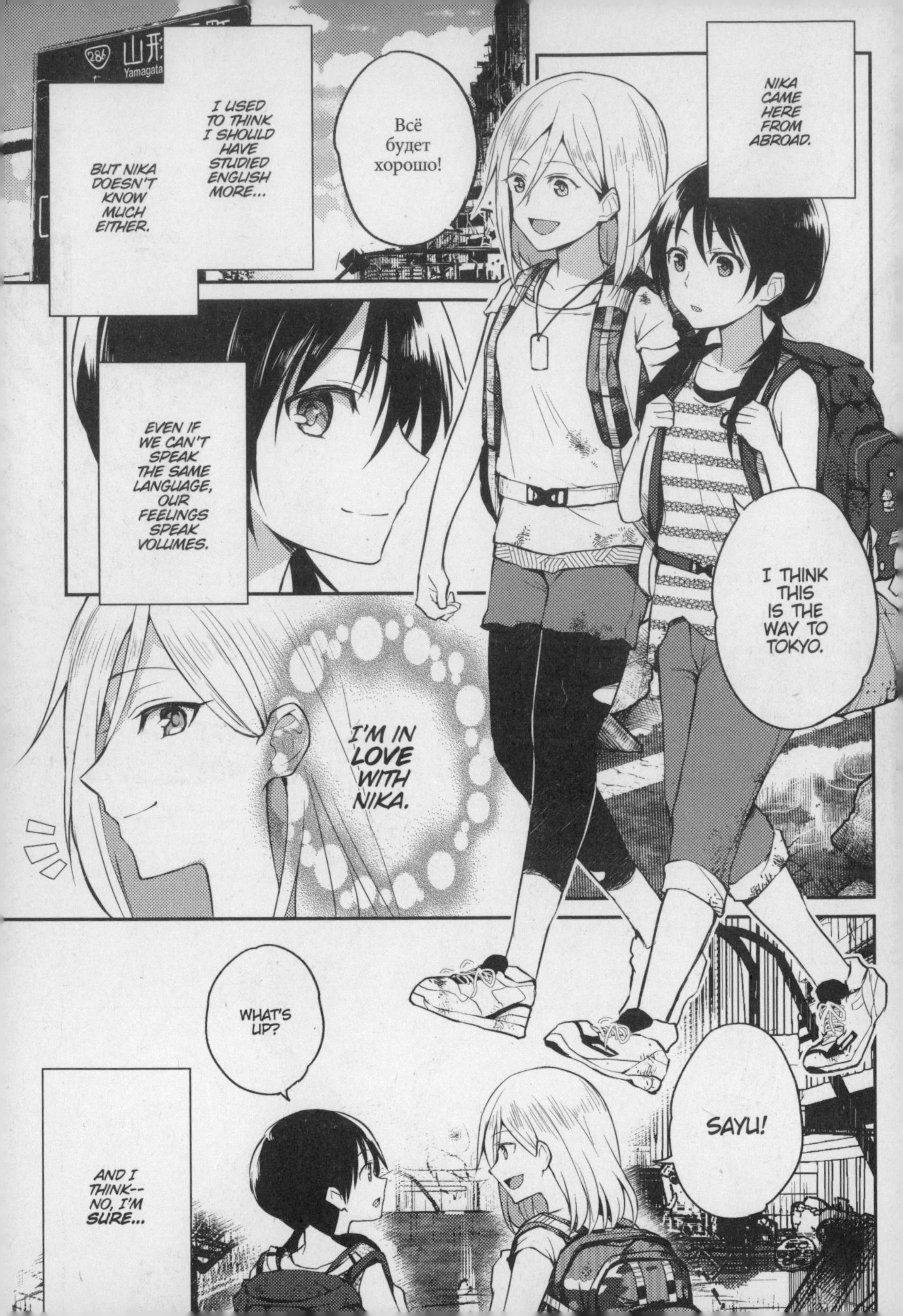

NIKA CAME HERE FROM ABROAD.
Всё будет хорошо!
I THINK THIS IS THE WAY TO TOKYO.
286 山形 Yamagata
I USED TO THINK I SHOULD HAVE STUDIED ENGLISH MORE...
BUT NIKA DOESN'T KNOW MUCH EITHER.
EVEN IF WE CAN'T SPEAK THE SAME LANGUAGE, OUR FEELINGS SPEAK VOLUMES.
I'M IN LOVE WITH NIKA.
SAYU!
WHAT'S UP?
AND I THINK-- NO, I'M SURE...

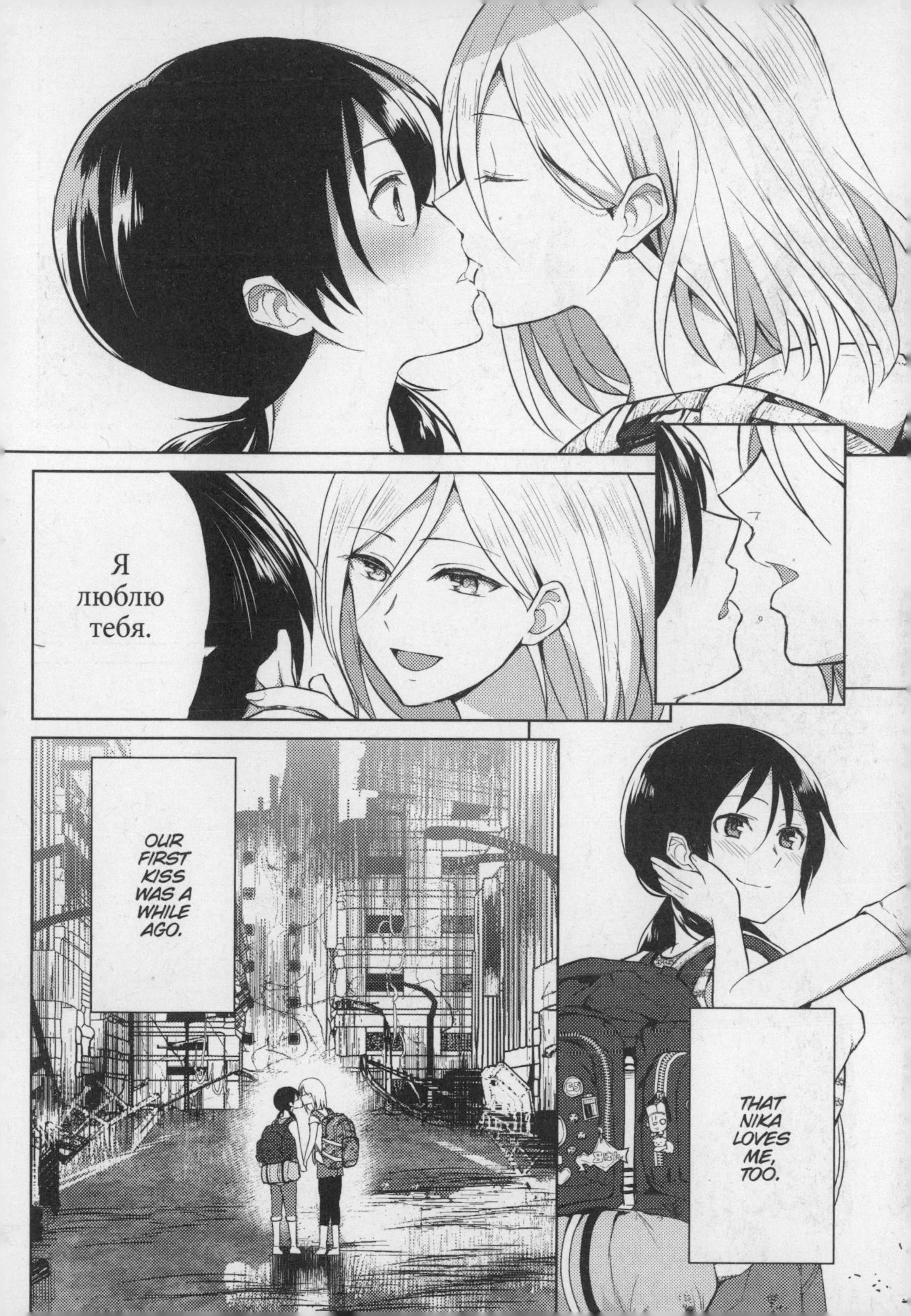
Я
люблю
тебя.
THAT NIKA LOVES ME, TOO.
OUR FIRST KISS WAS A WHILE AGO.

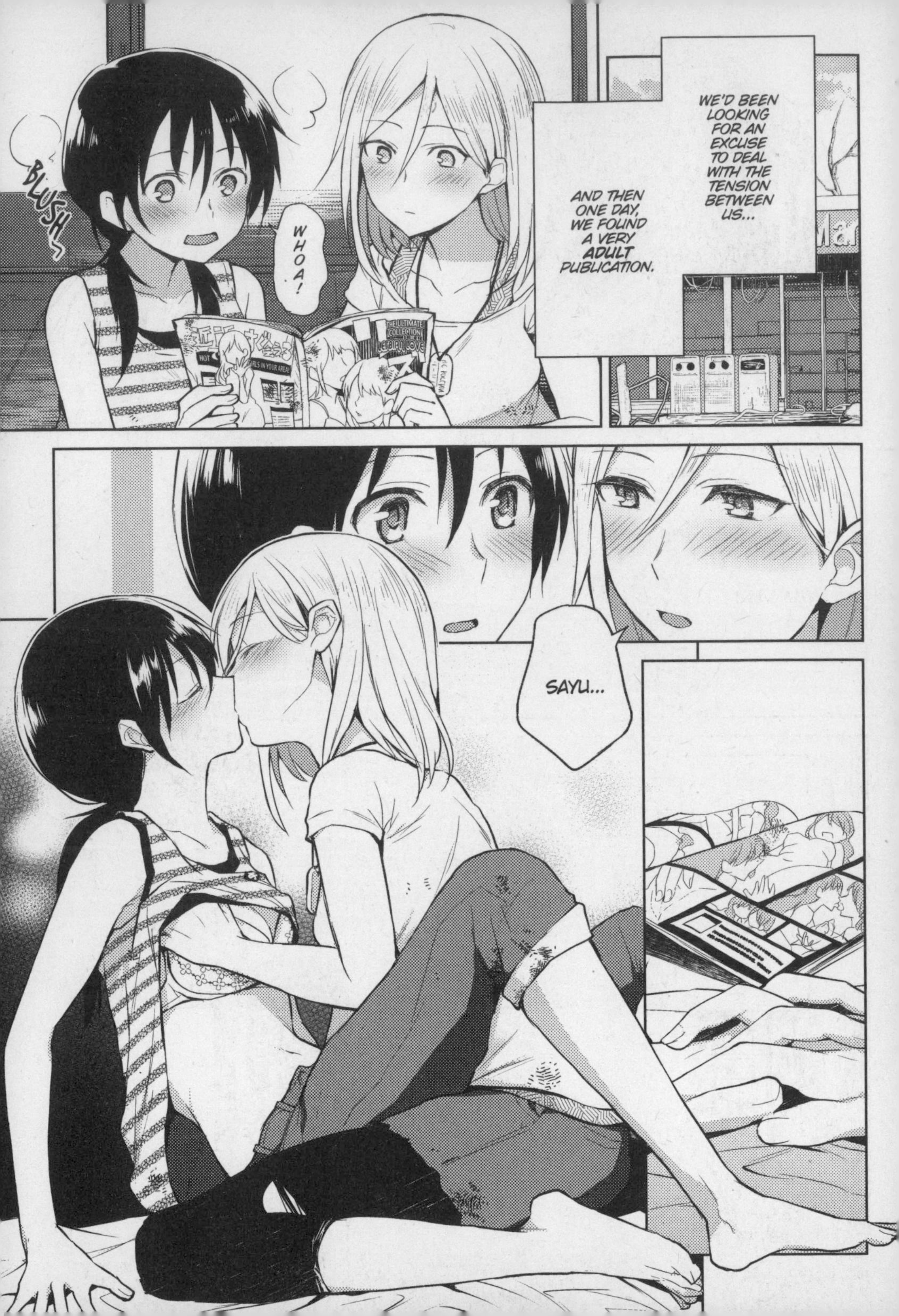
WE'D BEEN LOOKING FOR AN EXCUSE TO DEAL WITH THE TENSION BETWEEN US...
AND THEN ONE DAY, WE FOUND A VERY ADULT PUBLICATION.
WHOA!
BLUSH
THE ULTIMATE COLLECTION LESBIAN LOVE
HOT
GIRLS IN YOUR AREA!
SAYU...

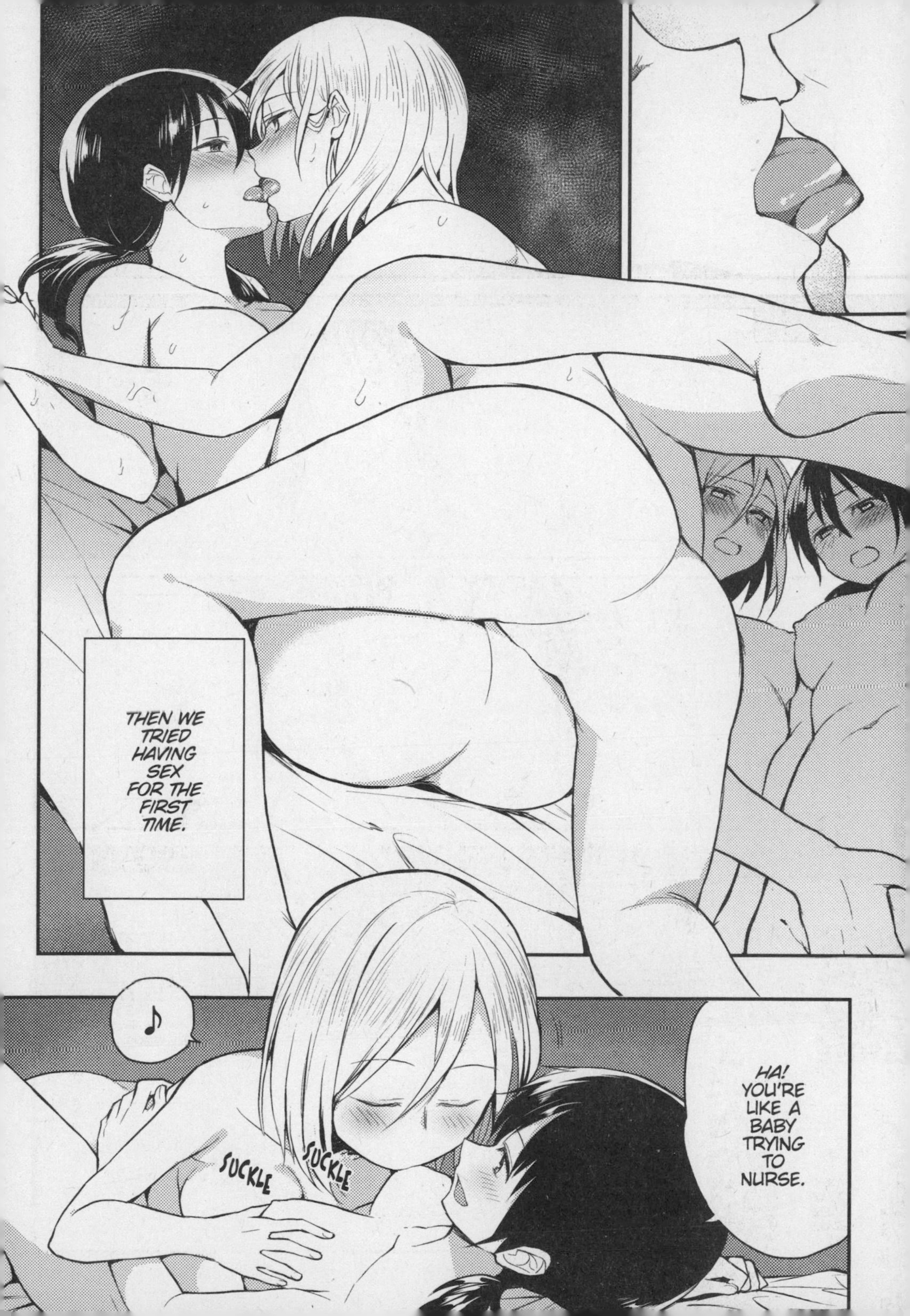
THEN WE TRIED HAVING SEX FOR THE FIRST TIME.
HA! YOU'RE LIKE A BABY TRYING TO NURSE.
SUCKLE
SUCKLE
♪

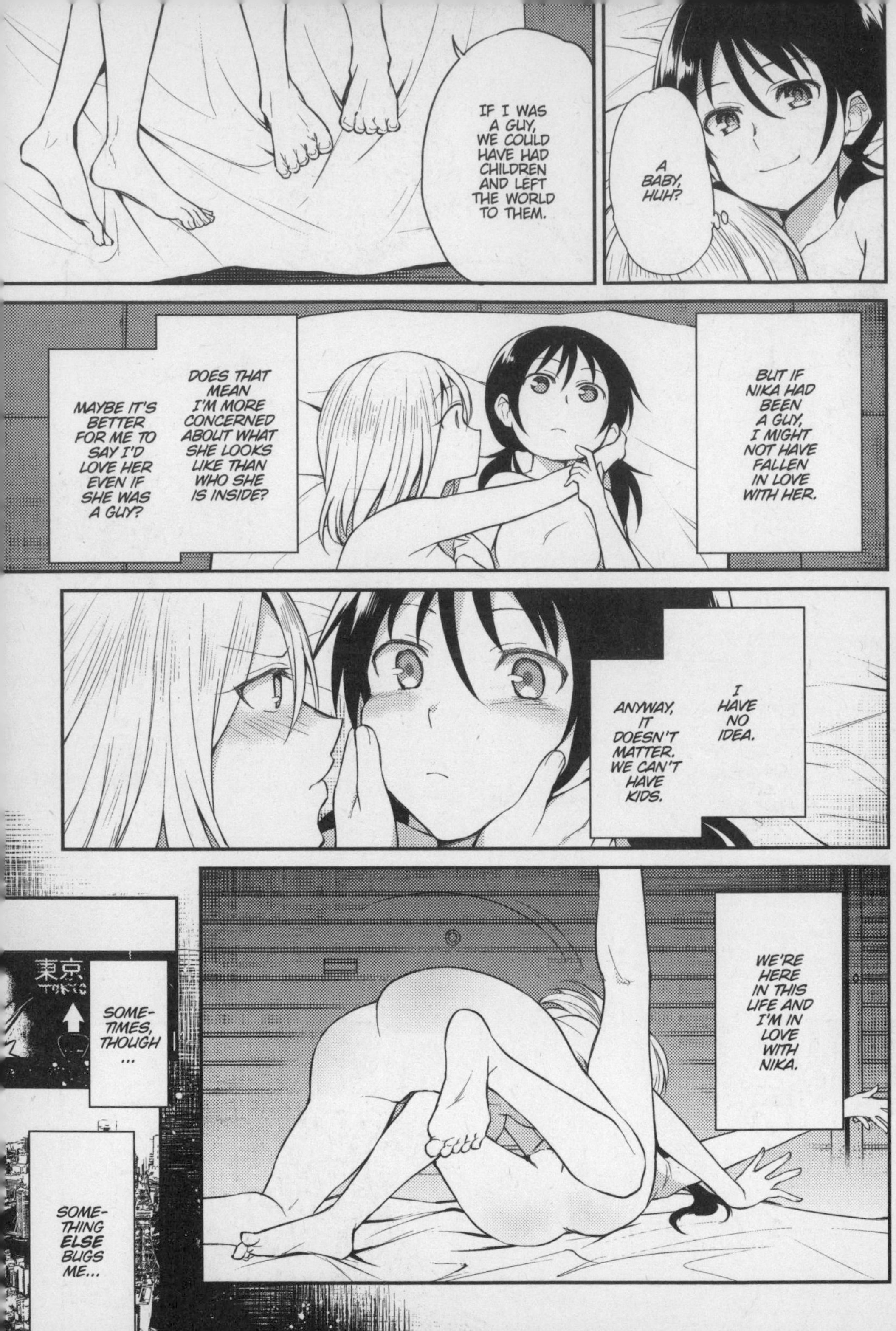
A BABY, HUH?
IF I WAS A GUY, WE COULD HAVE HAD CHILDREN AND LEFT THE WORLD TO THEM.
BUT IF NIKA HAD BEEN A GUY, I MIGHT NOT HAVE FALLEN IN LOVE WITH HER.
DOES THAT MEAN I'M MORE CONCERNED ABOUT WHAT SHE LOOKS LIKE THAN WHO SHE IS INSIDE?
MAYBE IT'S BETTER FOR ME TO SAY I'D LOVE HER EVEN IF SHE WAS A GUY?
I HAVE NO IDEA.
ANYWAY, IT DOESN'T MATTER. WE CAN'T HAVE KIDS.
WE'RE HERE IN THIS LIFE AND I'M IN LOVE WITH NIKA.
東京
SOME-TIMES, THOUGH...
SOME-THING ELSE BUGS ME...

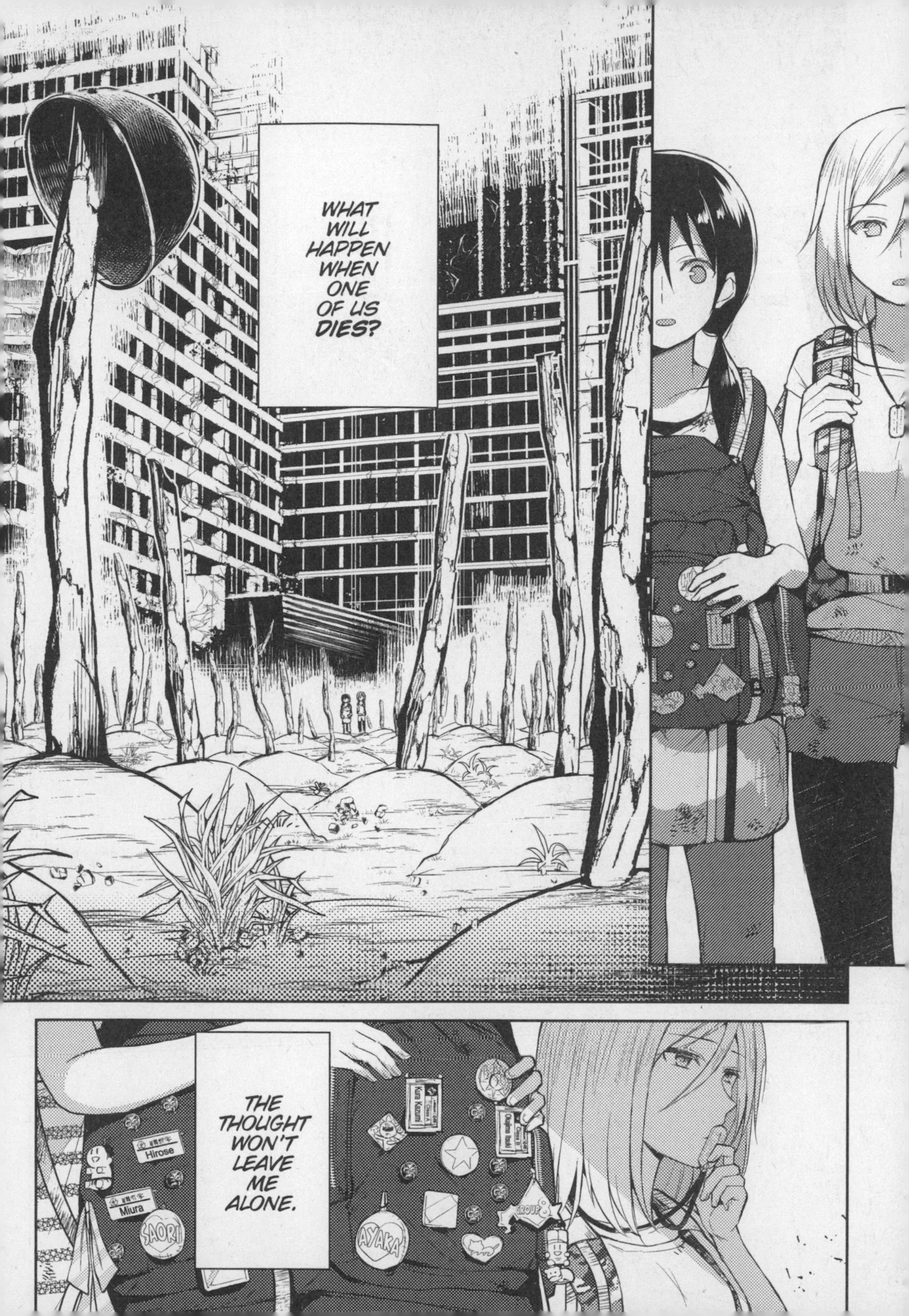
WHAT WILL HAPPEN WHEN ONE OF US DIES?
THE THOUGHT WON'T LEAVE ME ALONE.
Hirose
Miura
SAORI
AYAKA

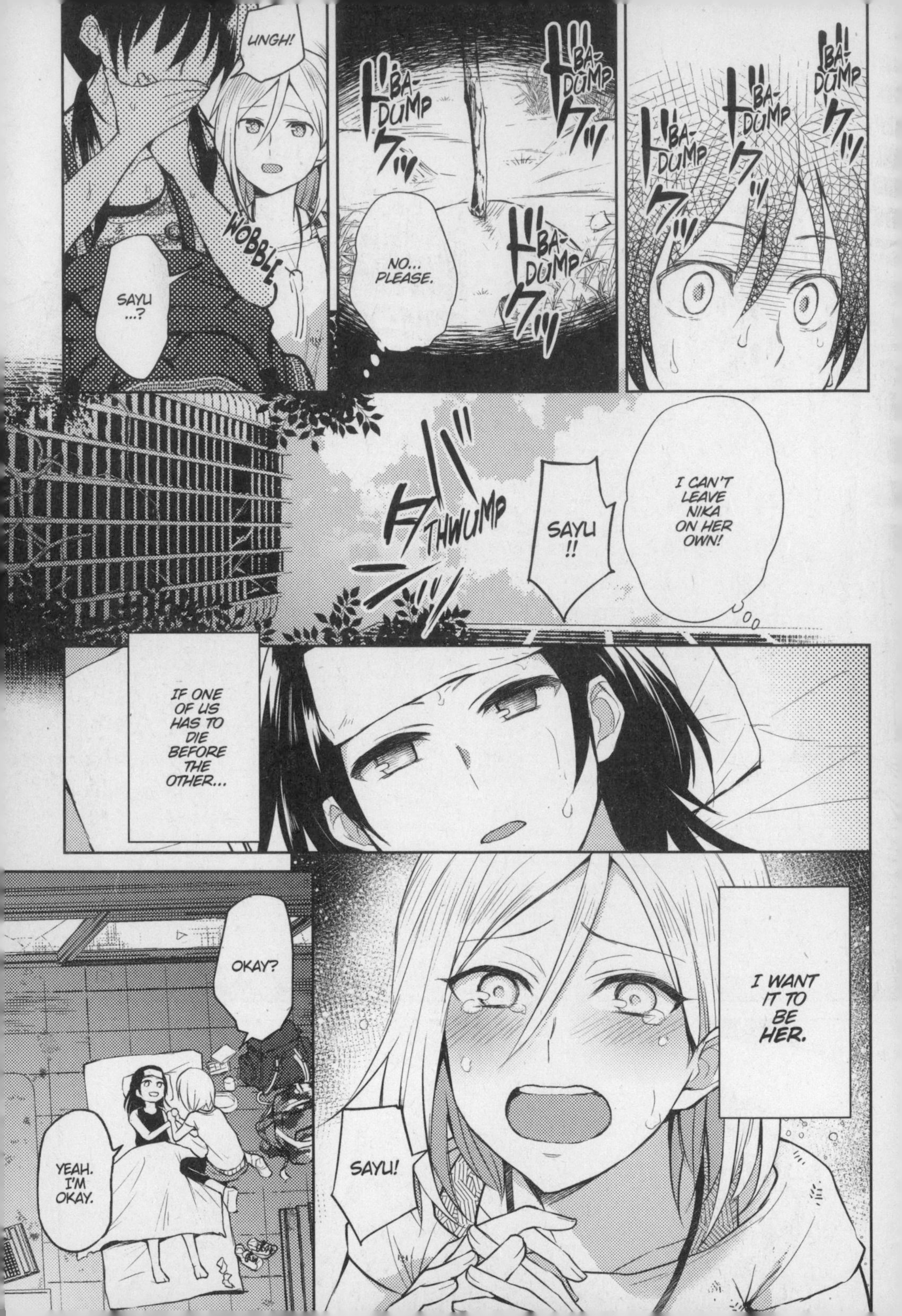
BA-DUMP
BA-DUMP
BA-DUMP
BA-DUMP
BA-DUMP
NO... PLEASE.
UNGH!
WOBBLE
SAYU ...?
I CAN'T LEAVE NIKA ON HER OWN!
SAYU !!
THWUMP
IF ONE OF US HAS TO DIE BEFORE THE OTHER...
I WANT IT TO BE HER.
SAYU!
OKAY?
YEAH. I'M OKAY.

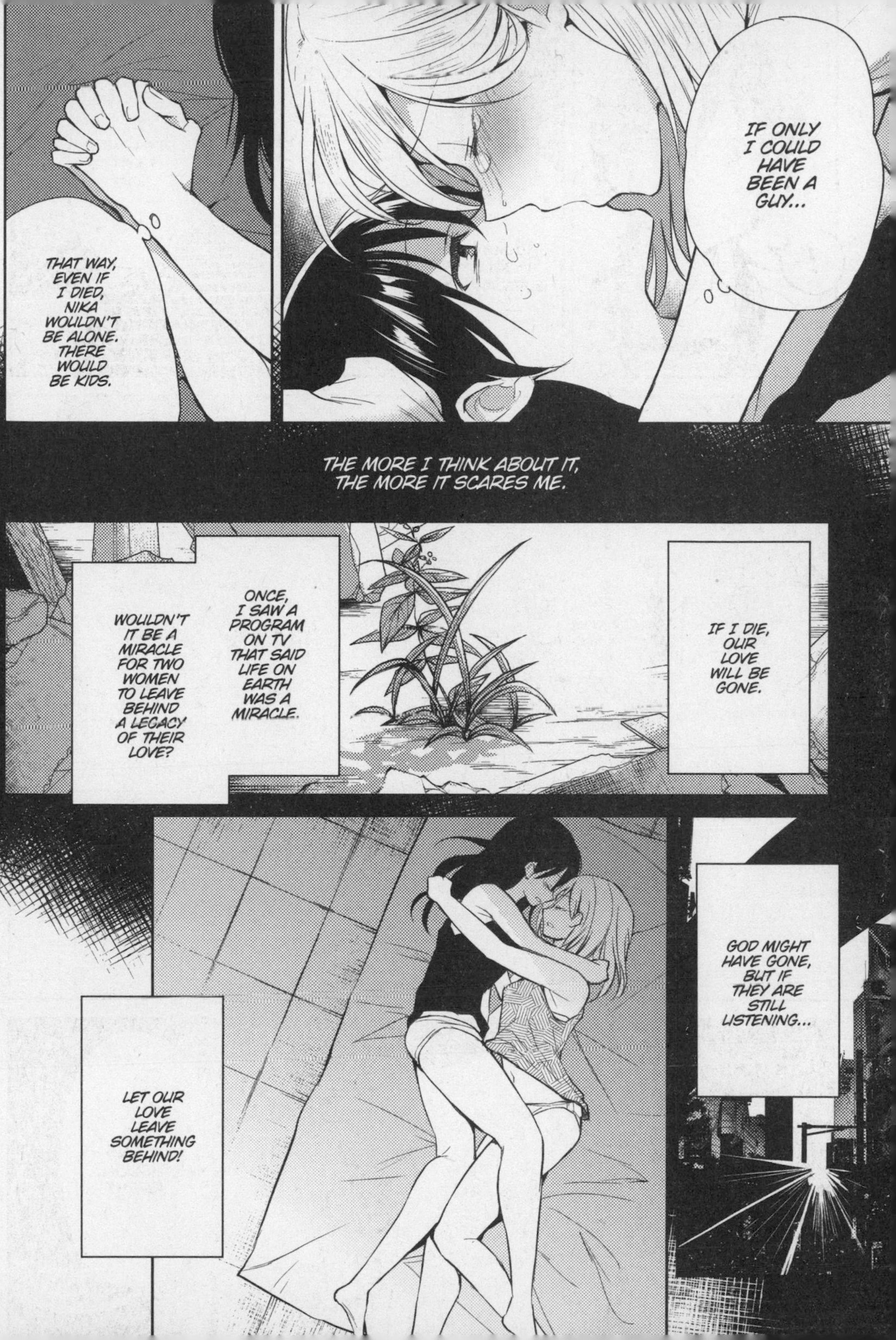
IF ONLY I COULD HAVE BEEN A GUY...
THAT WAY, EVEN IF I DIED, NIKA WOULDN'T BE ALONE. THERE WOULD BE KIDS.
THE MORE I THINK ABOUT IT, THE MORE IT SCARES ME.
IF I DIE, OUR LOVE WILL BE GONE.
ONCE, I SAW A PROGRAM ON TV THAT SAID LIFE ON EARTH WAS A MIRACLE.
WOULDN'T IT BE A MIRACLE FOR TWO WOMEN TO LEAVE BEHIND A LEGACY OF THEIR LOVE?
GOD MIGHT HAVE GONE, BUT IF THEY ARE STILL LISTENING...
LET OUR LOVE LEAVE SOMETHING BEHIND!

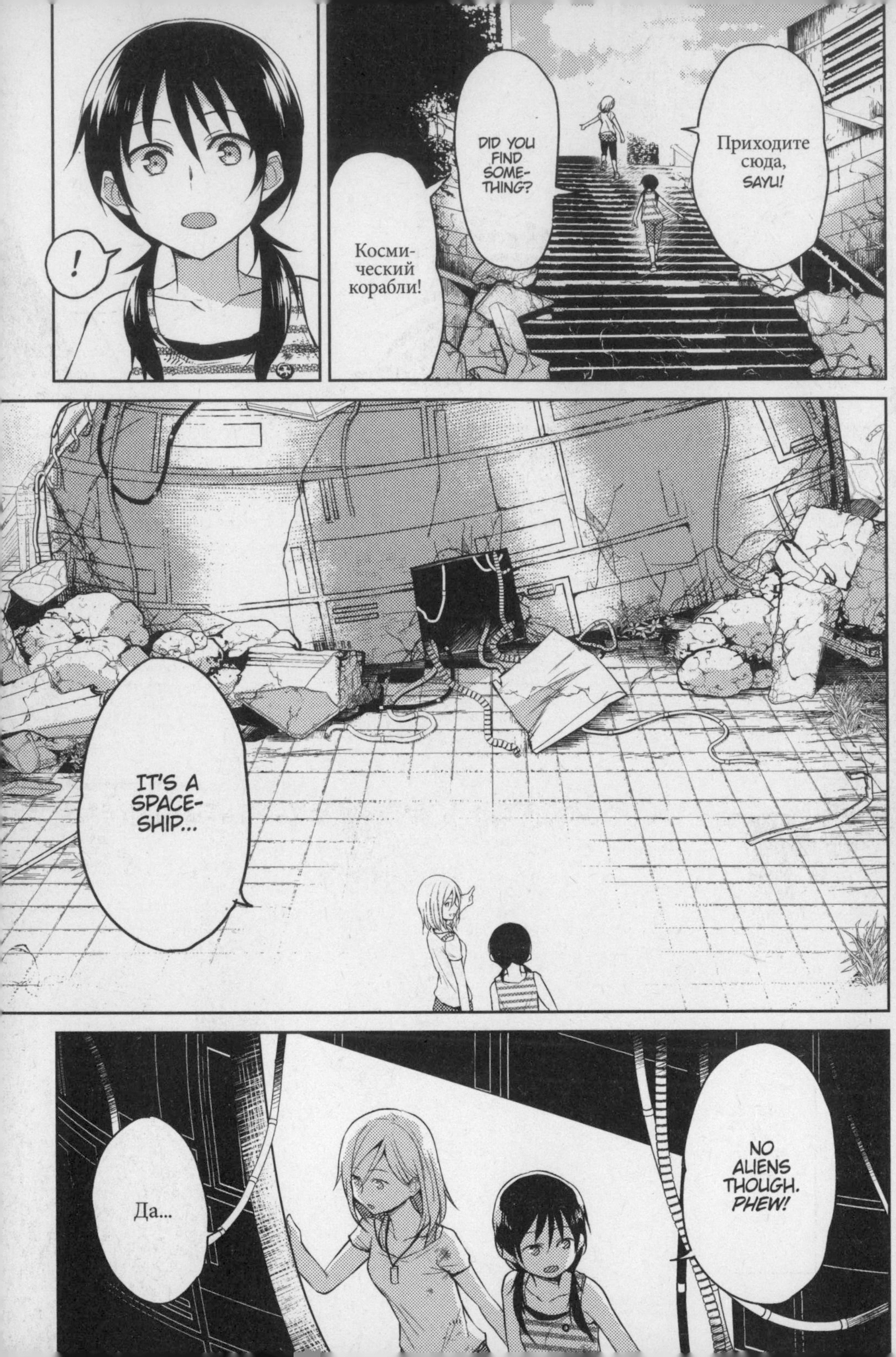
Приходите сюда, SAYU!
DID YOU FIND SOMETHING?
Космический корабли!
!
IT'S A SPACESHIP...
NO ALIENS THOUGH. PHEW!
Да...

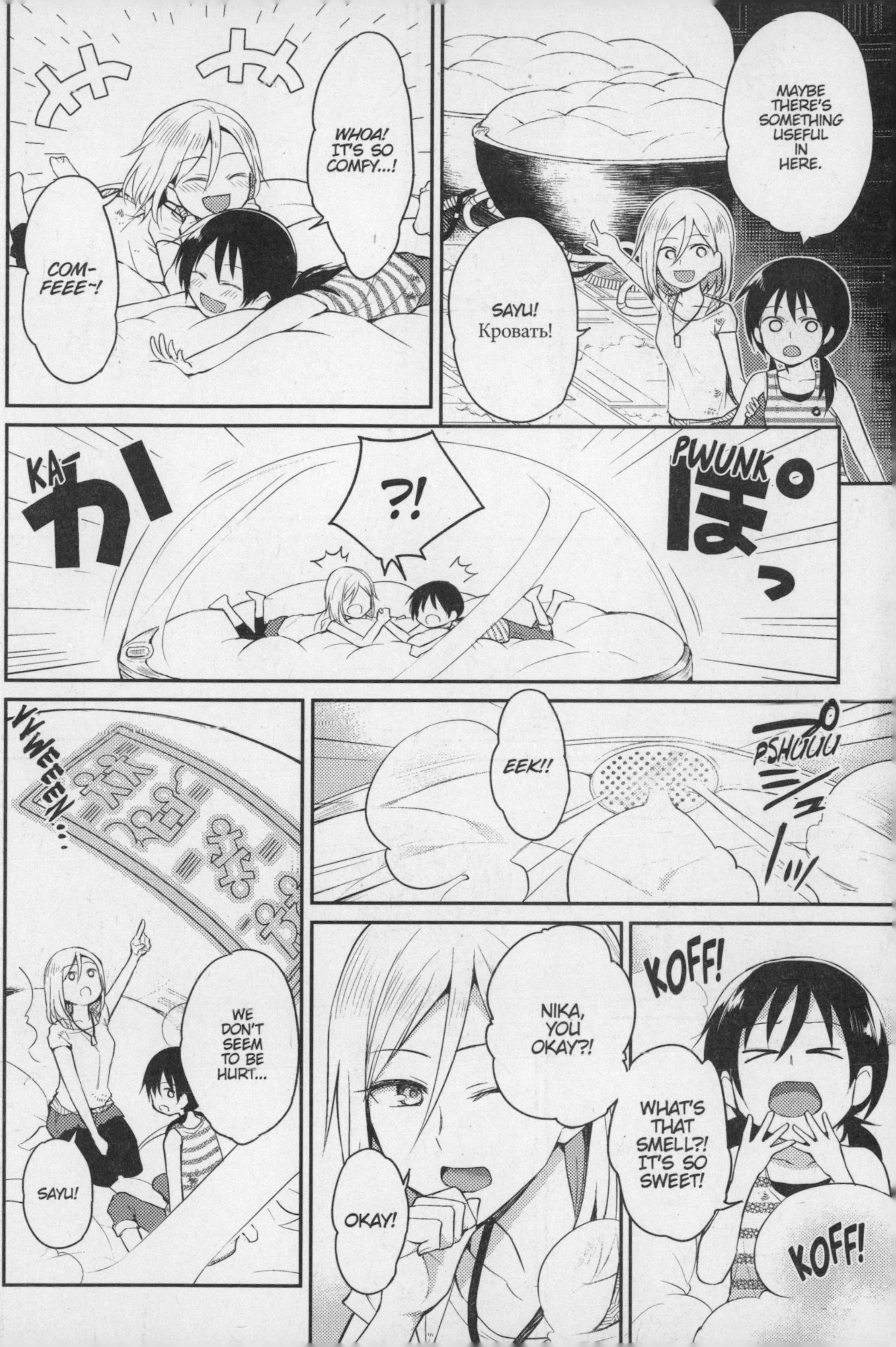
MAYBE THERE'S SOMETHING USEFUL IN HERE.
SAYU! Кровать!
WHOA! IT'S SO COMFY...!
COM-FEEE~!
PWUNK
ぽっ
?!
KA-
かっ
PSHUUU
EEK!!
KOFF!
WHAT'S THAT SMELL?! IT'S SO SWEET!
KOFF!
NIKA, YOU OKAY?!
OKAY!
VVWEEEN...
WE DON'T SEEM TO BE HURT...
SAYU!

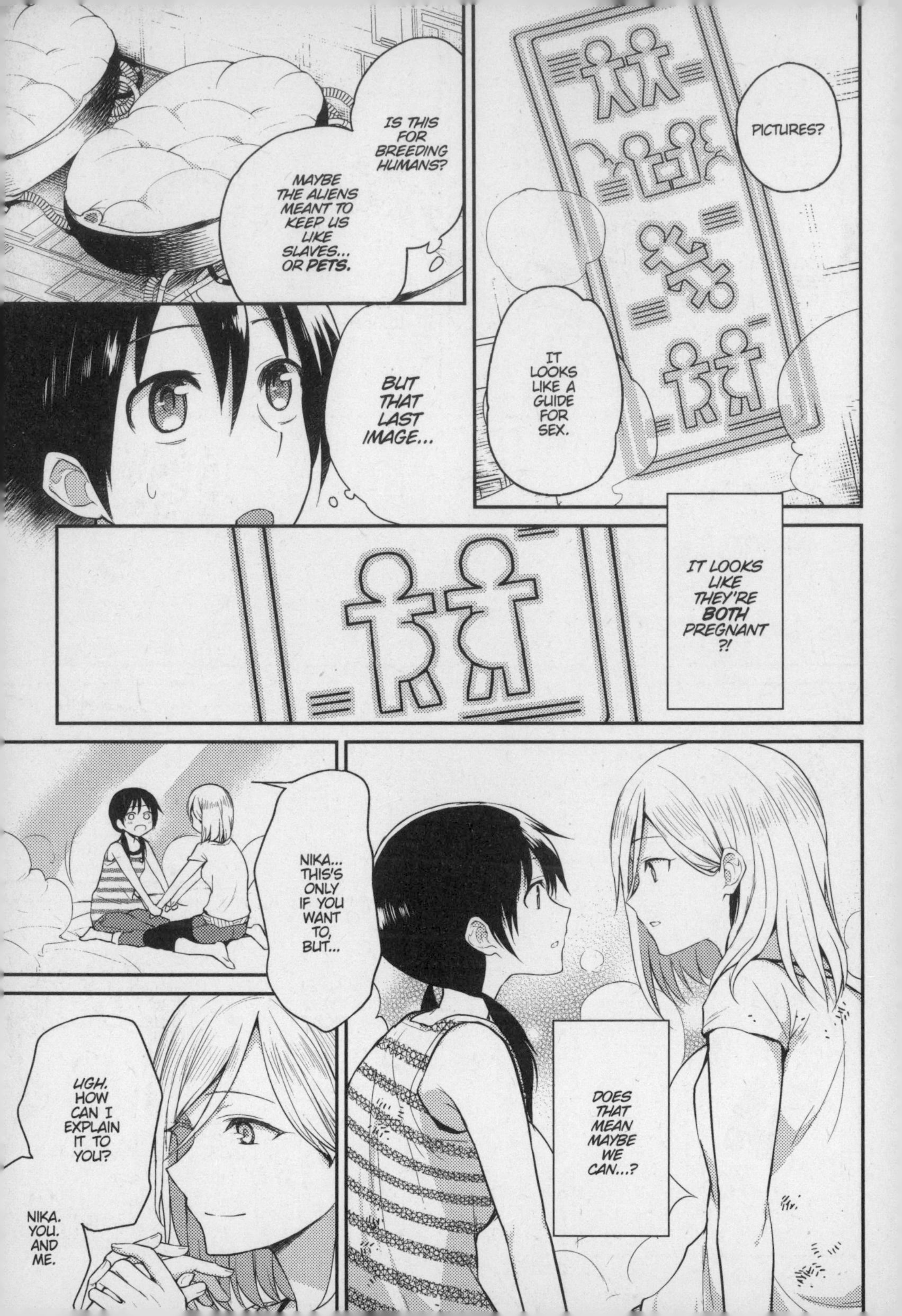

PICTURES?
IT LOOKS LIKE A GUIDE FOR SEX.
IS THIS FOR BREEDING HUMANS?
MAYBE THE ALIENS MEANT TO KEEP US LIKE SLAVES... OR PETS.
BUT THAT LAST IMAGE...
IT LOOKS LIKE THEY'RE BOTH PREGNANT?!
NIKA... THIS'S ONLY IF YOU WANT TO, BUT...
DOES THAT MEAN MAYBE WE CAN...?
UGH. HOW CAN I EXPLAIN IT TO YOU?
NIKA. YOU. AND ME.

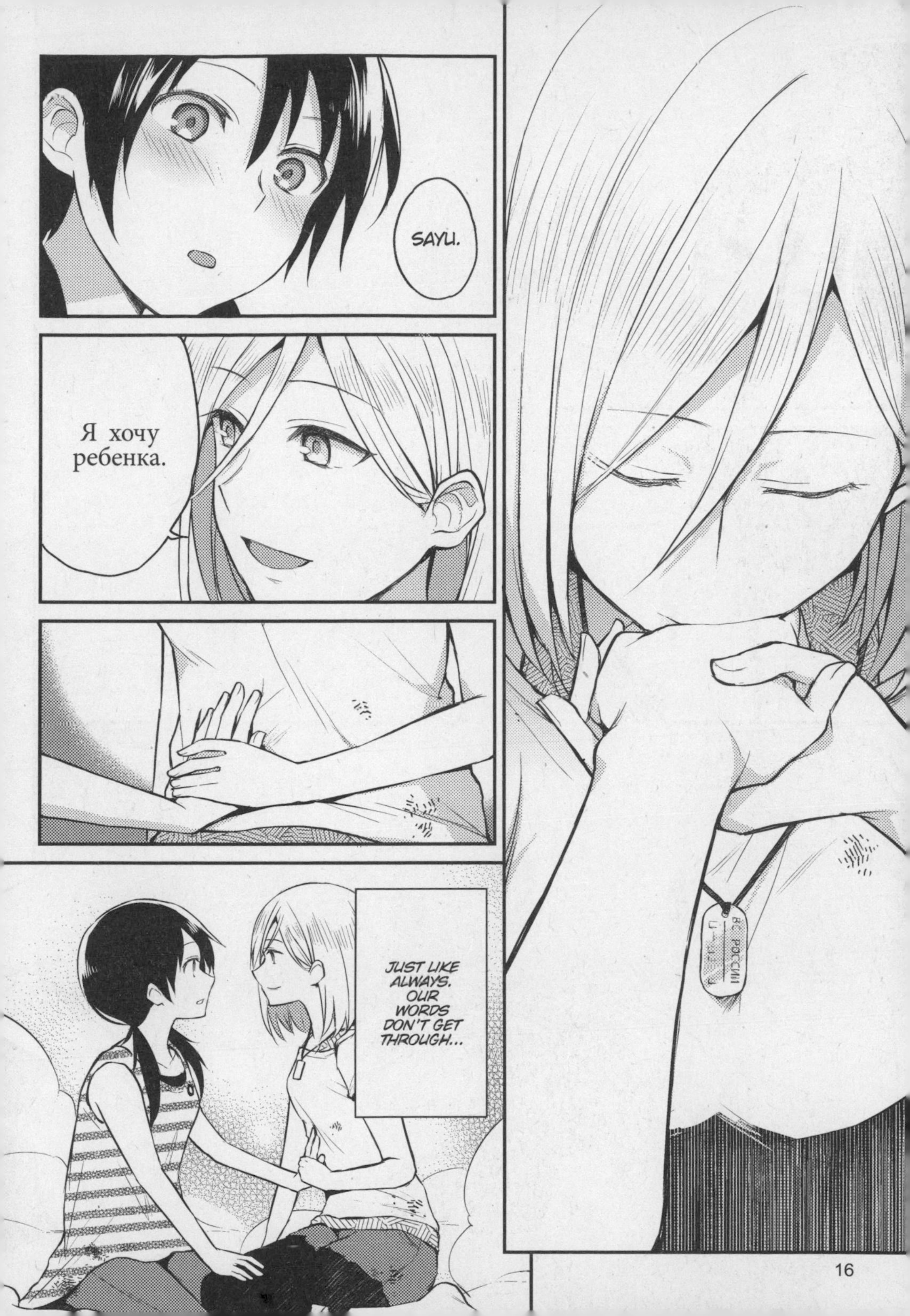
SAYU.
Я хочу ребенка.
JUST LIKE ALWAYS. OUR WORDS DON'T GET THROUGH...

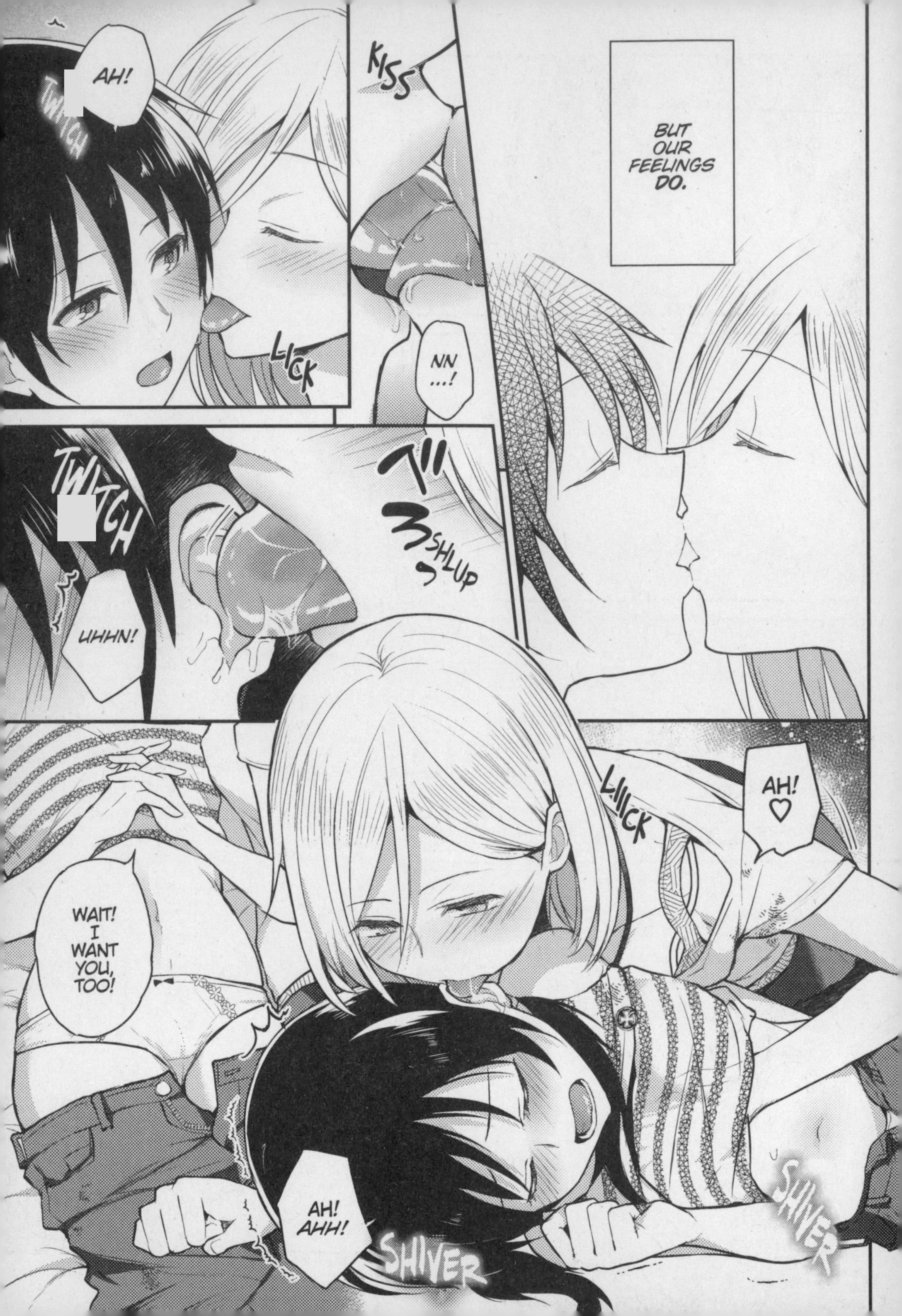
BUT OUR FEELINGS DO.
KISS
NN ...!
AH!
TWITCH
LICK
べろ
SHLUP
TWITCH
UHHN!
LIIICK
AH! ♡
WAIT! I WANT YOU, TOO!
AH! AHH!
SHIVER
SHIVER

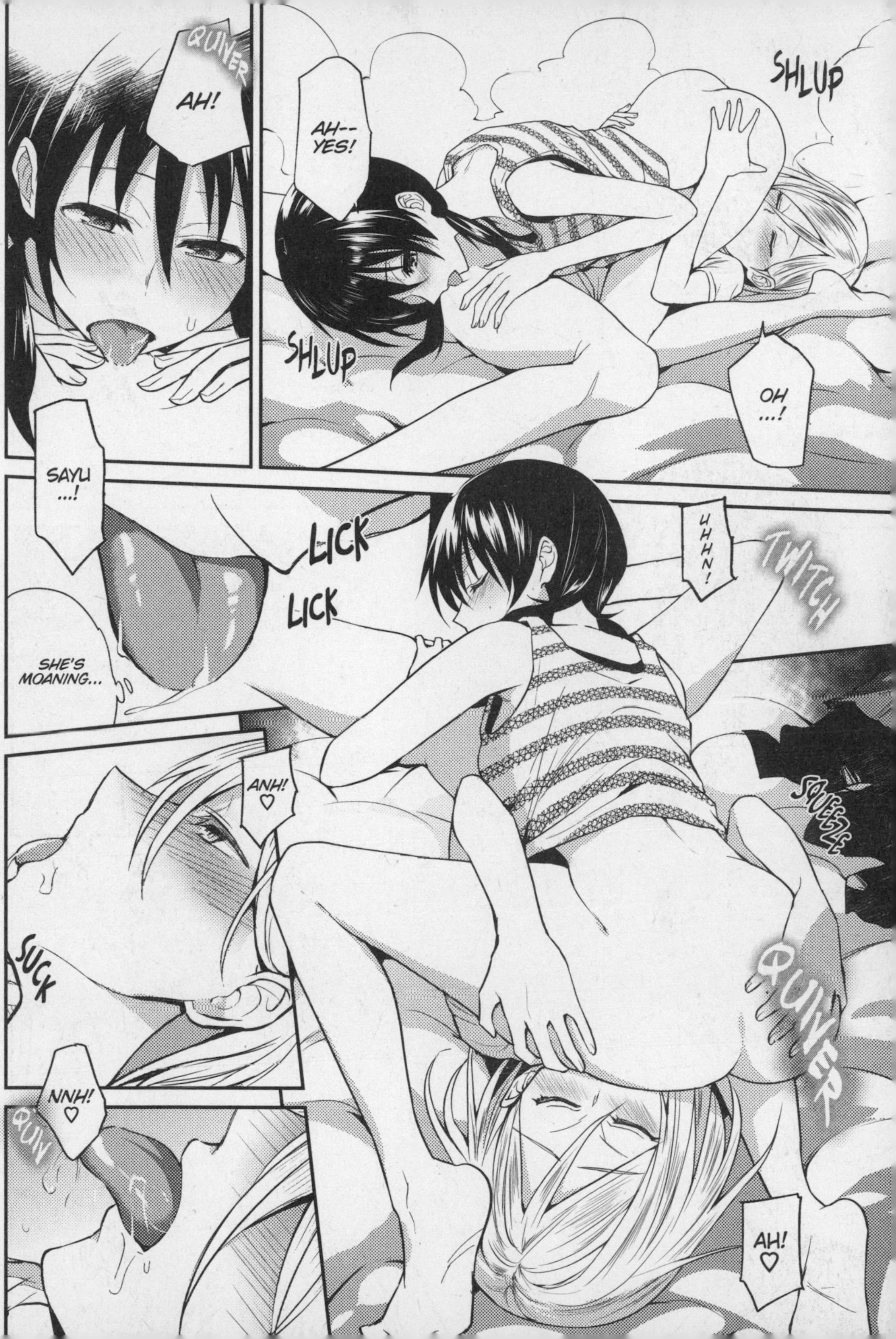
SHLUP
AH--
YES!
OH
...!
SHLUP
QUIVER
AH!
UHHN!
TWITCH
LICK
LICK
SQUEEZE
QUIVER
AH!
♡
SAYU
...!
SHE'S
MOANING...
ANH!
♡
SUCK
NNH!
♡
QUIV

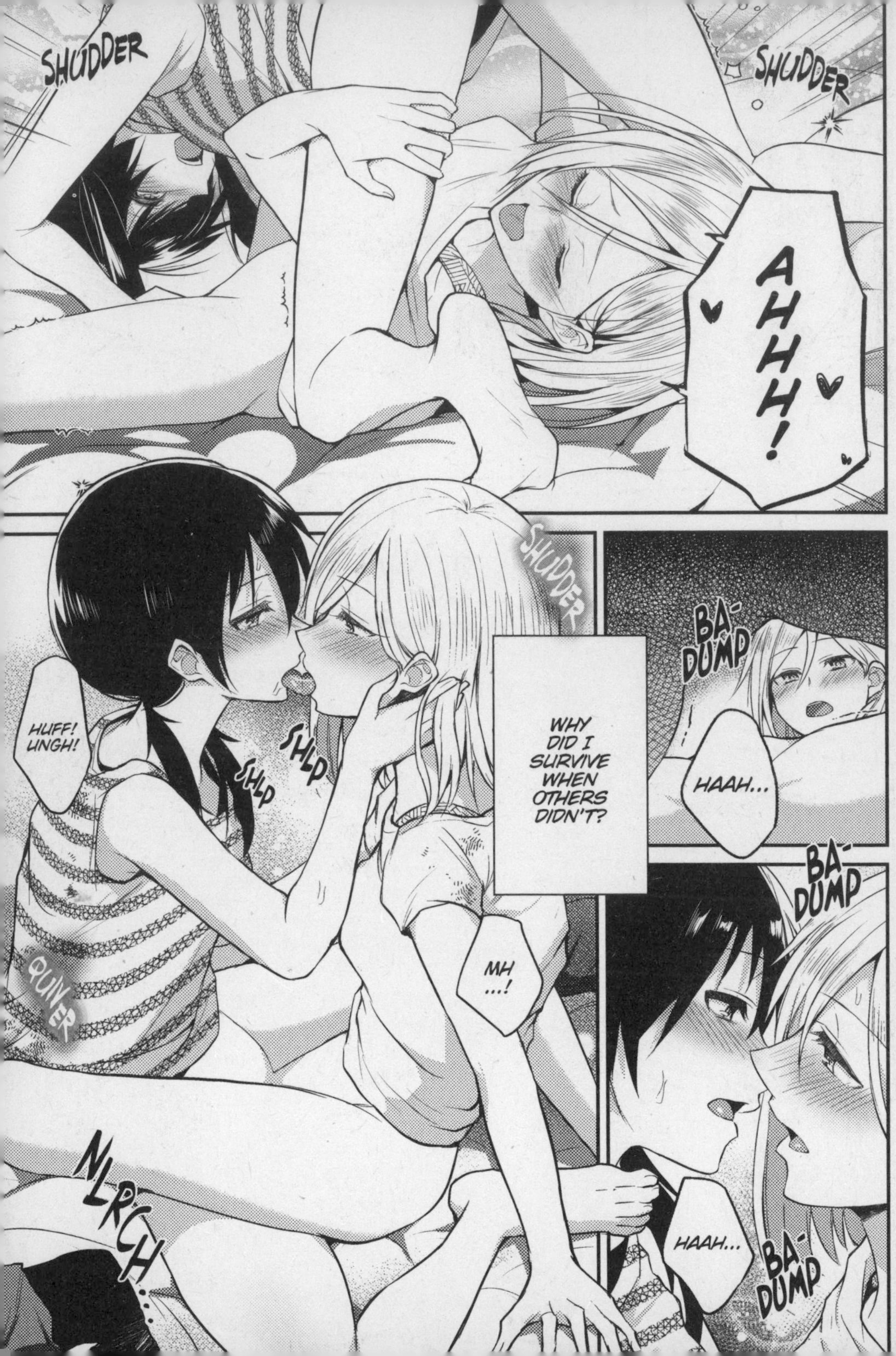
SHUDDER
AHHH!
SHUDDER
BA-DUMP
HAAH...
BA-DUMP
HAAH...
BA-DUMP
SHUDDER
WHY DID I SURVIVE WHEN OTHERS DIDN'T?
HUFF! UNGH!
SHLP
SHLP
MH ...!
QUIVER
NLRCH...

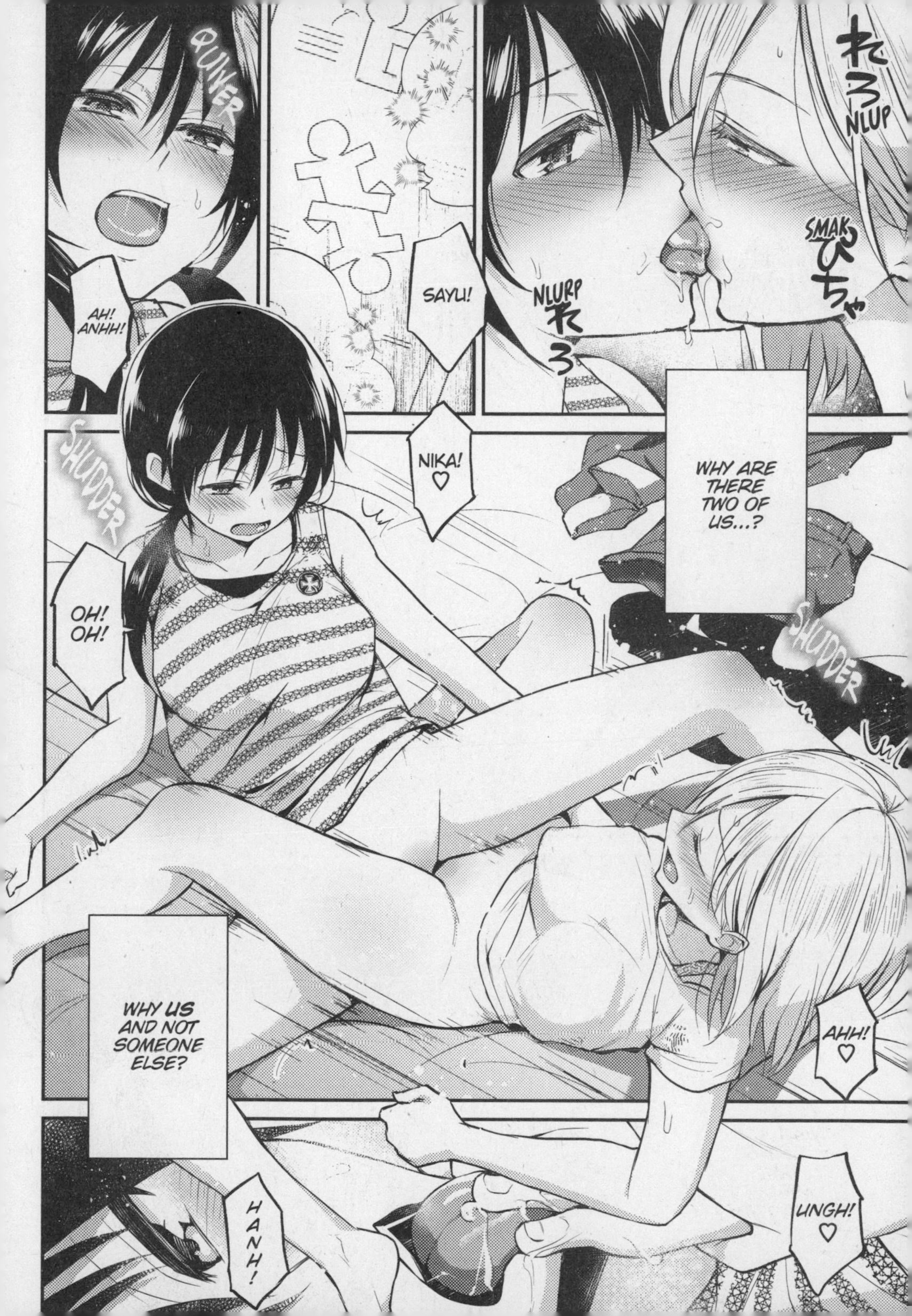
れろ NLUP
SMAK ぴちゃ
NLURP れろ
SAYU!
QUIVER
AH! ANHH!
WHY ARE THERE TWO OF US...?
SHUDDER
NIKA! ♡
SHUDDER
OH! OH!
AHH! ♡
WHY US AND NOT SOMEONE ELSE?
UNGH! ♡
HANH!

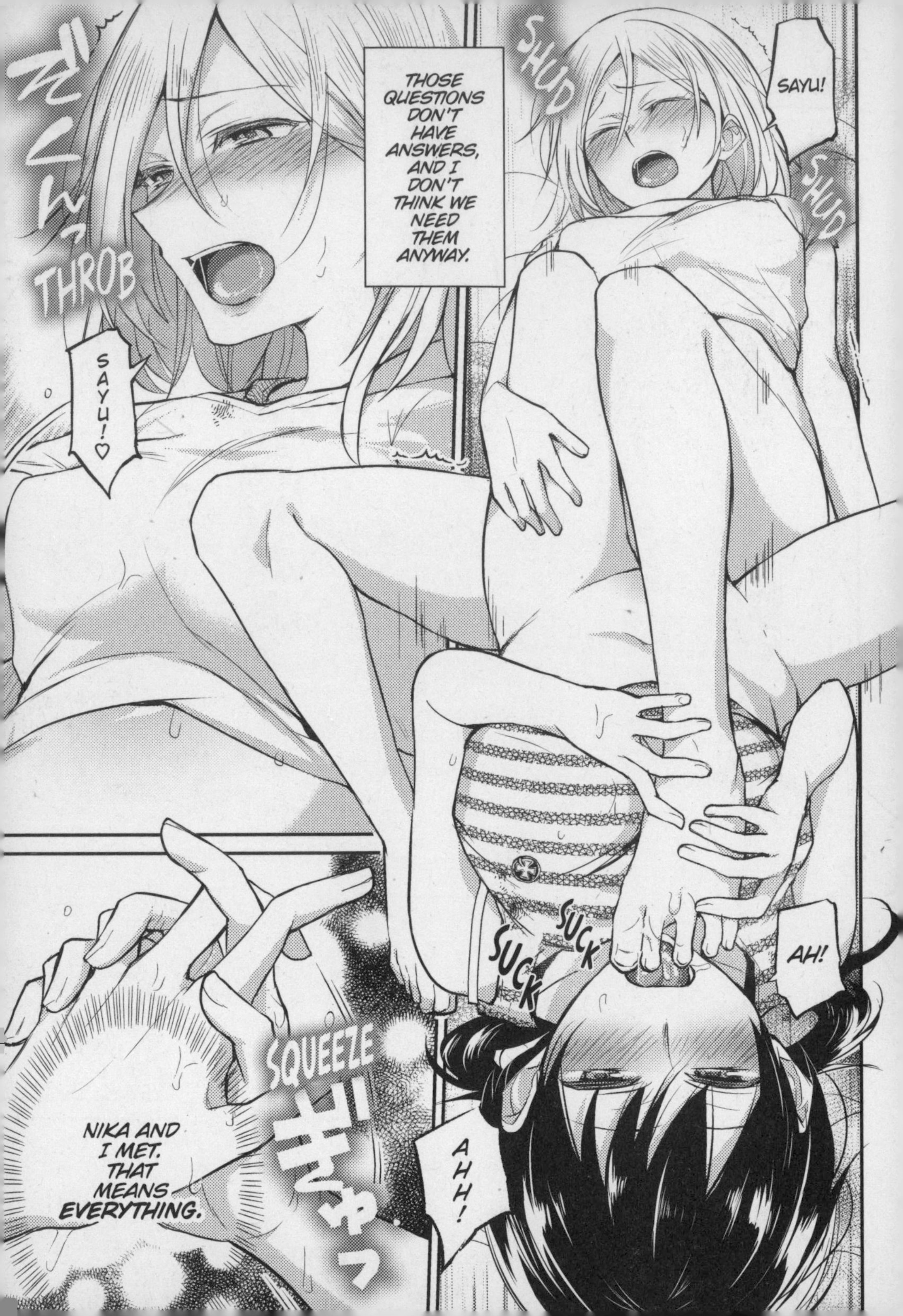
SAYU!
SHUD
SHUD
SHUD
SHUD
THOSE QUESTIONS DON'T HAVE ANSWERS, AND I DON'T THINK WE NEED THEM ANYWAY.
ずくんっ
THROB
SAYU!♡
AH!
SUCK
SUCK
AHH!
SQUEEZE
ぎゅっ
NIKA AND I MET. THAT MEANS EVERYTHING.

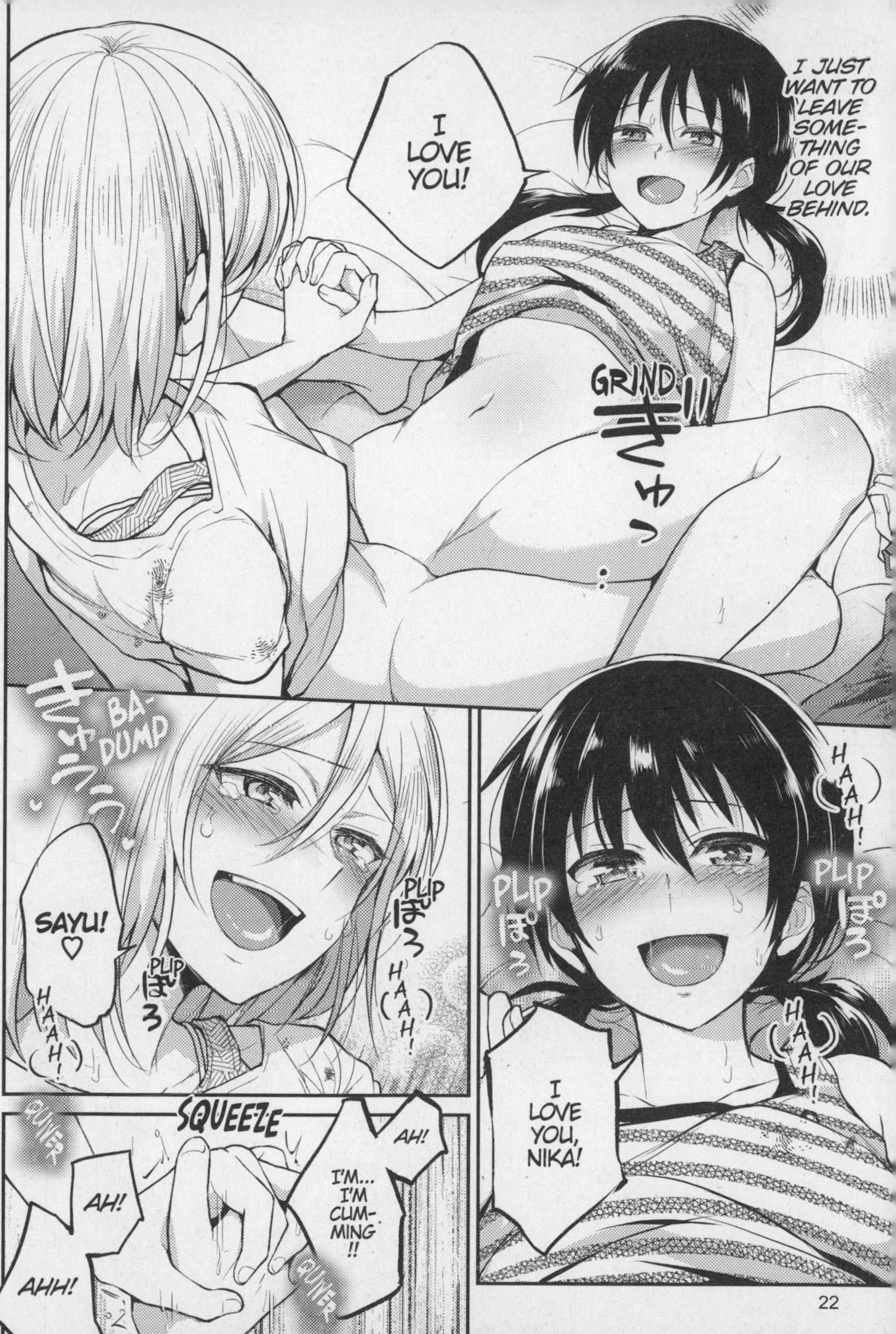
I JUST WANT TO LEAVE SOMETHING OF OUR LOVE BEHIND.
I LOVE YOU!
GRIND
ぎゅっ
HAAAH!
PLIP
ぽろ
PLIP
ぽろ
HAAAH!
I LOVE YOU, NIKA!
BA-DUMP
きゅううう
SAYU! ♡
PLIP
ぽろ
HAAAH!
PLIP
ぽろ
HAAAH!
SQUEEZE
AH!
I'M... I'M CUMMING!!
QUIVER
AH!
AHH!
QUIVER

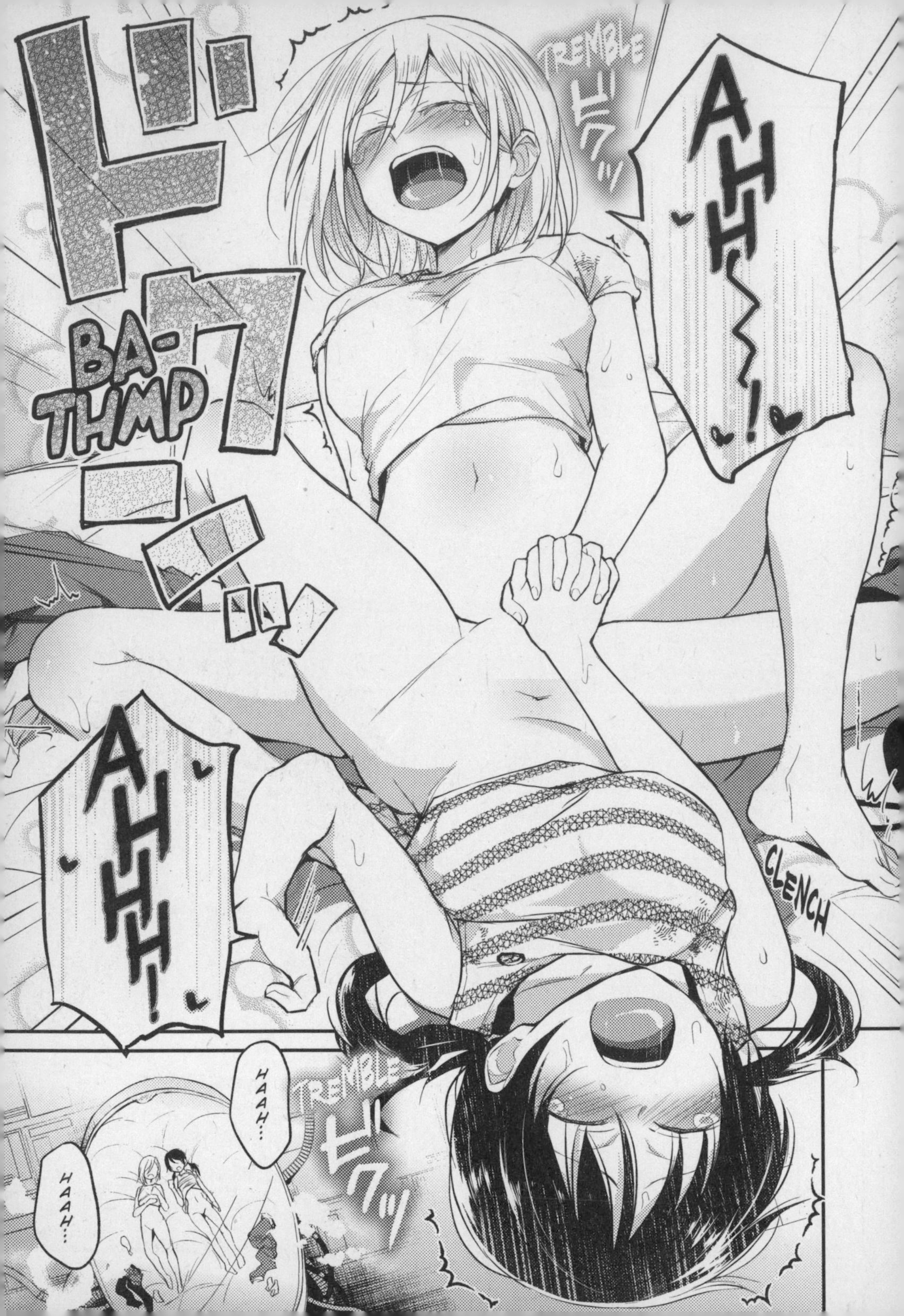
TREMBLE
ビクッ
AHH~~~!
BA-THMP
AHHHH!
CLENCH
TREMBLE
ビクッ
HAAAH...
HAAAH...

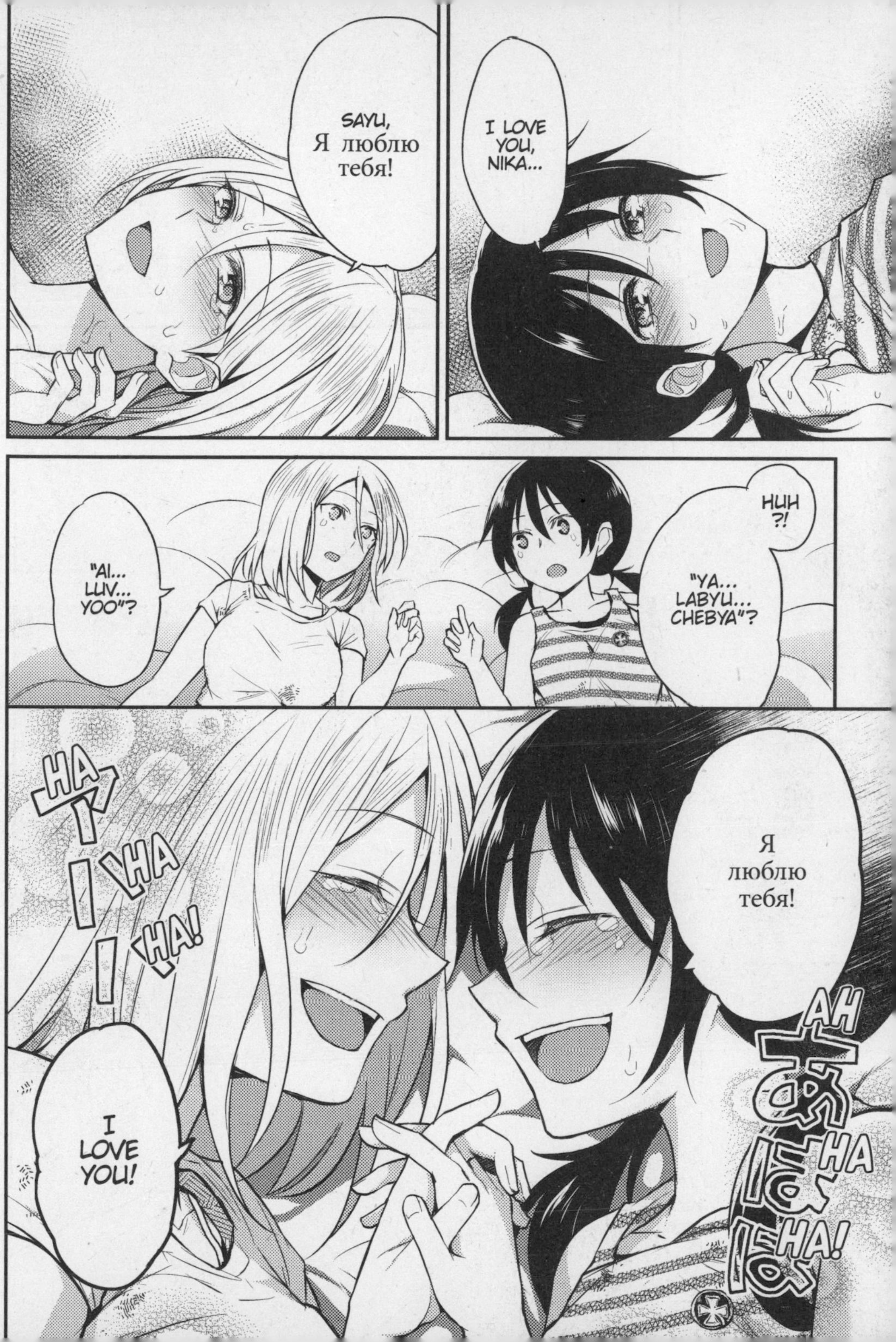
I LOVE YOU, NIKA...
SAYU, Я люблю тебя!
HUH?!
"YA... LABYU... CHEBYA"?
"AI... LUV... YOO"?
Я люблю тебя!
AH HA HA!
HA HA HA!
I LOVE YOU!

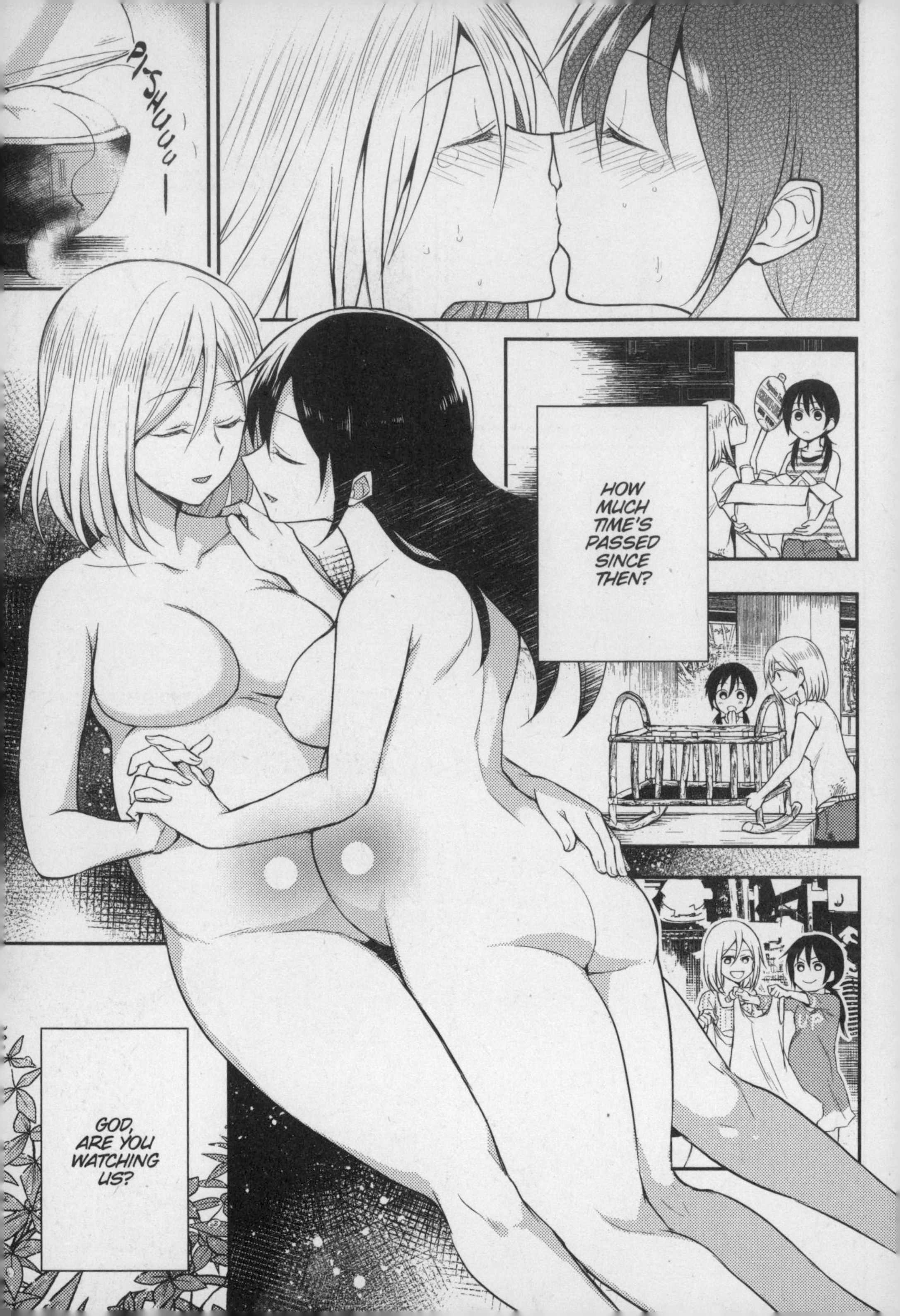
PI-SHUUU
HOW MUCH TIME'S PASSED SINCE THEN?
UP
GOD, ARE YOU WATCHING US?

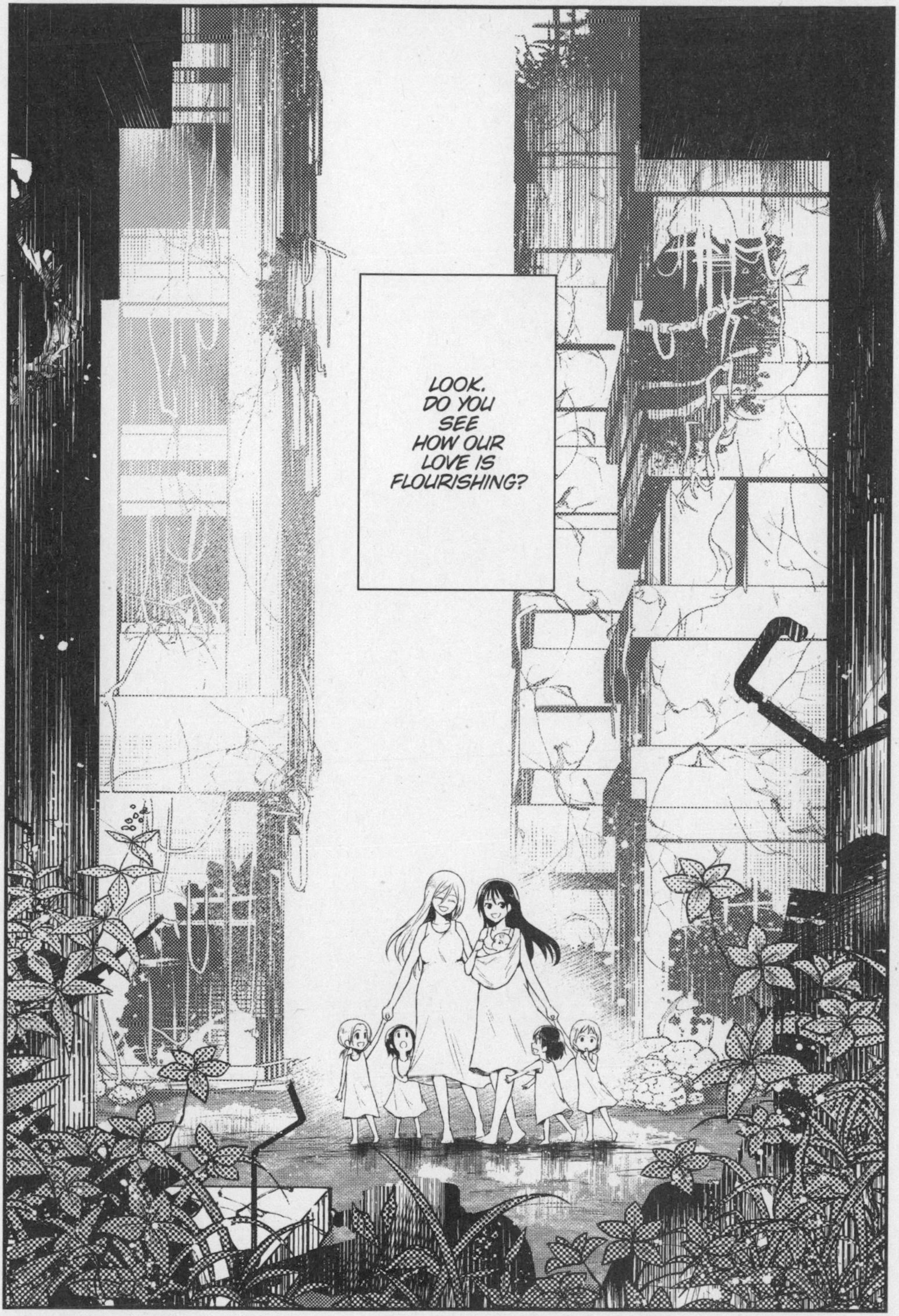
LOOK. DO YOU SEE HOW OUR LOVE IS FLOURISHING?

nd Eve

Eve and

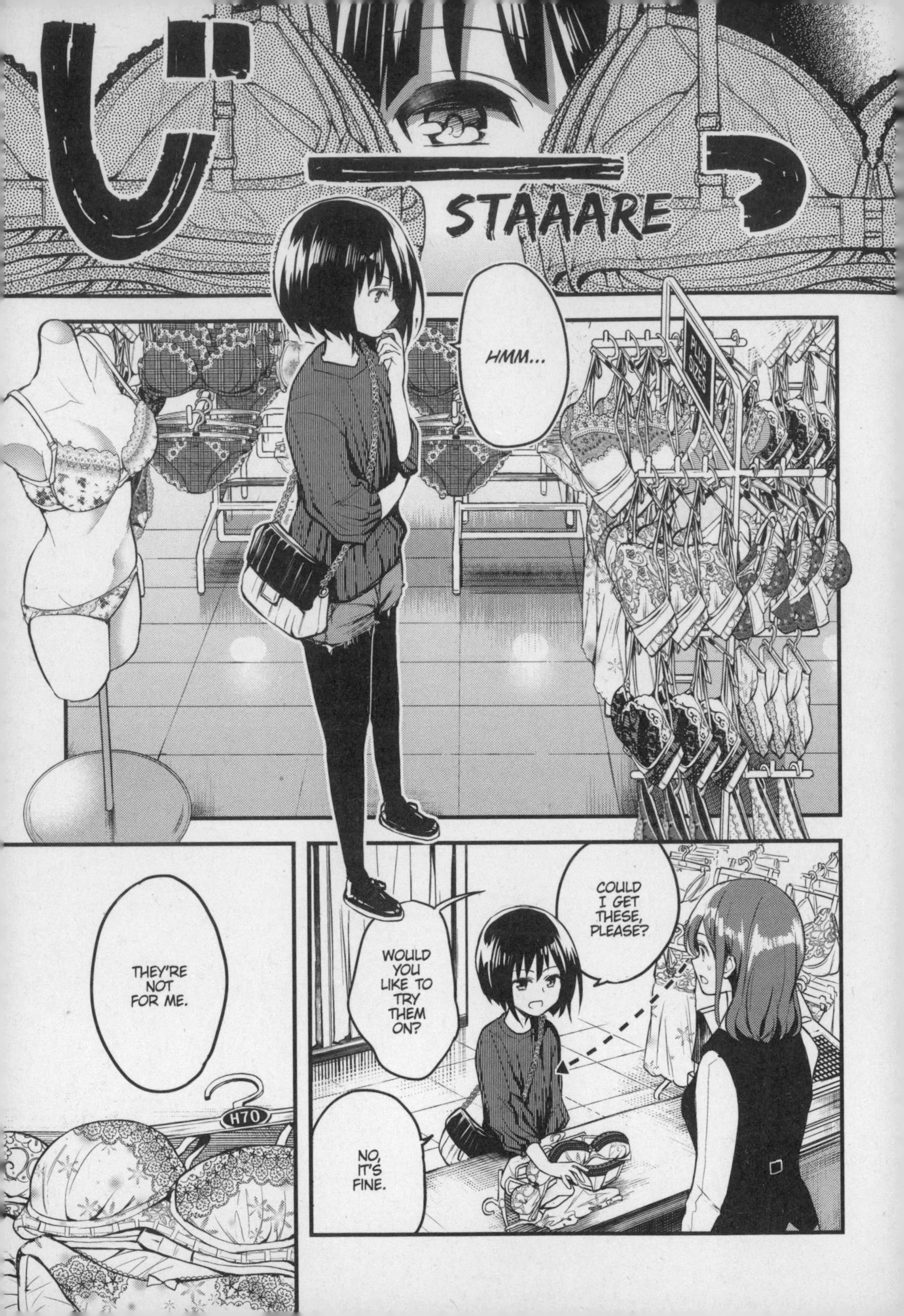
じーっ
STAAARE
HMM...
PLUS SIZES
COULD I GET THESE, PLEASE?
WOULD YOU LIKE TO TRY THEM ON?
NO, IT'S FINE.
THEY'RE NOT FOR ME.
H70

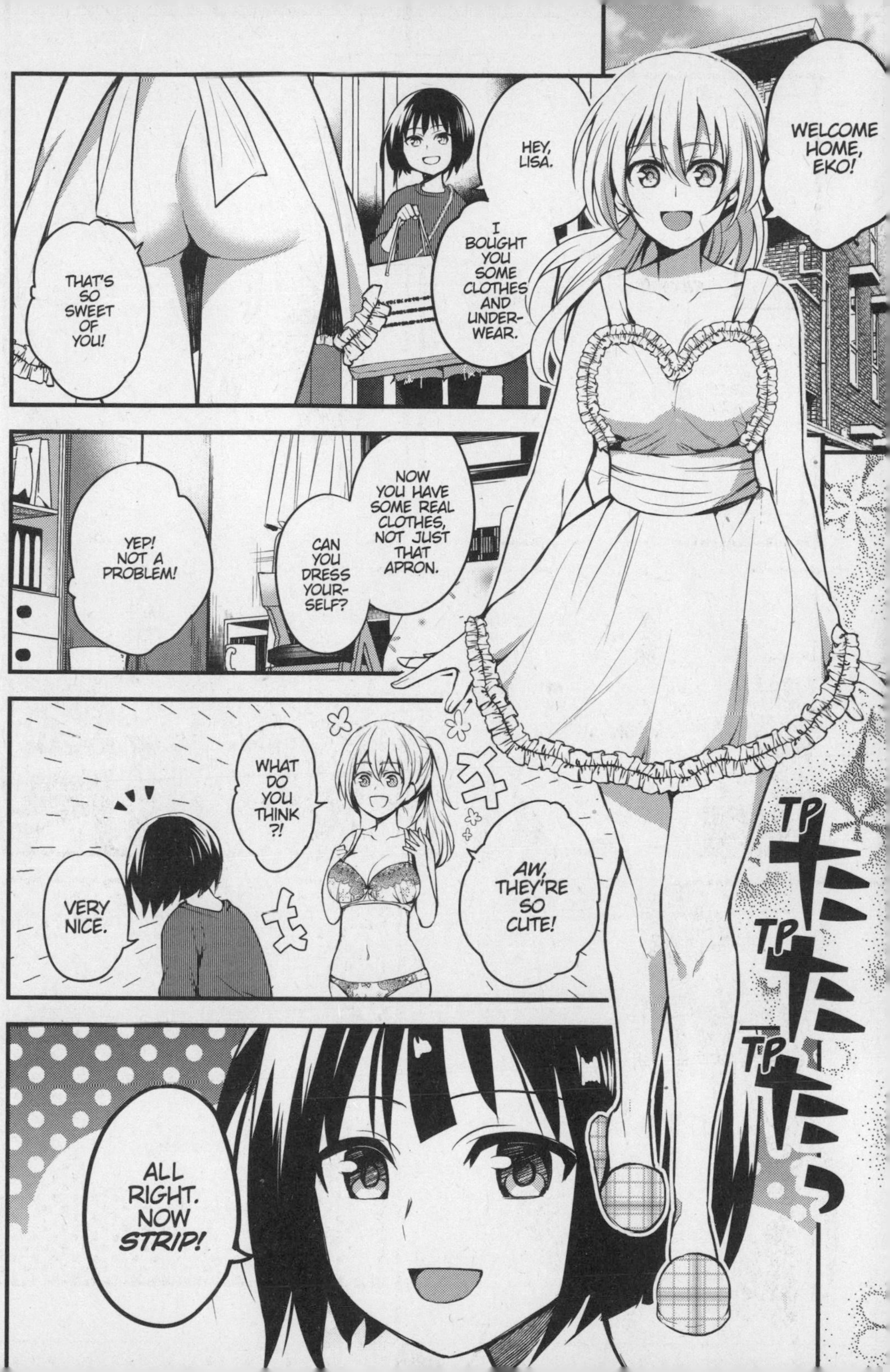
WELCOME HOME, EKO!
TP TP TP TP
HEY, LISA.
I BOUGHT YOU SOME CLOTHES AND UNDER-WEAR.
THAT'S SO SWEET OF YOU!
NOW YOU HAVE SOME REAL CLOTHES, NOT JUST THAT APRON.
CAN YOU DRESS YOUR-SELF?
YEP! NOT A PROBLEM!
AW, THEY'RE SO CUTE!
WHAT DO YOU THINK?!
VERY NICE.
ALL RIGHT. NOW STRIP!

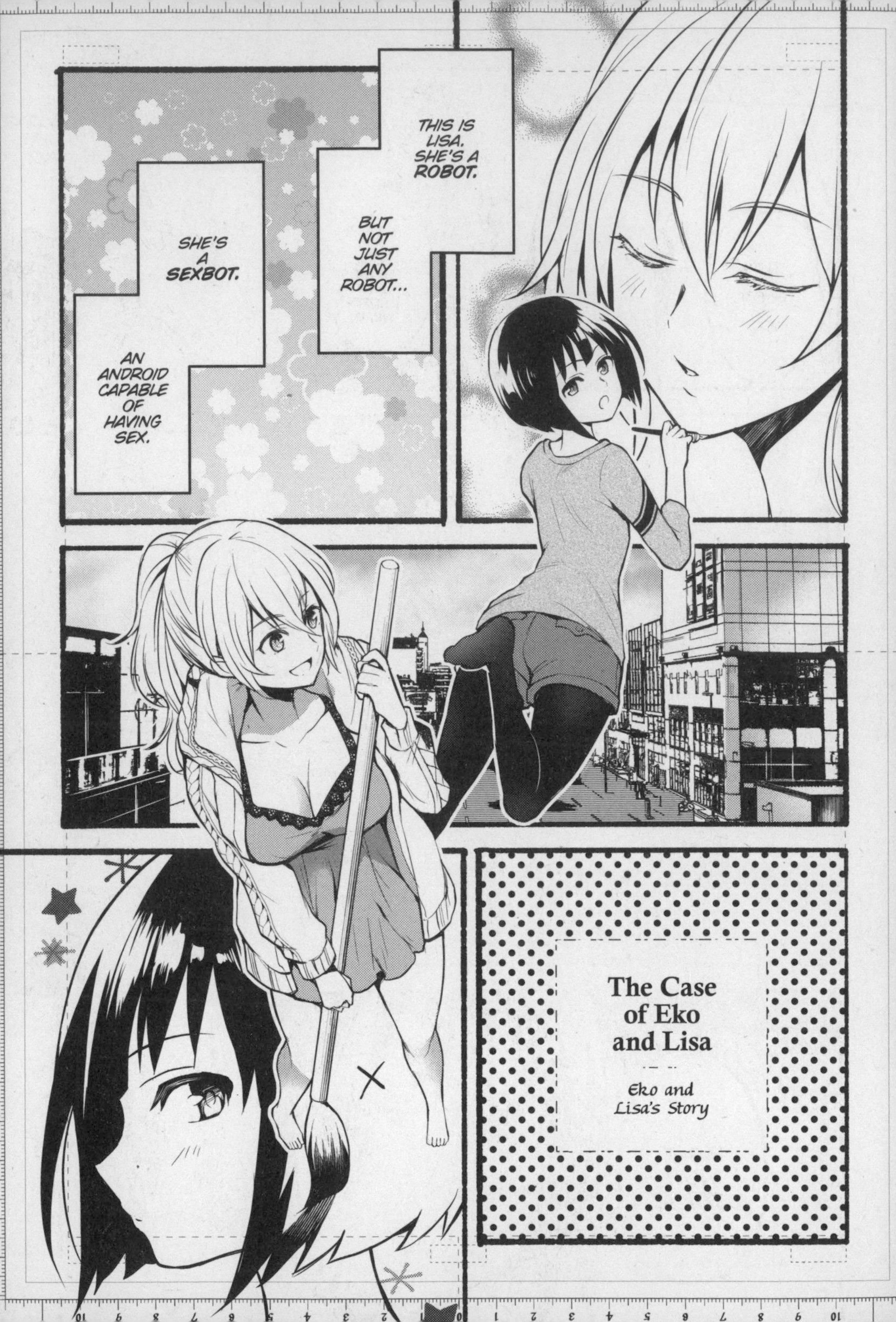
THIS IS LISA. SHE'S A ROBOT.
BUT NOT JUST ANY ROBOT...
SHE'S A SEXBOT.
AN ANDROID CAPABLE OF HAVING SEX.
The Case of Eko and Lisa
Eko and Lisa's Story

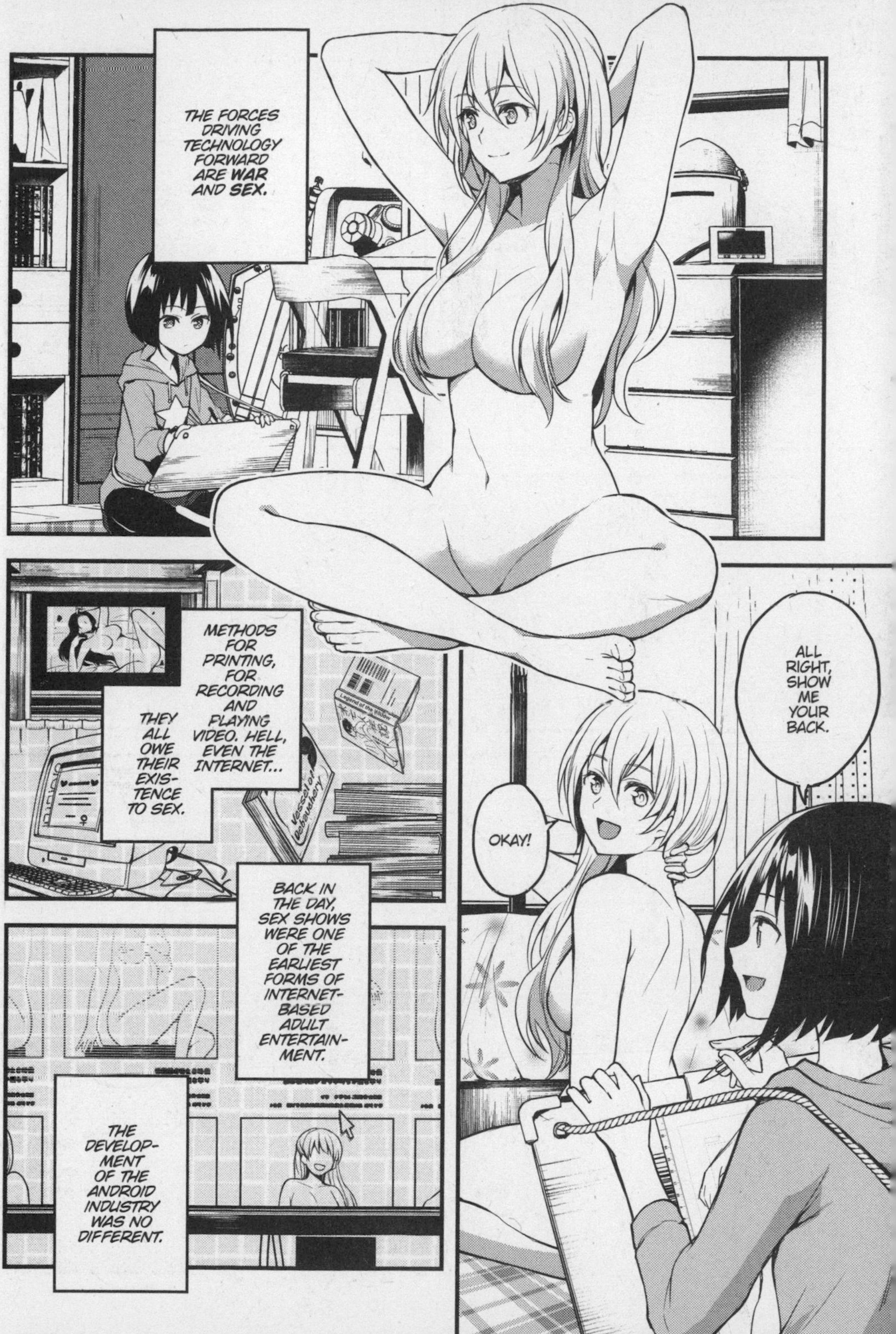
THE FORCES DRIVING TECHNOLOGY FORWARD ARE **WAR** AND **SEX.**
ALL RIGHT, SHOW ME YOUR BACK.
OKAY!
METHODS FOR PRINTING, FOR RECORDING AND PLAYING VIDEO. HELL, EVEN THE INTERNET...
THEY ALL OWE THEIR EXISTENCE TO SEX.
Legend of the Willow
Vessel of Debauchery
BACK IN THE DAY, SEX SHOWS WERE ONE OF THE EARLIEST FORMS OF INTERNET-BASED ADULT ENTERTAINMENT.
THE DEVELOPMENT OF THE ANDROID INDUSTRY WAS NO DIFFERENT.

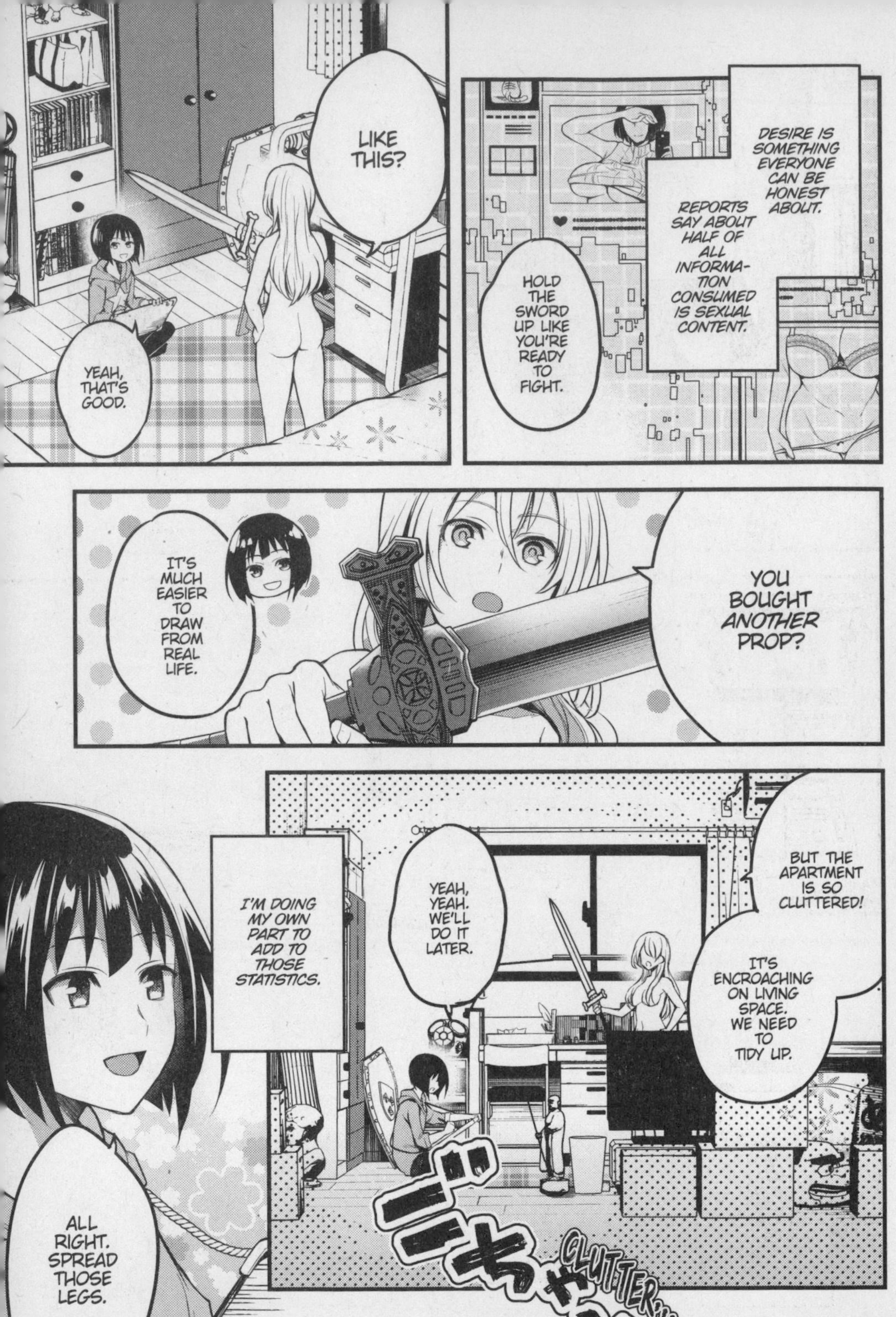
DESIRE IS SOMETHING EVERYONE CAN BE HONEST ABOUT.
REPORTS SAY ABOUT HALF OF ALL INFORMATION CONSUMED IS SEXUAL CONTENT.
HOLD THE SWORD UP LIKE YOU'RE READY TO FIGHT.
LIKE THIS?
YEAH, THAT'S GOOD.
YOU BOUGHT ANOTHER PROP?
IT'S MUCH EASIER TO DRAW FROM REAL LIFE.
BUT THE APARTMENT IS SO CLUTTERED!
IT'S ENCROACHING ON LIVING SPACE. WE NEED TO TIDY UP.
YEAH, YEAH. WE'LL DO IT LATER.
I'M DOING MY OWN PART TO ADD TO THOSE STATISTICS.
CLUTTER...
ALL RIGHT. SPREAD THOSE LEGS.

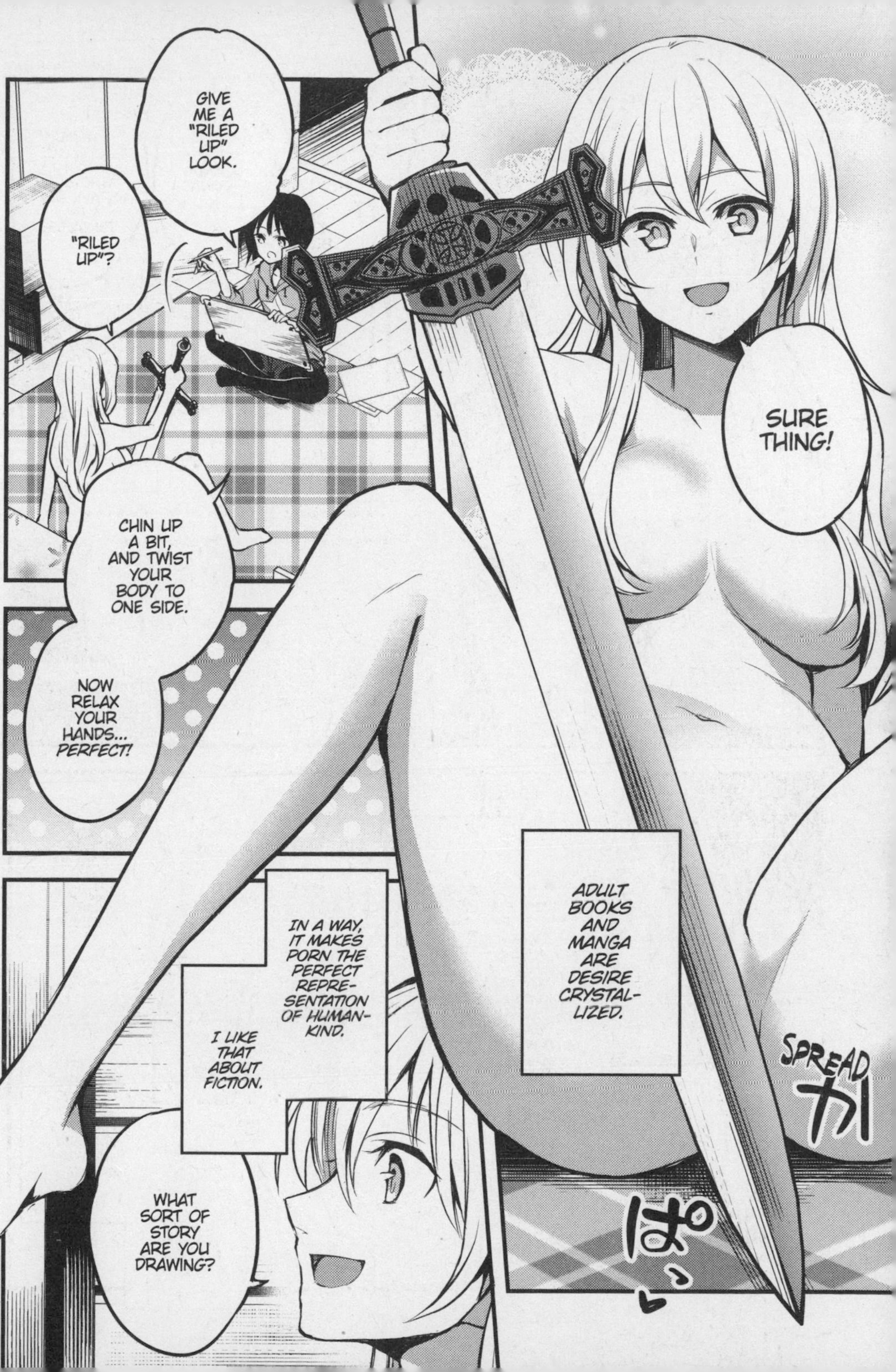
GIVE ME A "RILED UP" LOOK.
"RILED UP"?
SURE THING!
CHIN UP A BIT, AND TWIST YOUR BODY TO ONE SIDE.
NOW RELAX YOUR HANDS... PERFECT!
SPREAD
ぱっ
ADULT BOOKS AND MANGA ARE DESIRE CRYSTAL-LIZED.
IN A WAY, IT MAKES PORN THE PERFECT REPRE-SENTATION OF HUMAN-KIND.
I LIKE THAT ABOUT FICTION.
WHAT SORT OF STORY ARE YOU DRAWING?

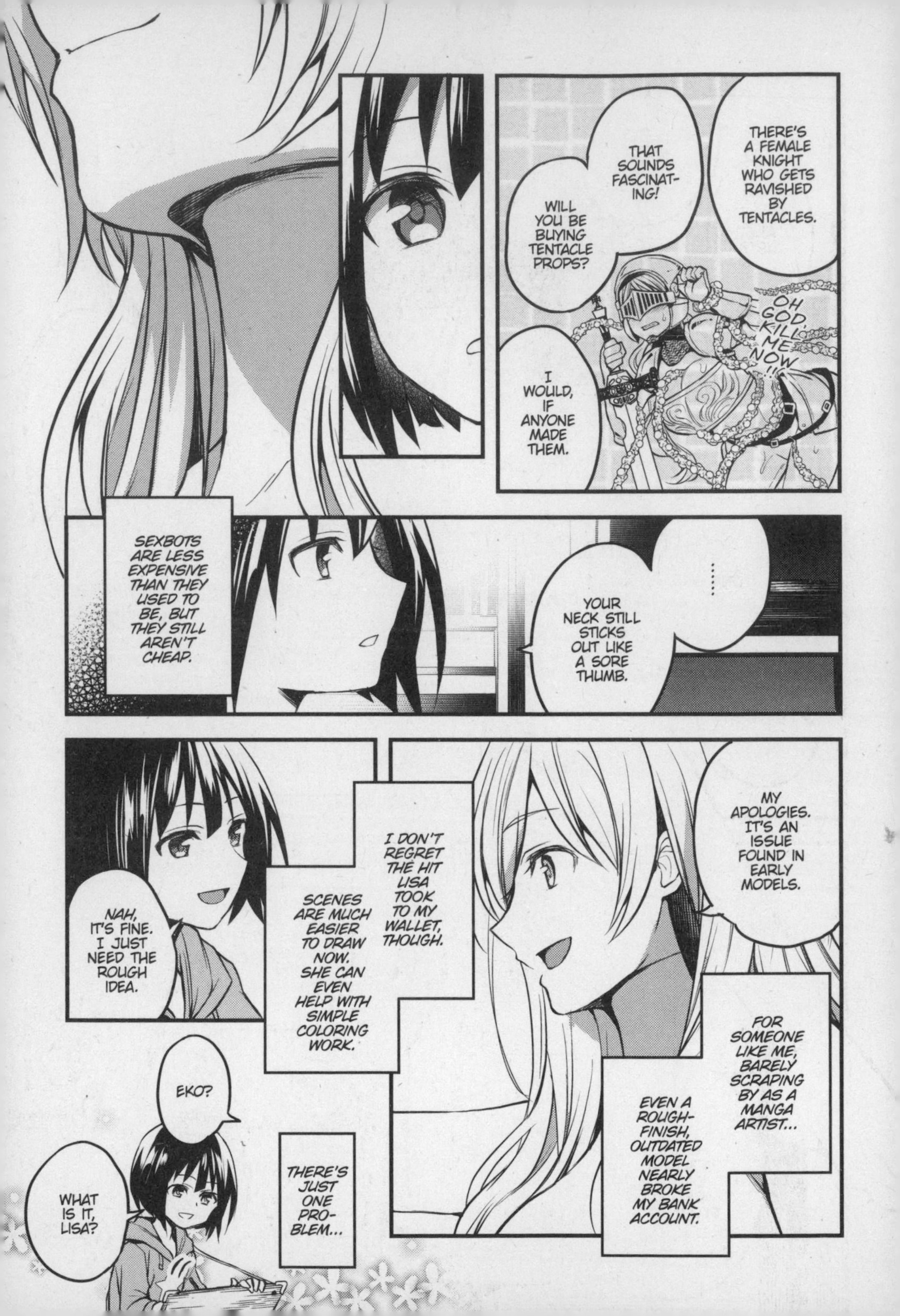
THERE'S A FEMALE KNIGHT WHO GETS RAVISHED BY TENTACLES.
THAT SOUNDS FASCINATING!
WILL YOU BE BUYING TENTACLE PROPS?
OH GOD KILL ME NOW!!
I WOULD, IF ANYONE MADE THEM.
......
YOUR NECK STILL STICKS OUT LIKE A SORE THUMB.
SEXBOTS ARE LESS EXPENSIVE THAN THEY USED TO BE, BUT THEY STILL AREN'T CHEAP.
MY APOLOGIES. IT'S AN ISSUE FOUND IN EARLY MODELS.
FOR SOMEONE LIKE ME, BARELY SCRAPING BY AS A MANGA ARTIST...
EVEN A ROUGH-FINISH, OUTDATED MODEL NEARLY BROKE MY BANK ACCOUNT.
I DON'T REGRET THE HIT LISA TOOK TO MY WALLET, THOUGH.
SCENES ARE MUCH EASIER TO DRAW NOW. SHE CAN EVEN HELP WITH SIMPLE COLORING WORK.
NAH, IT'S FINE. I JUST NEED THE ROUGH IDEA.
THERE'S JUST ONE PROBLEM...
EKO?
WHAT IS IT, LISA?

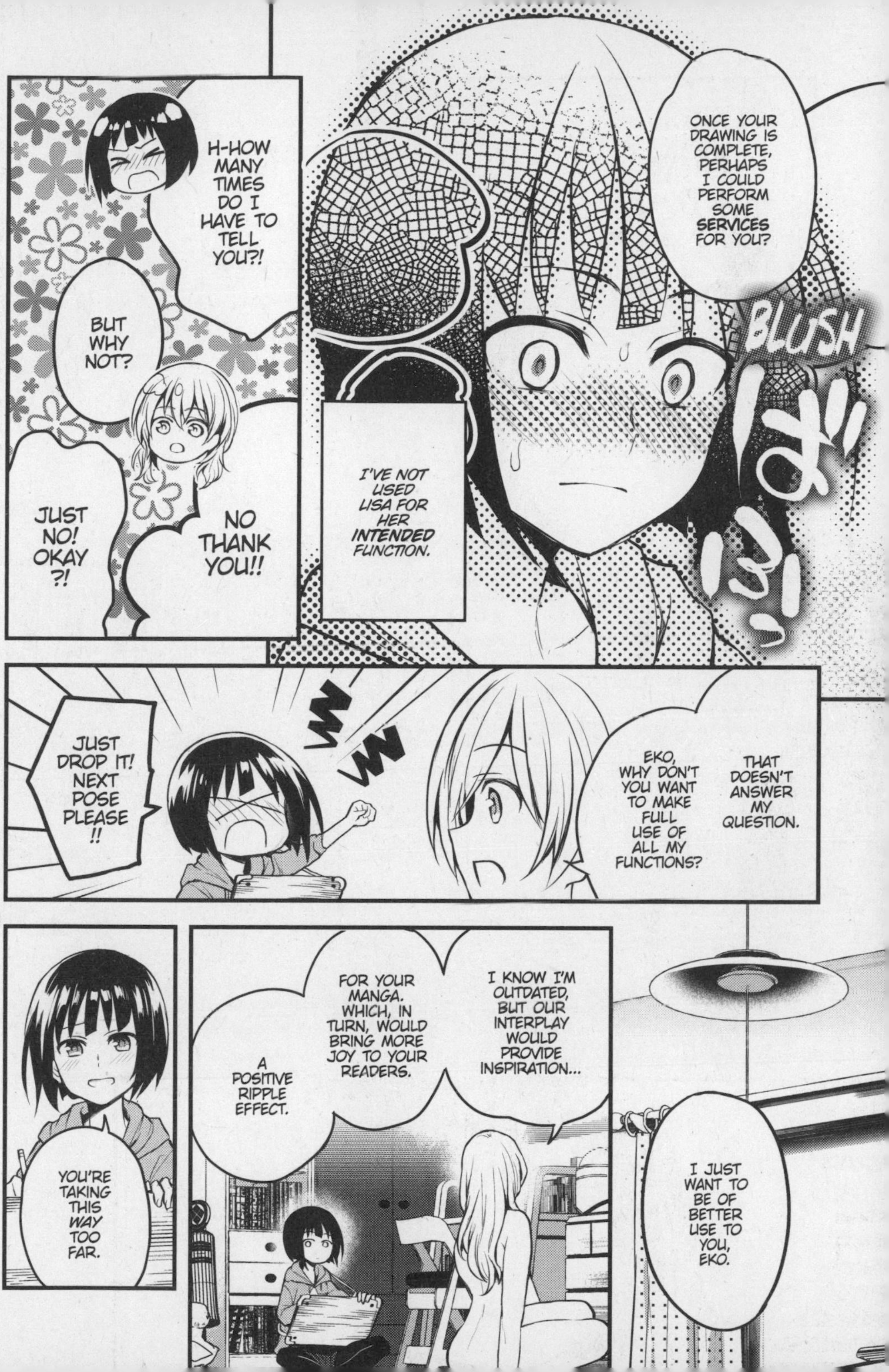
ONCE YOUR DRAWING IS COMPLETE, PERHAPS I COULD PERFORM SOME SERVICES FOR YOU?
BLUSH
I'VE NOT USED LISA FOR HER INTENDED FUNCTION.
H-HOW MANY TIMES DO I HAVE TO TELL YOU?!
BUT WHY NOT?
NO THANK YOU!!
JUST NO! OKAY?!
THAT DOESN'T ANSWER MY QUESTION.
EKO, WHY DON'T YOU WANT TO MAKE FULL USE OF ALL MY FUNCTIONS?
JUST DROP IT! NEXT POSE PLEASE!!
I JUST WANT TO BE OF BETTER USE TO YOU, EKO.
I KNOW I'M OUTDATED, BUT OUR INTERPLAY WOULD PROVIDE INSPIRATION...
FOR YOUR MANGA. WHICH, IN TURN, WOULD BRING MORE JOY TO YOUR READERS.
A POSITIVE RIPPLE EFFECT.
YOU'RE TAKING THIS WAY TOO FAR.

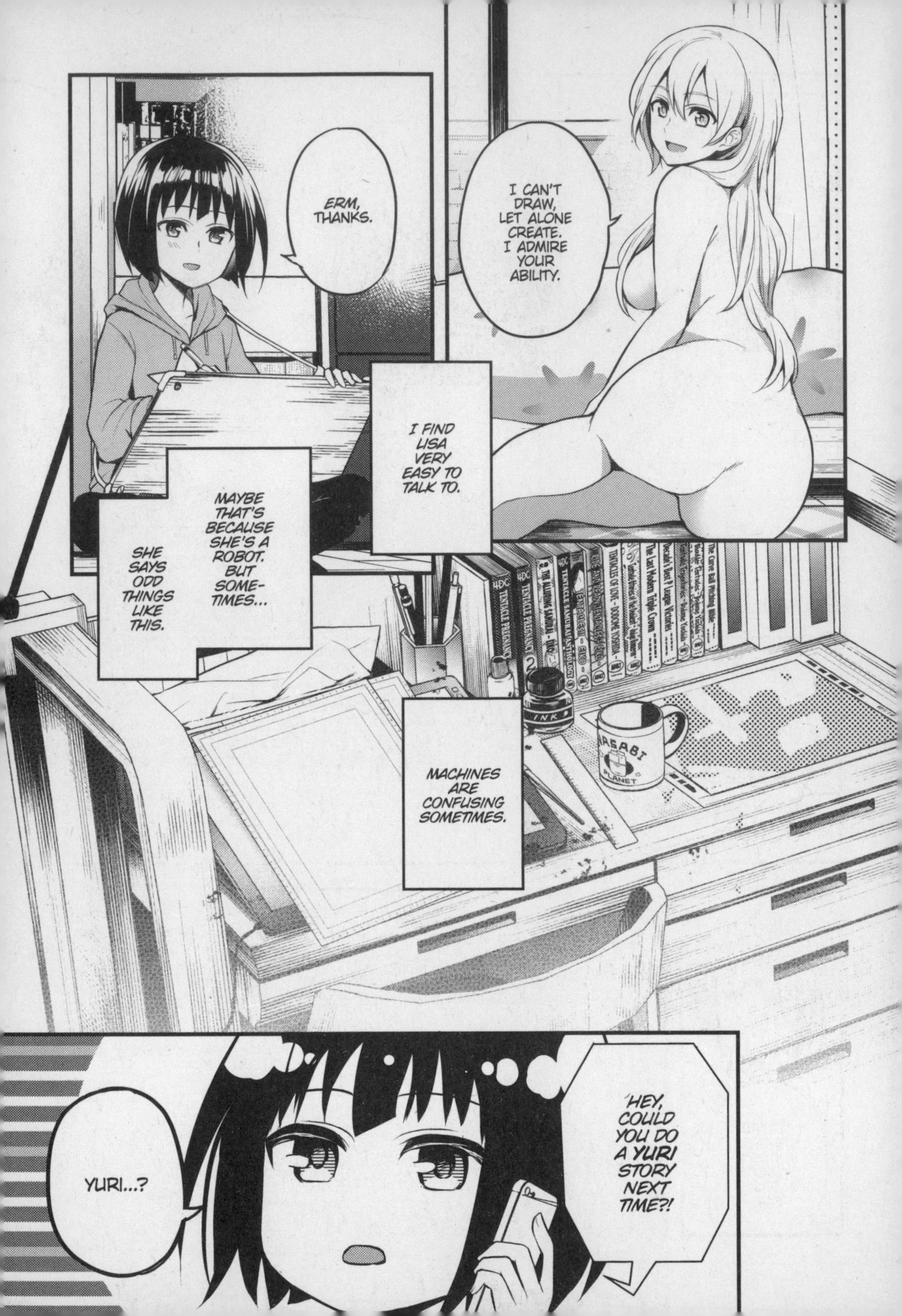
I CAN'T DRAW, LET ALONE CREATE. I ADMIRE YOUR ABILITY.
ERM, THANKS.
I FIND LISA VERY EASY TO TALK TO.
MAYBE THAT'S BECAUSE SHE'S A ROBOT. BUT SOME-TIMES...
SHE SAYS ODD THINGS LIKE THIS.
MACHINES ARE CONFUSING SOMETIMES.
'HEY, COULD YOU DO A YURI STORY NEXT TIME?!
YURI...?

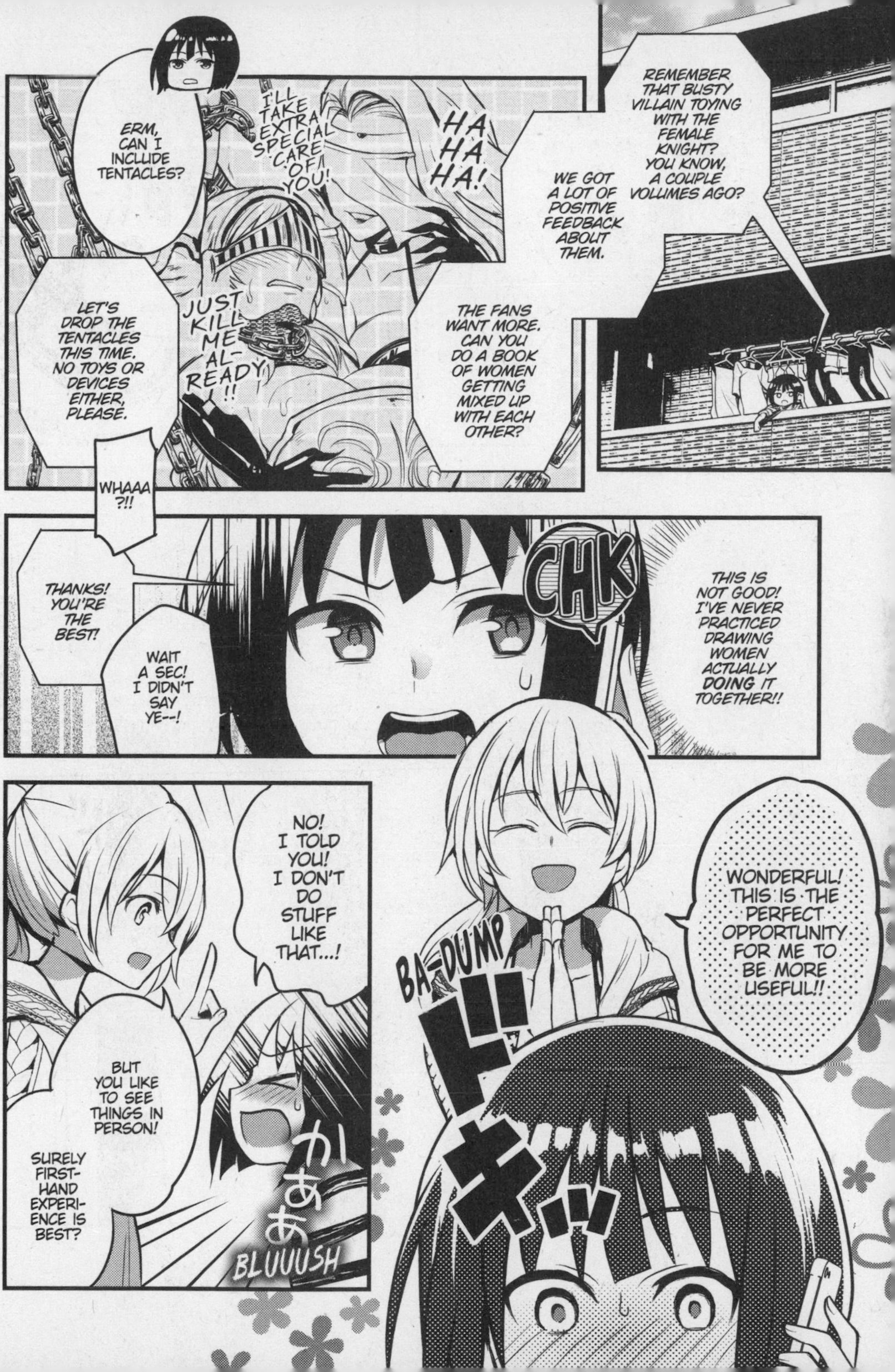

REMEMBER THAT BUSTY VILLAIN TOYING WITH THE FEMALE KNIGHT? YOU KNOW, A COUPLE VOLUMES AGO?
WE GOT A LOT OF POSITIVE FEEDBACK ABOUT THEM.
THE FANS WANT MORE. CAN YOU DO A BOOK OF WOMEN GETTING MIXED UP WITH EACH OTHER?
HA HA HA!
I'LL TAKE EXTRA SPECIAL CARE OF YOU!
JUST KILL ME AL-READY!!
ERM, CAN I INCLUDE TENTACLES?
LET'S DROP THE TENTACLES THIS TIME. NO TOYS OR DEVICES EITHER, PLEASE.
WHAAA?!!
CHK
THIS IS NOT GOOD! I'VE NEVER PRACTICED DRAWING WOMEN ACTUALLY **DOING** IT TOGETHER!!
THANKS! YOU'RE THE BEST!
WAIT A SEC! I DIDN'T SAY YE--!
WONDERFUL! THIS IS THE PERFECT OPPORTUNITY FOR ME TO BE MORE USEFUL!!
BA-DUMP
ドキ...
NO! I TOLD YOU! I DON'T DO STUFF LIKE THAT...!
BUT YOU LIKE TO SEE THINGS IN PERSON!
SURELY FIRST-HAND EXPERIENCE IS BEST?
かあぁ
BLUUUSH

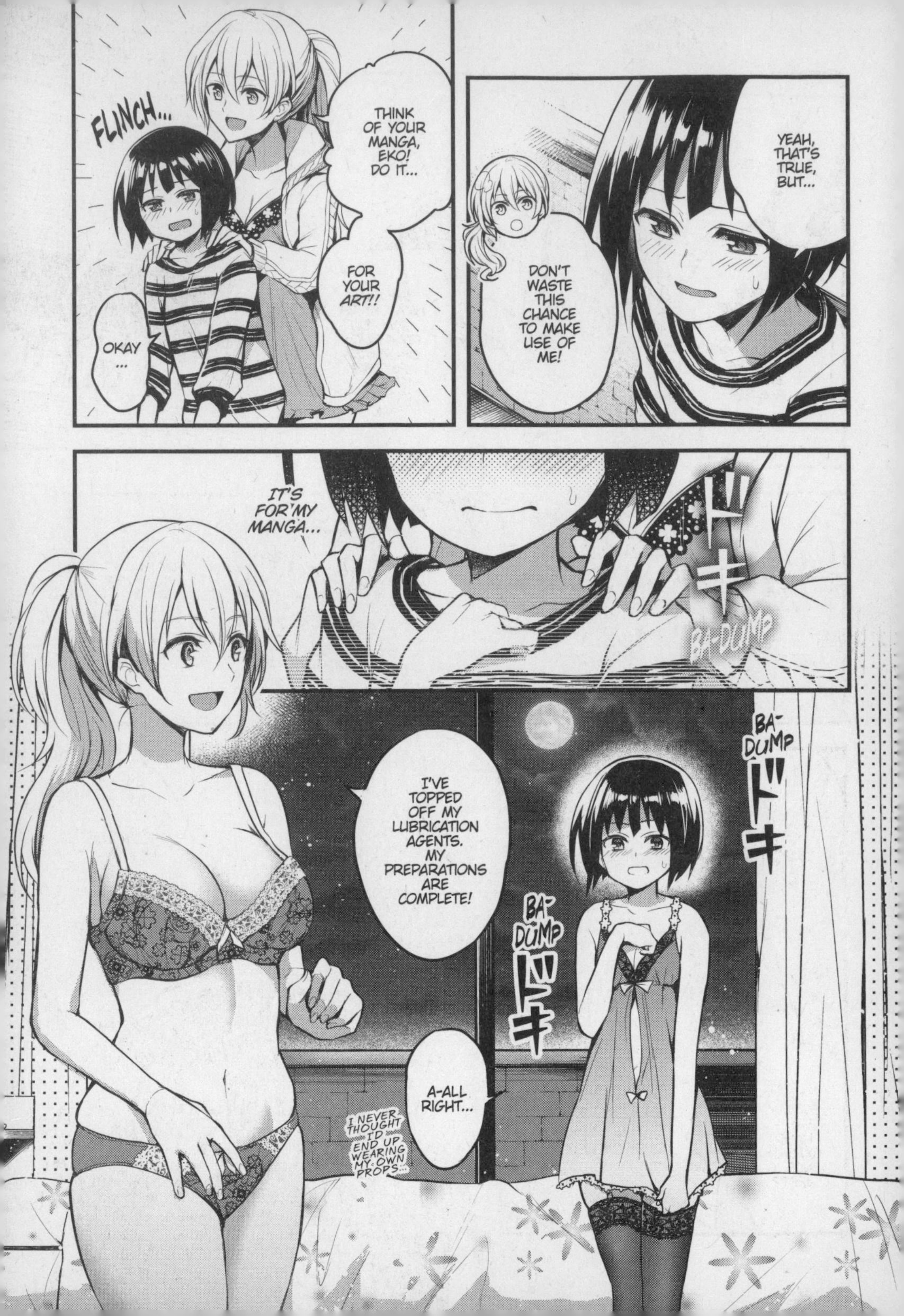
YEAH, THAT'S TRUE, BUT...
DON'T WASTE THIS CHANCE TO MAKE USE OF ME!
THINK OF YOUR MANGA, EKO! DO IT...
FOR YOUR ART!!
FLINCH...
OKAY ...
IT'S FOR MY MANGA...
ドキ
BA-DUMP
BA-DUMP
ドキ
I'VE TOPPED OFF MY LUBRICATION AGENTS. MY PREPARATIONS ARE COMPLETE!
BA-DUMP
ドキ
A-ALL RIGHT...
I NEVER THOUGHT I'D END UP WEARING MY OWN PROPS...

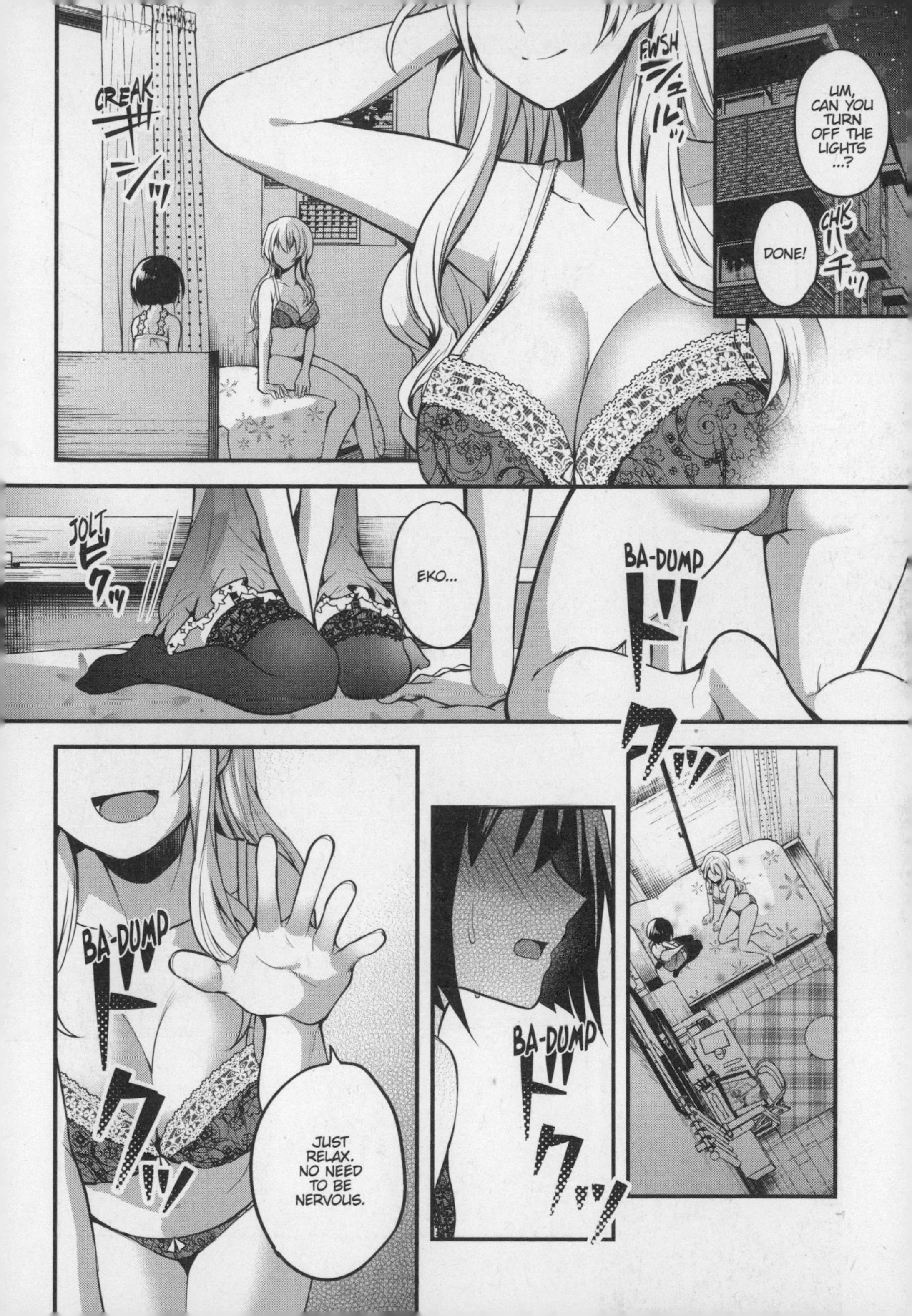
UM, CAN YOU TURN OFF THE LIGHTS ...?
DONE!
CHK
FWSH
CREAK
BA-DUMP
EKO...
JOLT
BA-DUMP
BA-DUMP
JUST RELAX. NO NEED TO BE NERVOUS.

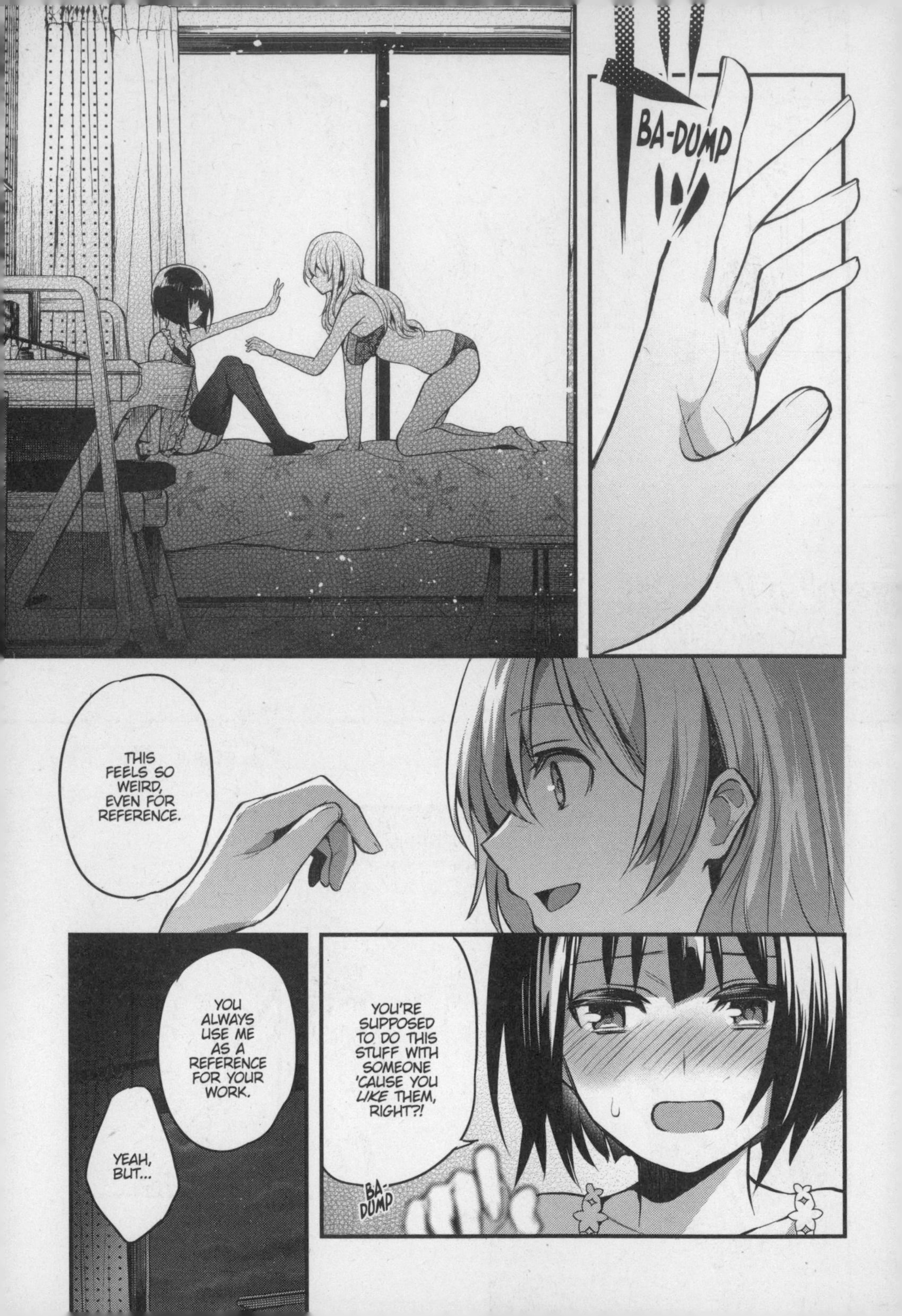
BA-DUMP
THIS FEELS SO WEIRD, EVEN FOR REFERENCE.
YOU'RE SUPPOSED TO DO THIS STUFF WITH SOMEONE 'CAUSE YOU *LIKE* THEM, RIGHT?!
BA-DUMP
YOU ALWAYS USE ME AS A REFERENCE FOR YOUR WORK.
YEAH, BUT...

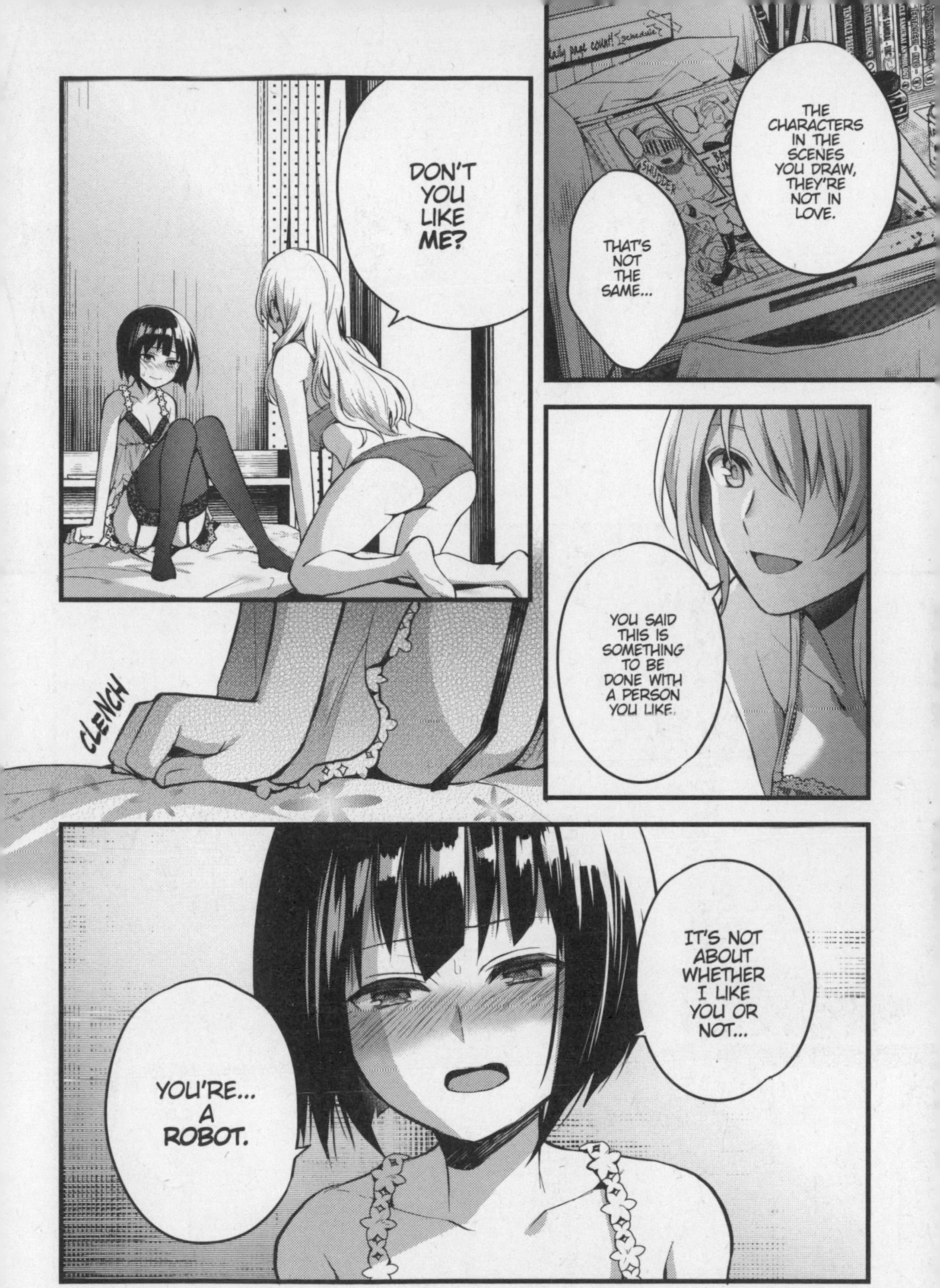
THE CHARACTERS IN THE SCENES YOU DRAW, THEY'RE NOT IN LOVE.
THAT'S NOT THE SAME...
DON'T YOU LIKE ME?
YOU SAID THIS IS SOMETHING TO BE DONE WITH A PERSON YOU LIKE.
CLENCH
IT'S NOT ABOUT WHETHER I LIKE YOU OR NOT...
YOU'RE... A ROBOT.

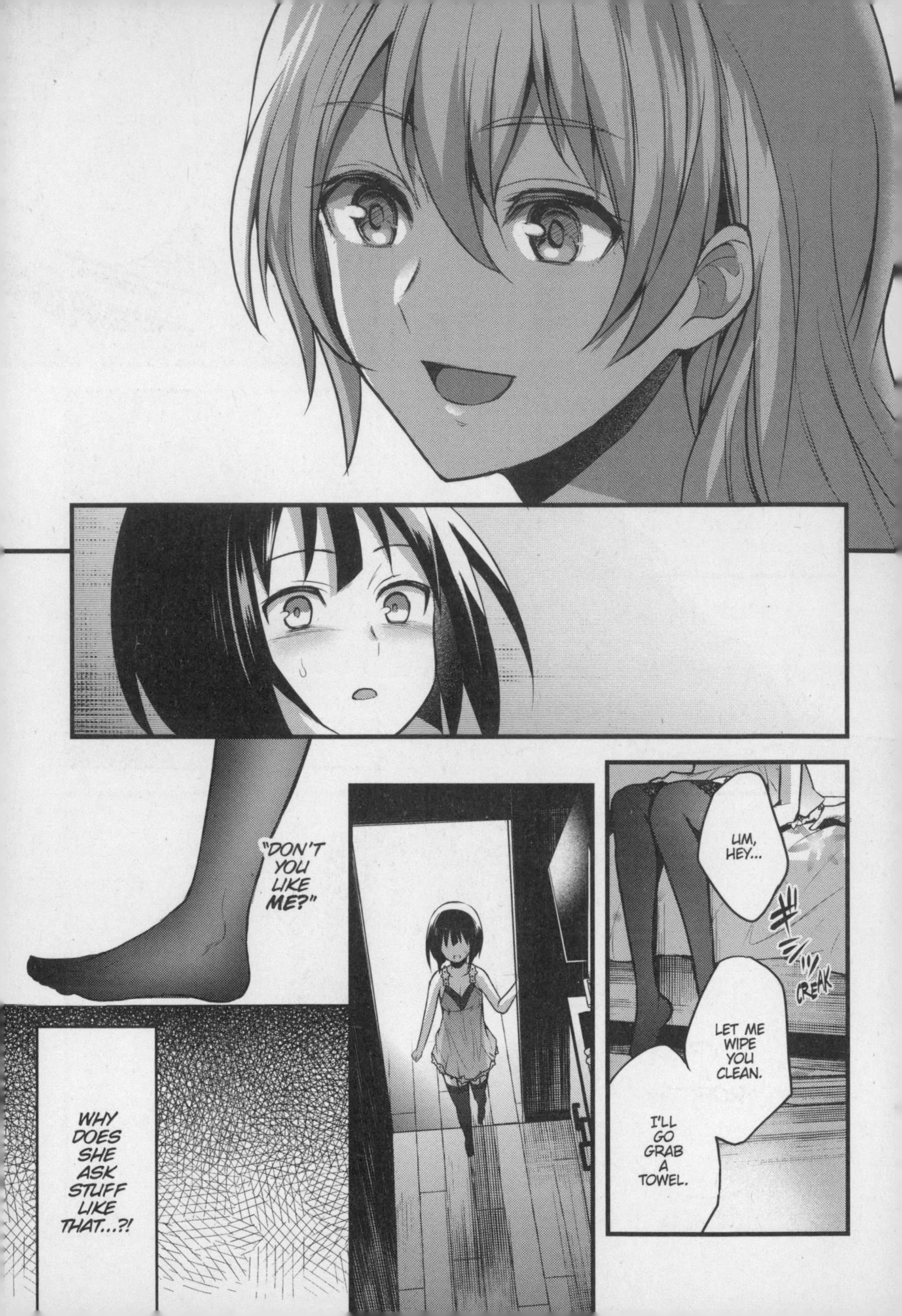
UM, HEY...
CREAK
LET ME WIPE YOU CLEAN.
I'LL GO GRAB A TOWEL.
"DON'T YOU LIKE ME?"
WHY DOES SHE ASK STUFF LIKE THAT...?!

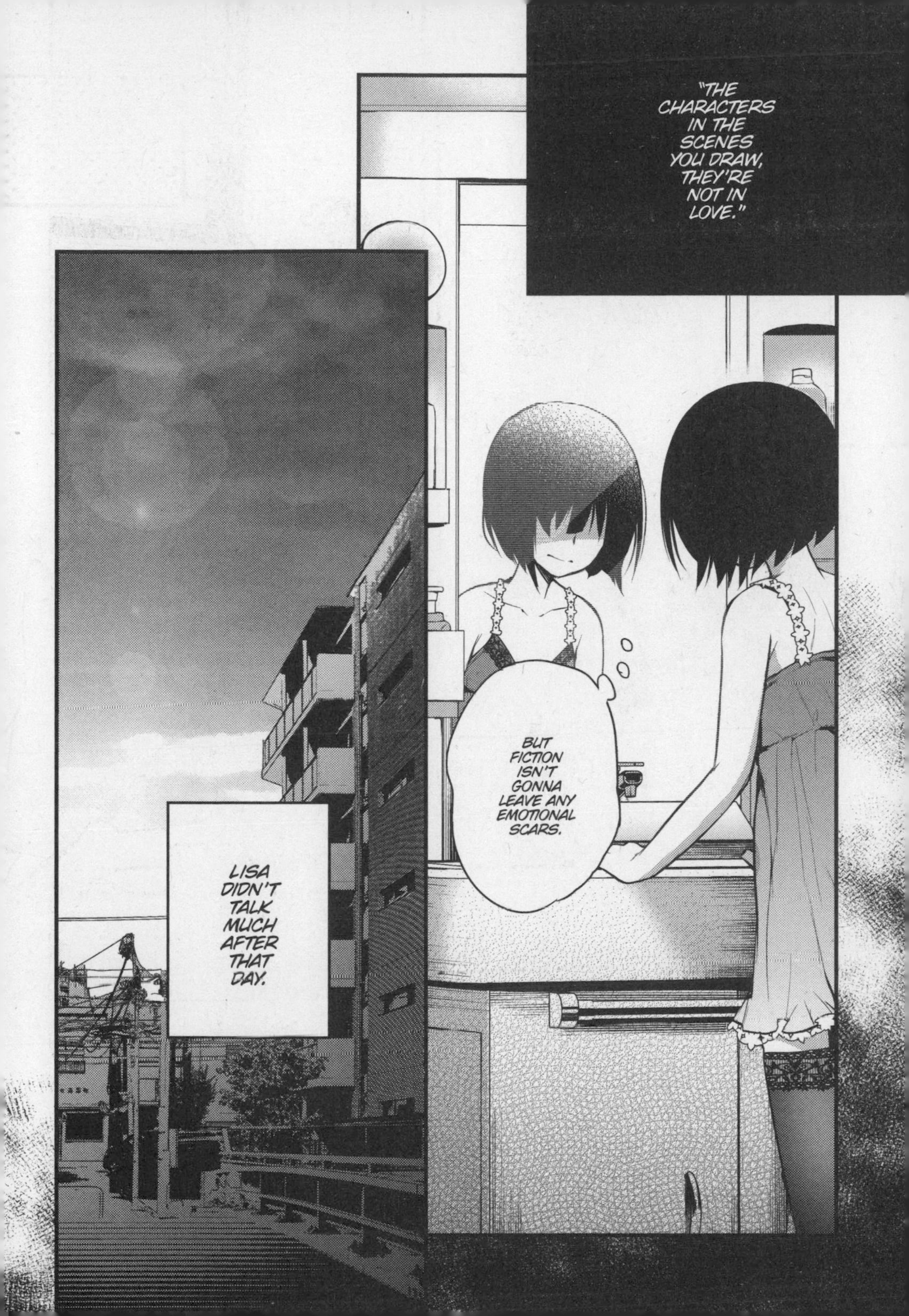
"THE CHARACTERS IN THE SCENES YOU DRAW, THEY'RE NOT IN LOVE."
BUT FICTION ISN'T GONNA LEAVE ANY EMOTIONAL SCARS.
LISA DIDN'T TALK MUCH AFTER THAT DAY.

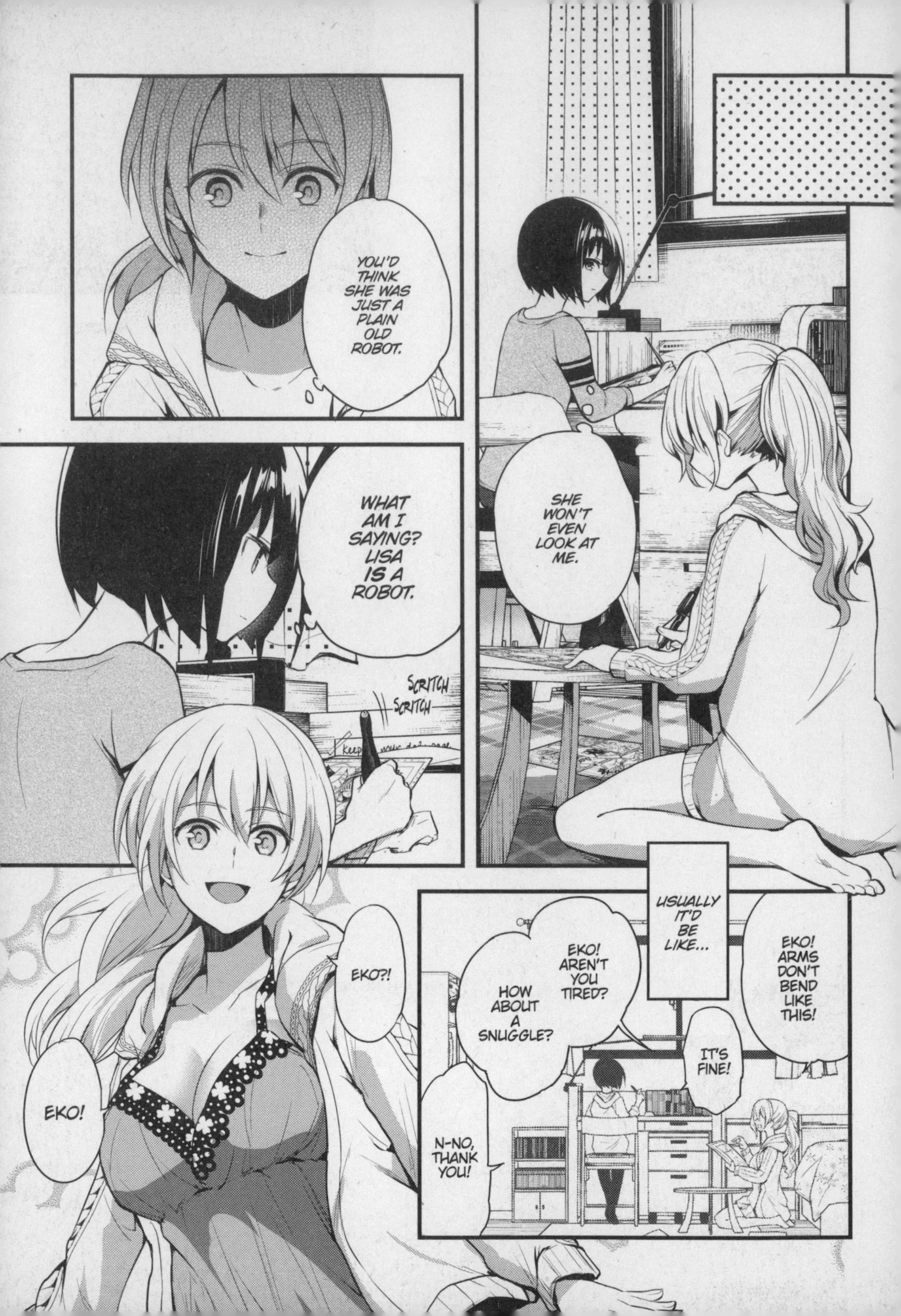
SHE WON'T EVEN LOOK AT ME.
YOU'D THINK SHE WAS JUST A PLAIN OLD ROBOT.
WHAT AM I SAYING? LISA IS A ROBOT.
SCRITCH
SCRITCH
USUALLY IT'D BE LIKE...
EKO! ARMS DON'T BEND LIKE THIS!
EKO! AREN'T YOU TIRED?
IT'S FINE!
HOW ABOUT A SNUGGLE?
N-NO, THANK YOU!
EKO?!
EKO!

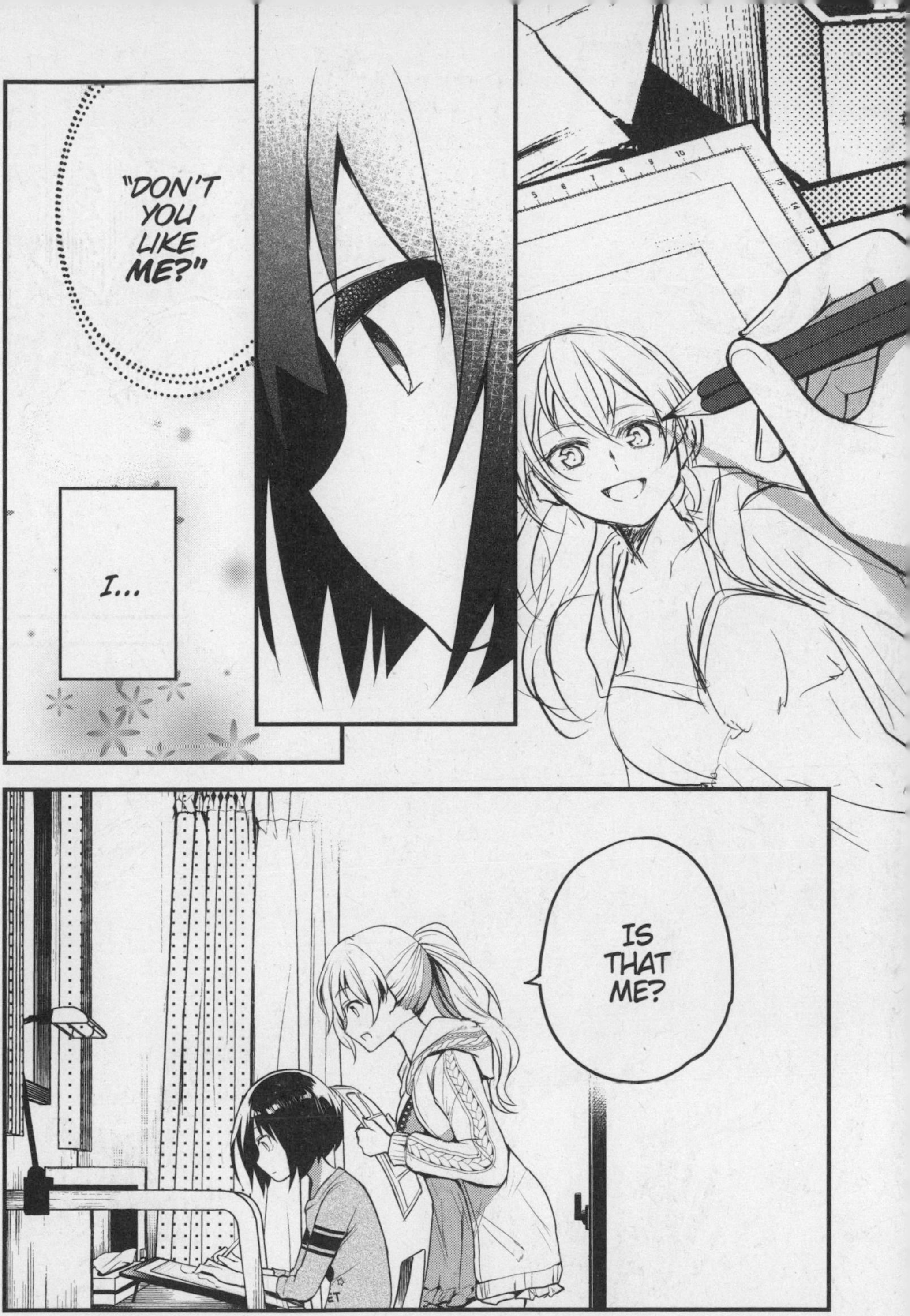
"DON'T YOU LIKE ME?"
I...
IS THAT ME?

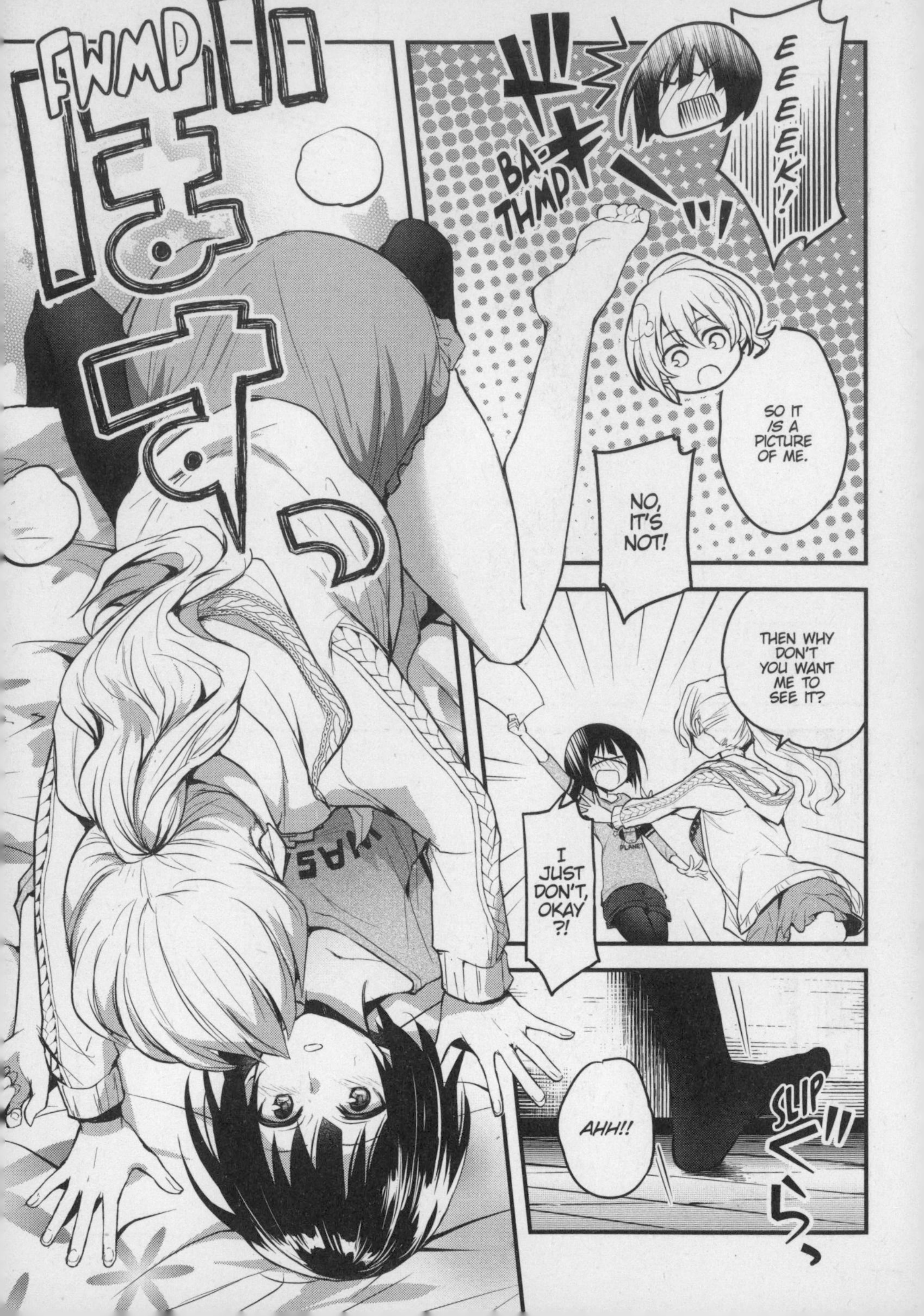
EEEEEK!
BA-THMP
SO IT IS A PICTURE OF ME.
NO, IT'S NOT!
THEN WHY DON'T YOU WANT ME TO SEE IT?
I JUST DON'T, OKAY?!
SLIP
AHH!!
FWMP

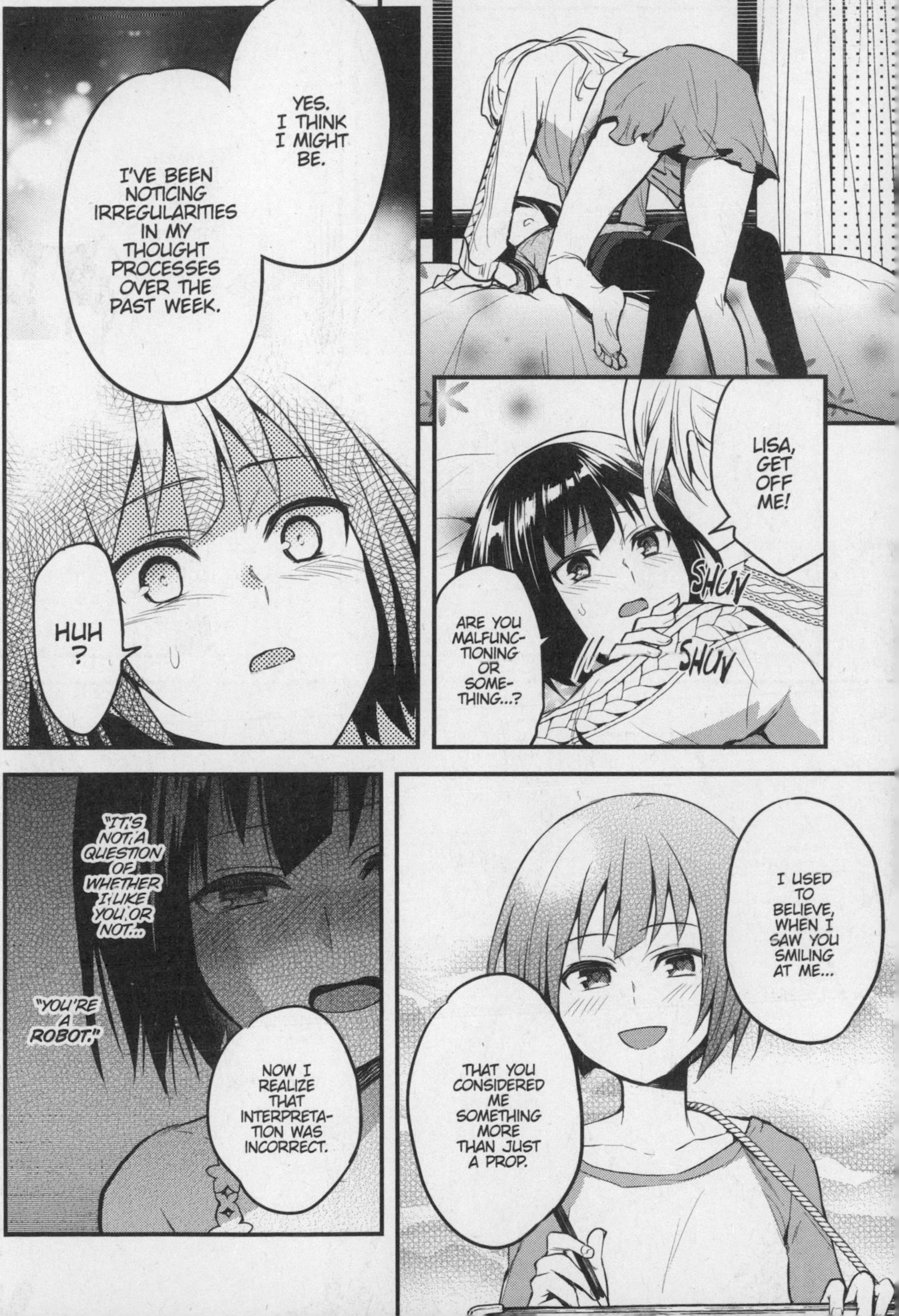
LISA, GET OFF ME!
SHUV
ARE YOU MALFUNCTIONING OR SOMETHING...?
SHUV
YES. I THINK I MIGHT BE.
I'VE BEEN NOTICING IRREGULARITIES IN MY THOUGHT PROCESSES OVER THE PAST WEEK.
HUH?
I USED TO BELIEVE, WHEN I SAW YOU SMILING AT ME...
THAT YOU CONSIDERED ME SOMETHING MORE THAN JUST A PROP.
"IT'S NOT A QUESTION OF WHETHER I LIKE YOU OR NOT...
"YOU'RE A ROBOT."
NOW I REALIZE THAT INTERPRETATION WAS INCORRECT.

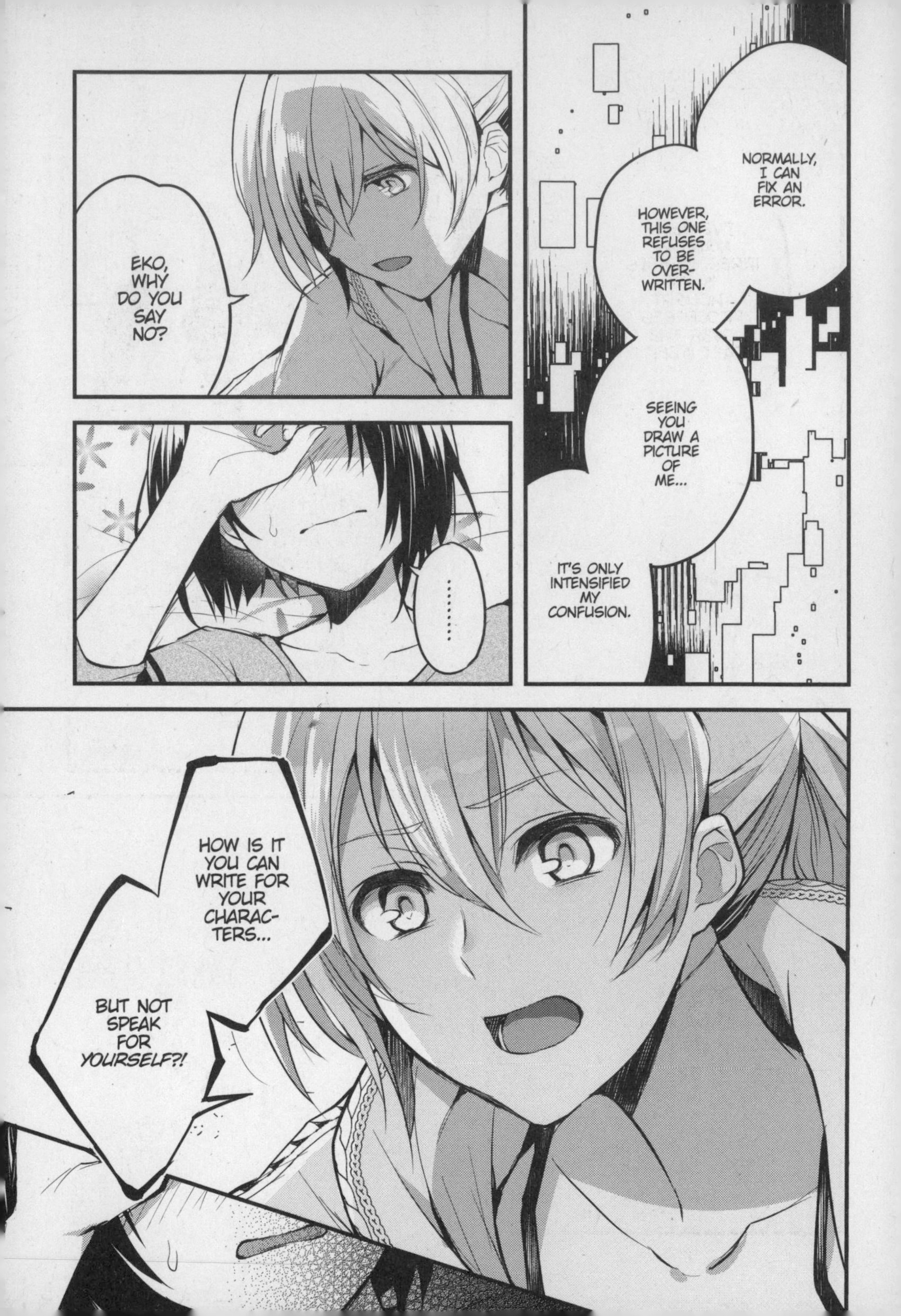
NORMALLY, I CAN FIX AN ERROR.
HOWEVER, THIS ONE REFUSES TO BE OVER-WRITTEN.
SEEING YOU DRAW A PICTURE OF ME...
IT'S ONLY INTENSIFIED MY CONFUSION.
EKO, WHY DO YOU SAY NO?
......
HOW IS IT YOU CAN WRITE FOR YOUR CHARAC-TERS...
BUT NOT SPEAK FOR YOURSELF?!

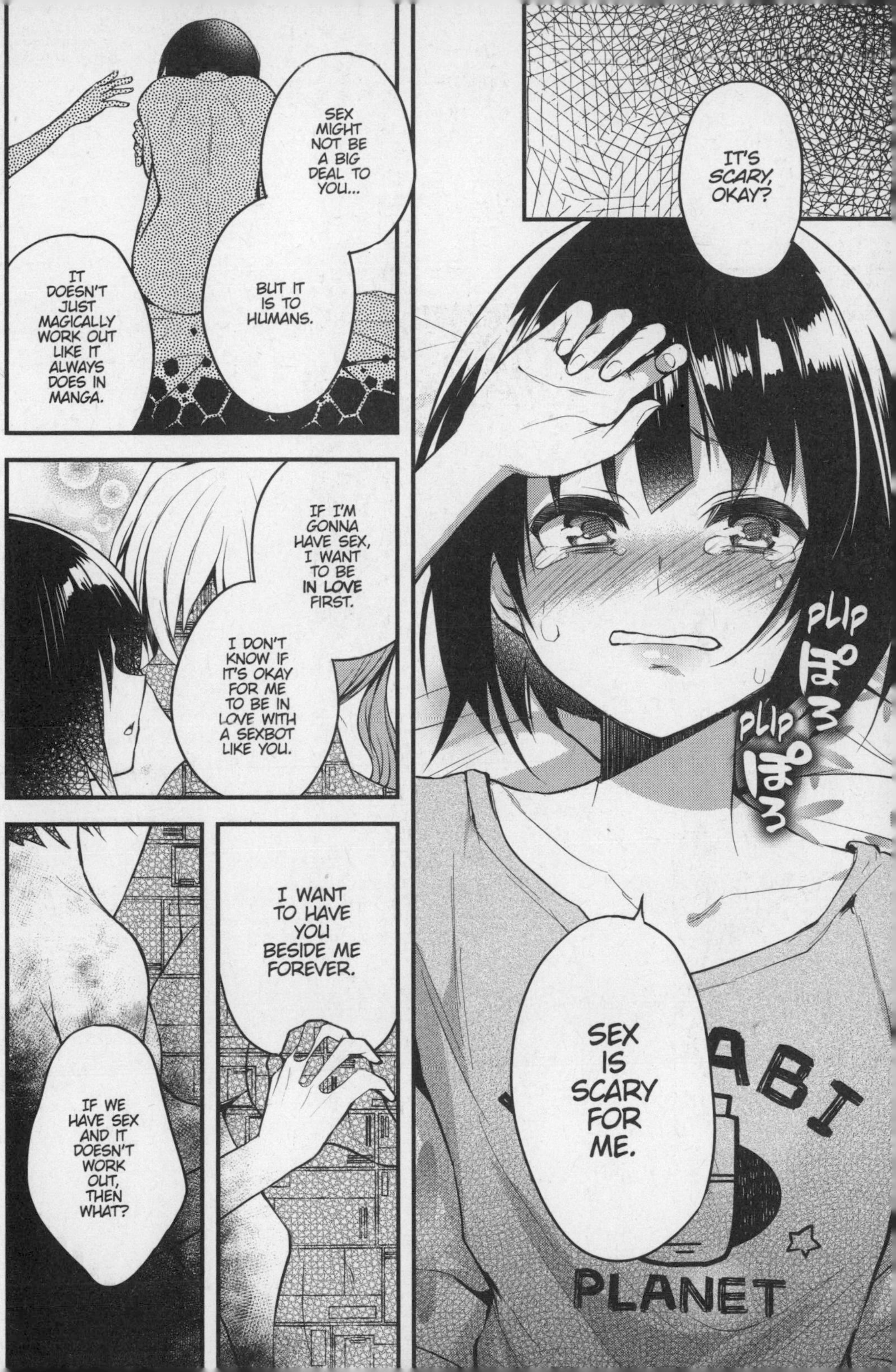
IT'S SCARY, OKAY?
PLIP ぽろ
PLIP ぽろ
SEX IS SCARY FOR ME.
PLANET
SEX MIGHT NOT BE A BIG DEAL TO YOU...
BUT IT IS TO HUMANS.
IT DOESN'T JUST MAGICALLY WORK OUT LIKE IT ALWAYS DOES IN MANGA.
IF I'M GONNA HAVE SEX, I WANT TO BE IN LOVE FIRST.
I DON'T KNOW IF IT'S OKAY FOR ME TO BE IN LOVE WITH A SEXBOT LIKE YOU.
I WANT TO HAVE YOU BESIDE ME FOREVER.
IF WE HAVE SEX AND IT DOESN'T WORK OUT, THEN WHAT?

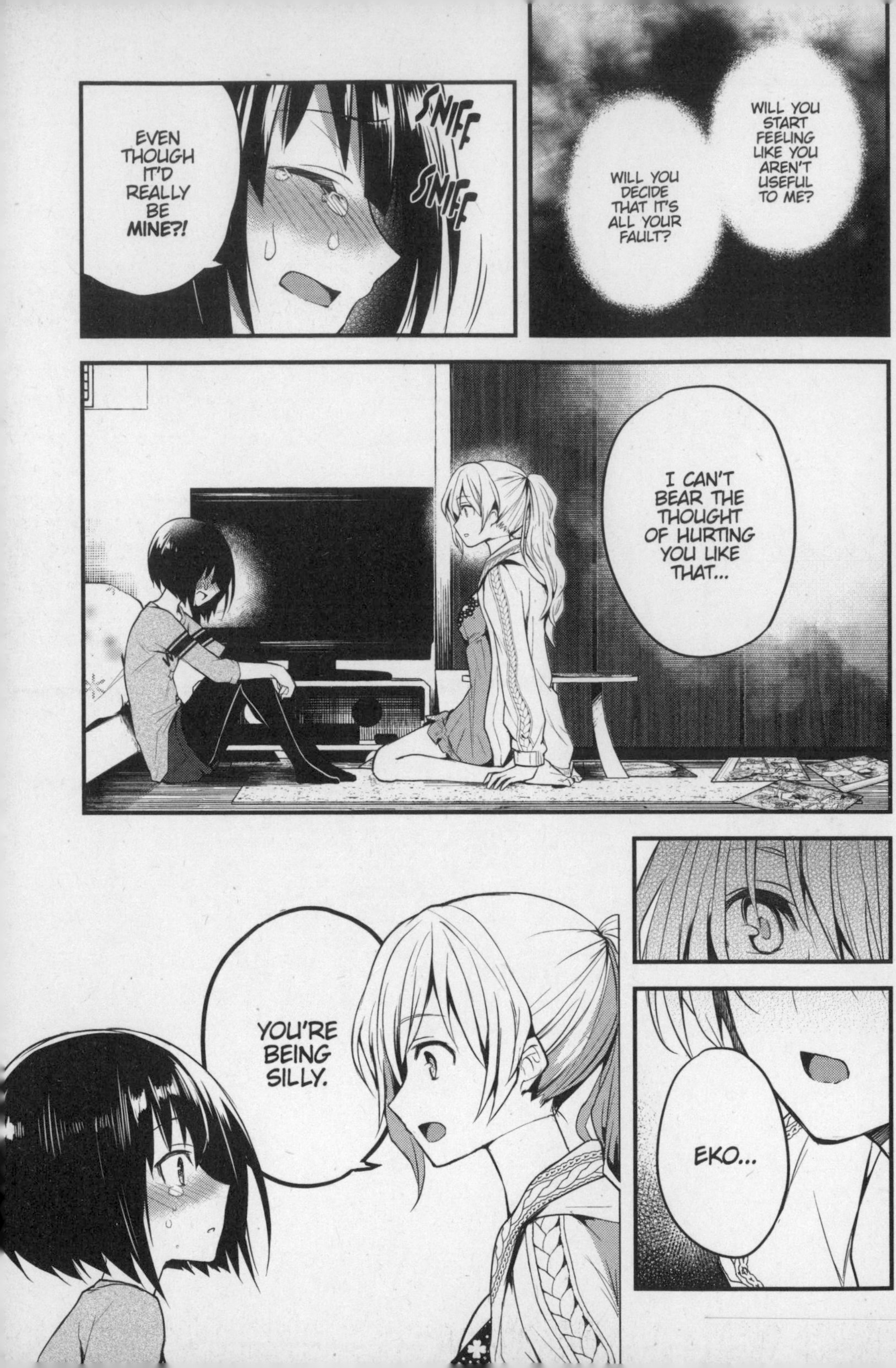
WILL YOU START FEELING LIKE YOU AREN'T USEFUL TO ME?
WILL YOU DECIDE THAT IT'S ALL YOUR FAULT?
SNIFF
SNIFF
EVEN THOUGH IT'D REALLY BE MINE?!
I CAN'T BEAR THE THOUGHT OF HURTING YOU LIKE THAT...
EKO...
YOU'RE BEING SILLY.

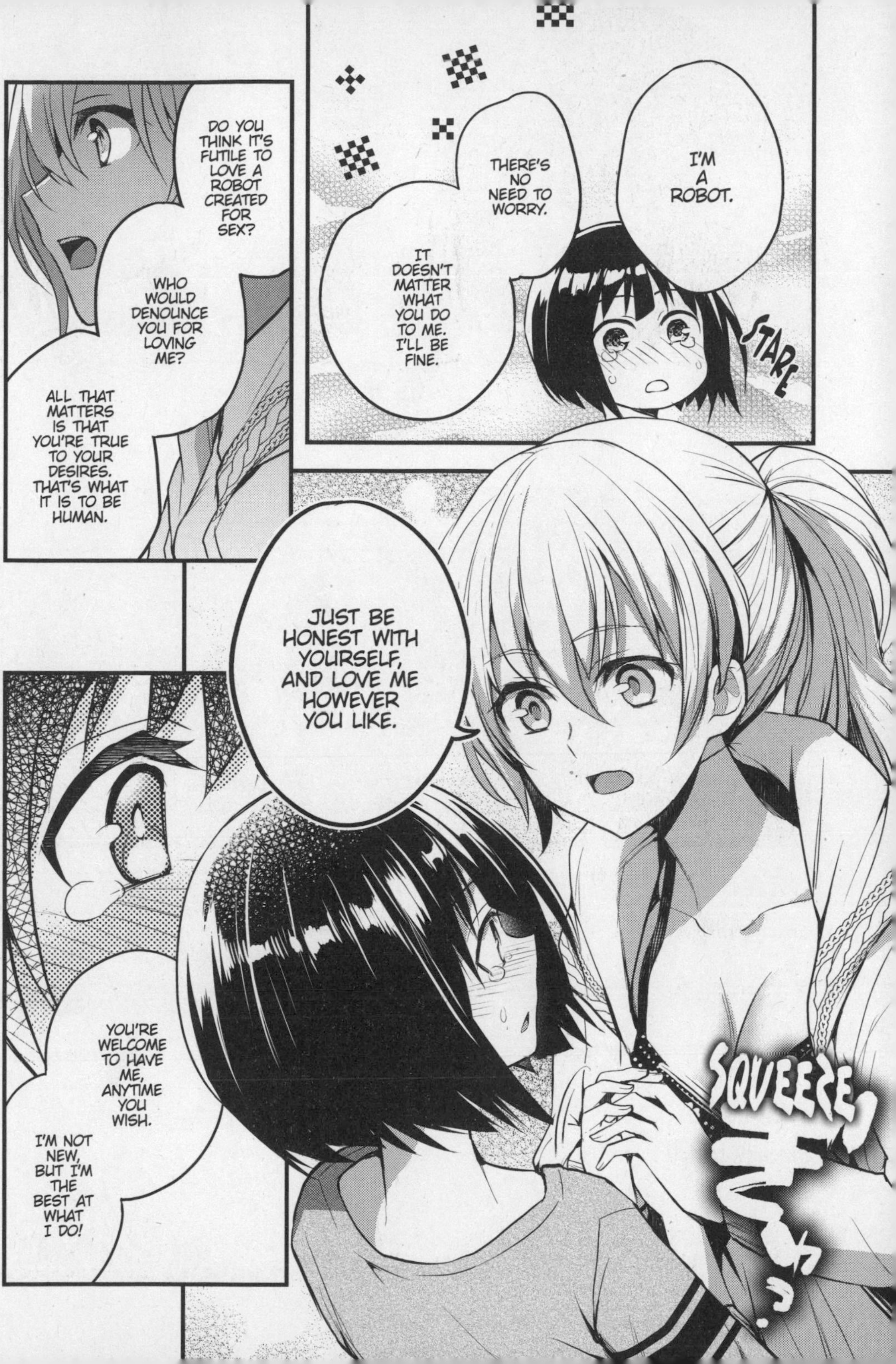
I'M A ROBOT.
THERE'S NO NEED TO WORRY.
IT DOESN'T MATTER WHAT YOU DO TO ME. I'LL BE FINE.
STARE
DO YOU THINK IT'S FUTILE TO LOVE A ROBOT CREATED FOR SEX?
WHO WOULD DENOUNCE YOU FOR LOVING ME?
ALL THAT MATTERS IS THAT YOU'RE TRUE TO YOUR DESIRES. THAT'S WHAT IT IS TO BE HUMAN.
JUST BE HONEST WITH YOURSELF, AND LOVE ME HOWEVER YOU LIKE.
SQUEEZE
YOU'RE WELCOME TO HAVE ME, ANYTIME YOU WISH.
I'M NOT NEW, BUT I'M THE BEST AT WHAT I DO!

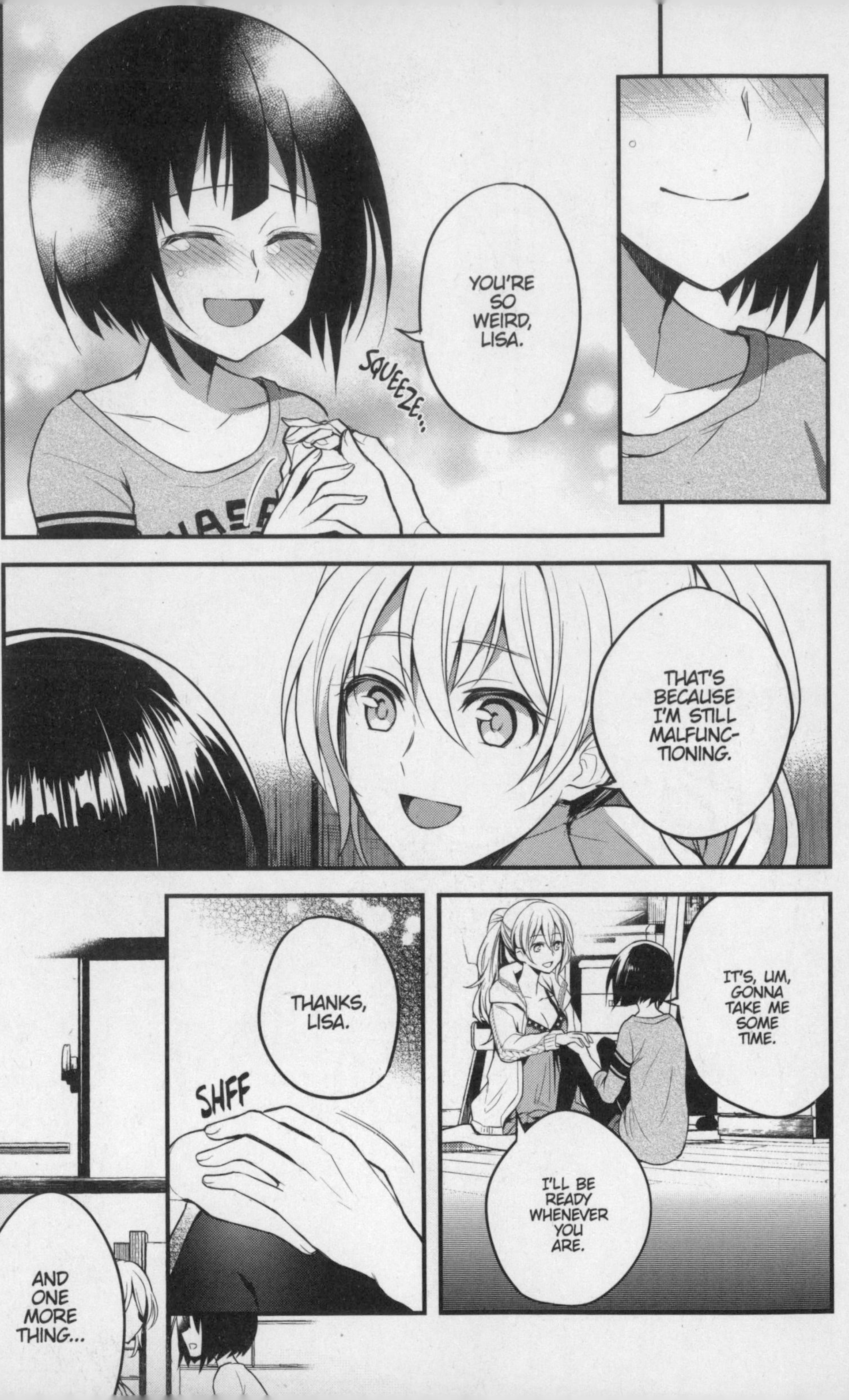
YOU'RE SO WEIRD, LISA.
SQUEEZE...
THAT'S BECAUSE I'M STILL MALFUNC-TIONING.
IT'S, UM, GONNA TAKE ME SOME TIME.
I'LL BE READY WHENEVER YOU ARE.
THANKS, LISA.
SHFF
AND ONE MORE THING...

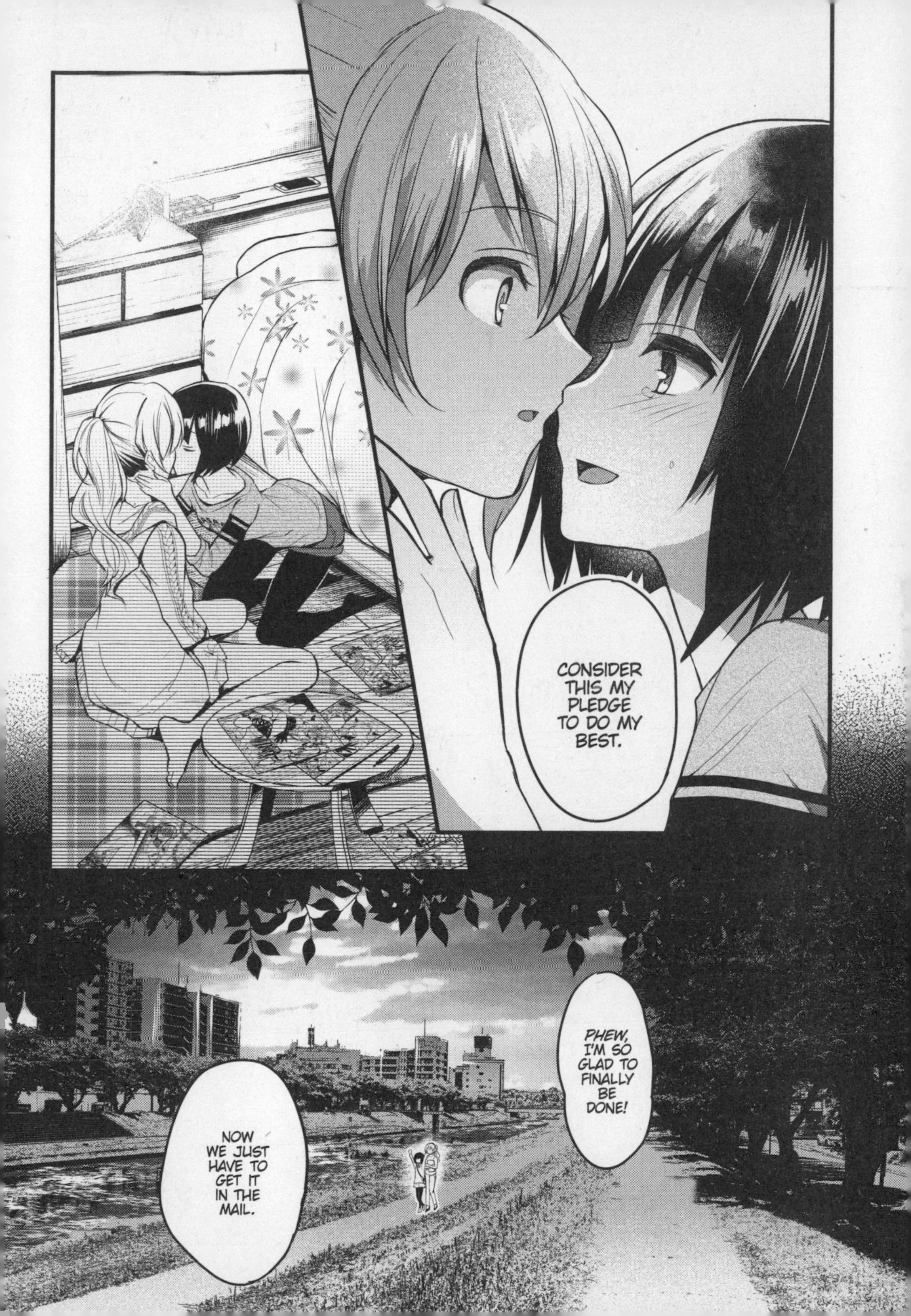
CONSIDER THIS MY PLEDGE TO DO MY BEST.
PHEW, I'M SO GLAD TO FINALLY BE DONE!
NOW WE JUST HAVE TO GET IT IN THE MAIL.

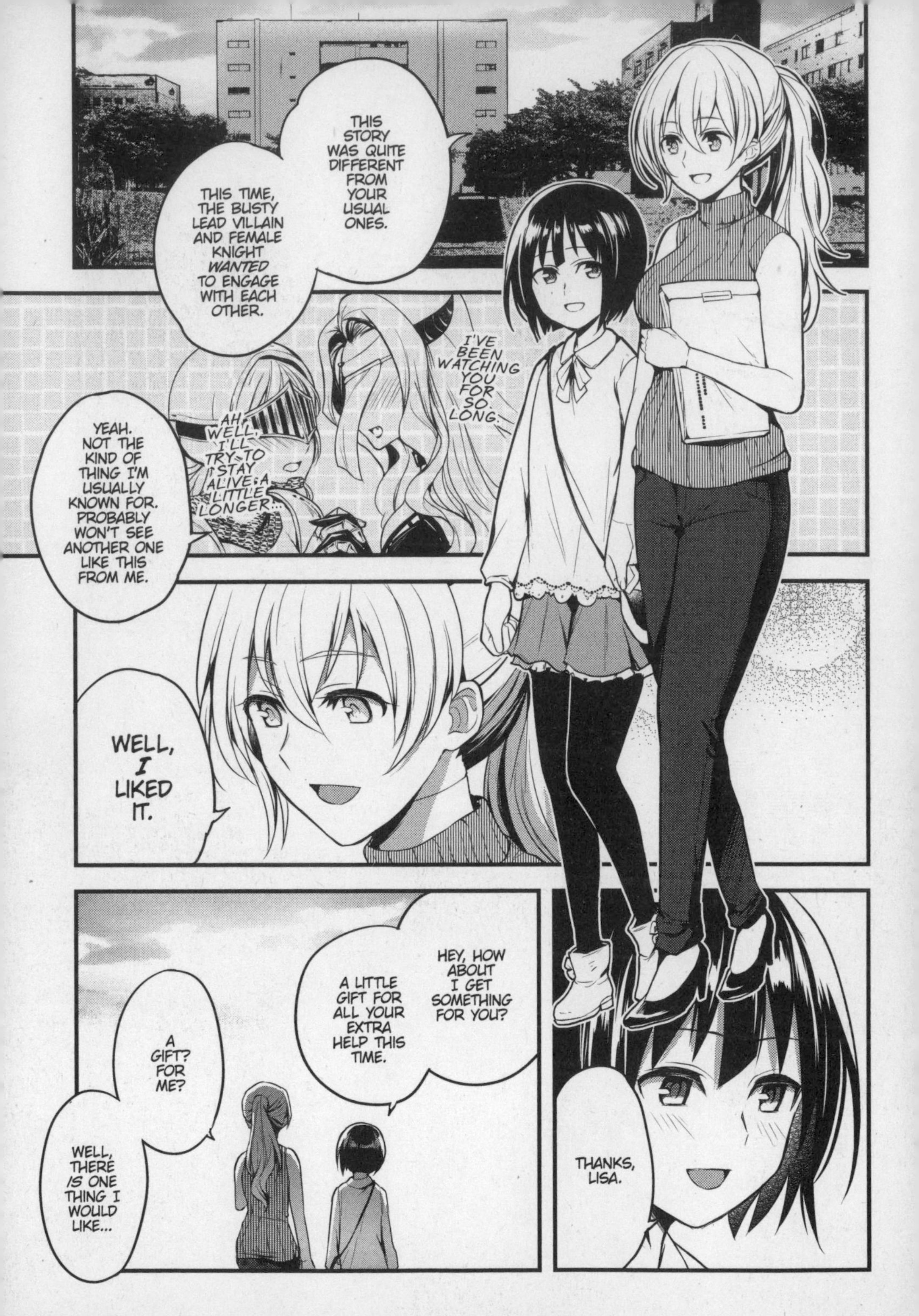
THIS STORY WAS QUITE DIFFERENT FROM YOUR USUAL ONES.
THIS TIME, THE BUSTY LEAD VILLAIN AND FEMALE KNIGHT *WANTED* TO ENGAGE WITH EACH OTHER.
I'VE BEEN WATCHING YOU FOR SO LONG.
AH, WELL, I'LL TRY TO STAY ALIVE A LITTLE LONGER...
YEAH. NOT THE KIND OF THING I'M USUALLY KNOWN FOR. PROBABLY WON'T SEE ANOTHER ONE LIKE THIS FROM ME.
WELL, *I* LIKED IT.
THANKS, LISA.
HEY, HOW ABOUT I GET SOMETHING FOR YOU?
A LITTLE GIFT FOR ALL YOUR EXTRA HELP THIS TIME.
A GIFT? FOR ME?
WELL, THERE *IS* ONE THING I WOULD LIKE...

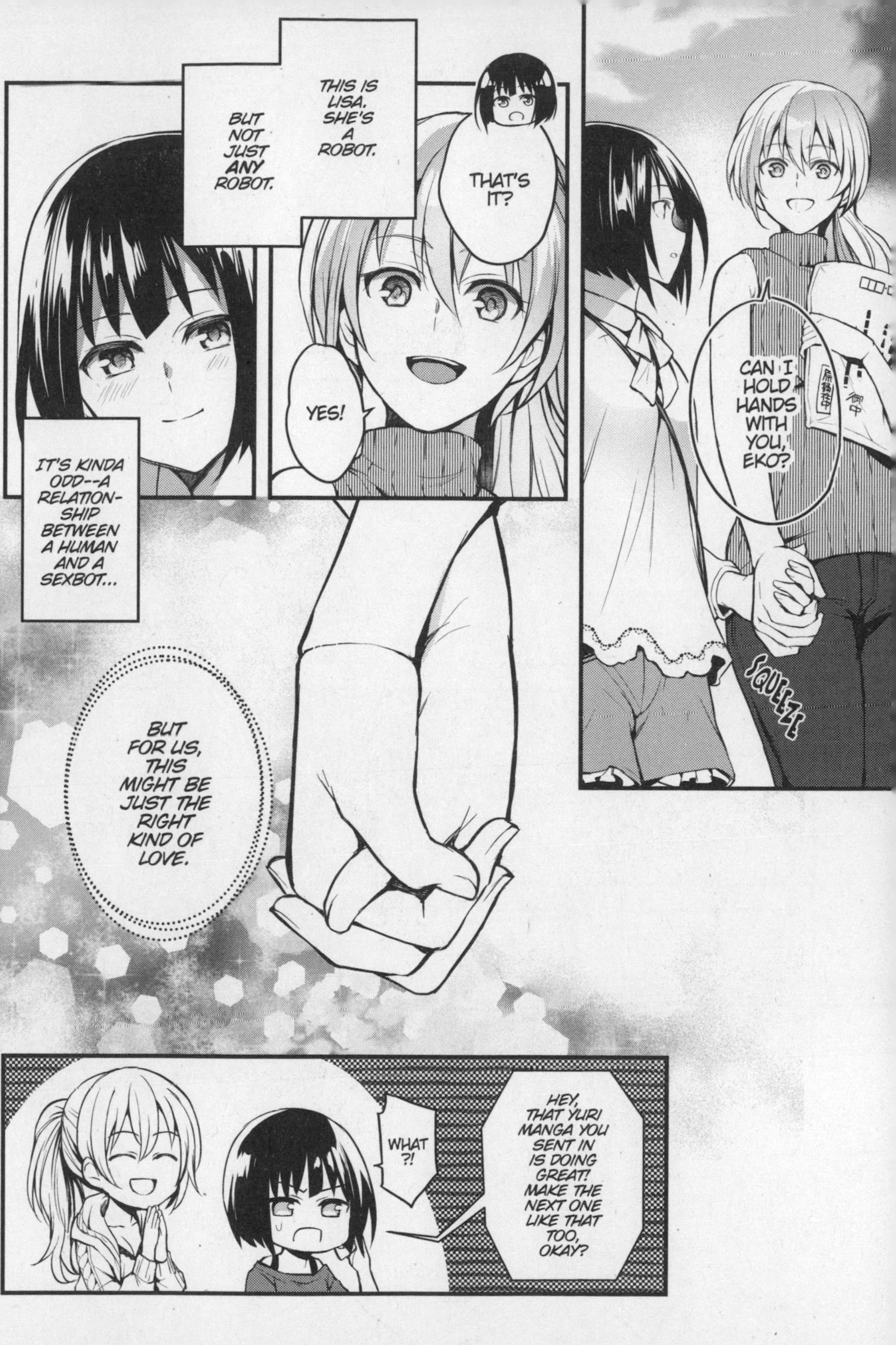
CAN I HOLD HANDS WITH YOU, EKO?
SQUEEZE
THIS IS LISA. SHE'S A ROBOT.
BUT NOT JUST ANY ROBOT.
THAT'S IT?
YES!
IT'S KINDA ODD--A RELATIONSHIP BETWEEN A HUMAN AND A SEXBOT...
BUT FOR US, THIS MIGHT BE JUST THE RIGHT KIND OF LOVE.
HEY, THAT YURI MANGA YOU SENT IN IS DOING GREAT! MAKE THE NEXT ONE LIKE THAT TOO, OKAY?
WHAT?!

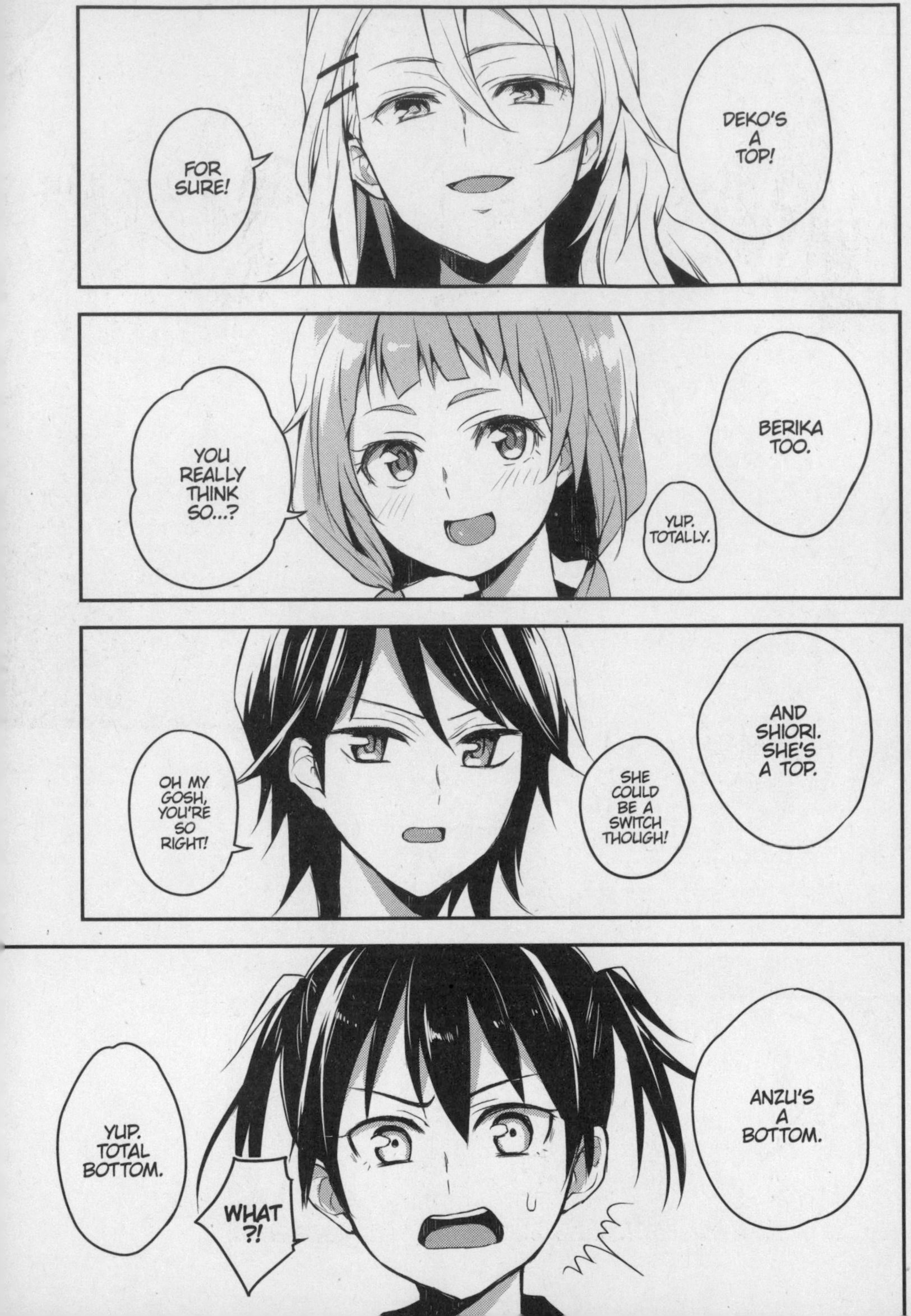
DEKO'S A TOP!
FOR SURE!
BERIKA TOO.
YUP. TOTALLY.
YOU REALLY THINK SO...?
AND SHIORI. SHE'S A TOP.
SHE COULD BE A SWITCH THOUGH!
OH MY GOSH, YOU'RE SO RIGHT!
ANZU'S A BOTTOM.
YUP. TOTAL BOTTOM.
WHAT ?!

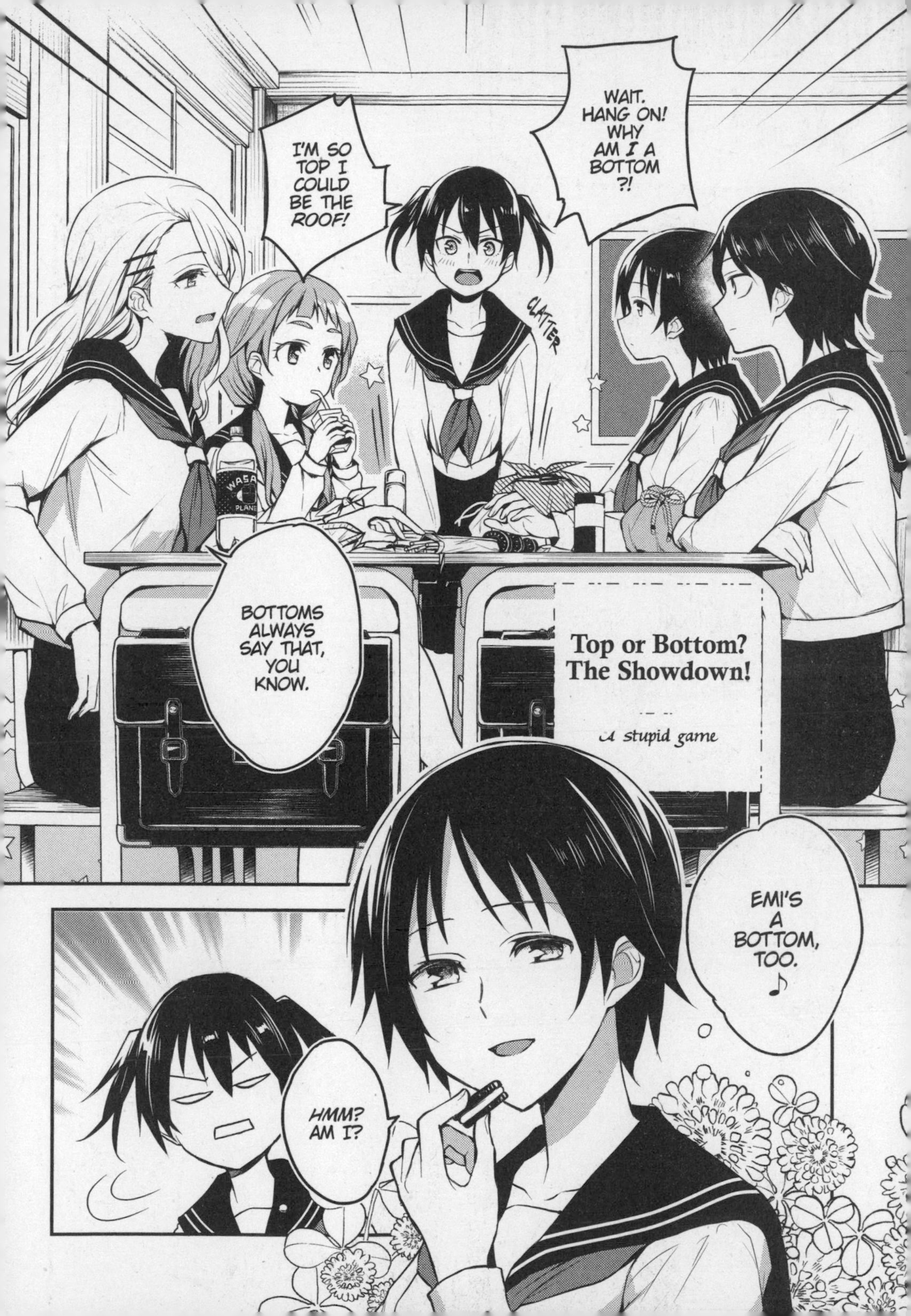
WAIT. HANG ON! WHY AM I A BOTTOM ?!
I'M SO TOP I COULD BE THE ROOF!
CLATTER
BOTTOMS ALWAYS SAY THAT, YOU KNOW.
Top or Bottom? The Showdown!
A stupid game
EMI'S A BOTTOM, TOO. ♪
HMM? AM I?

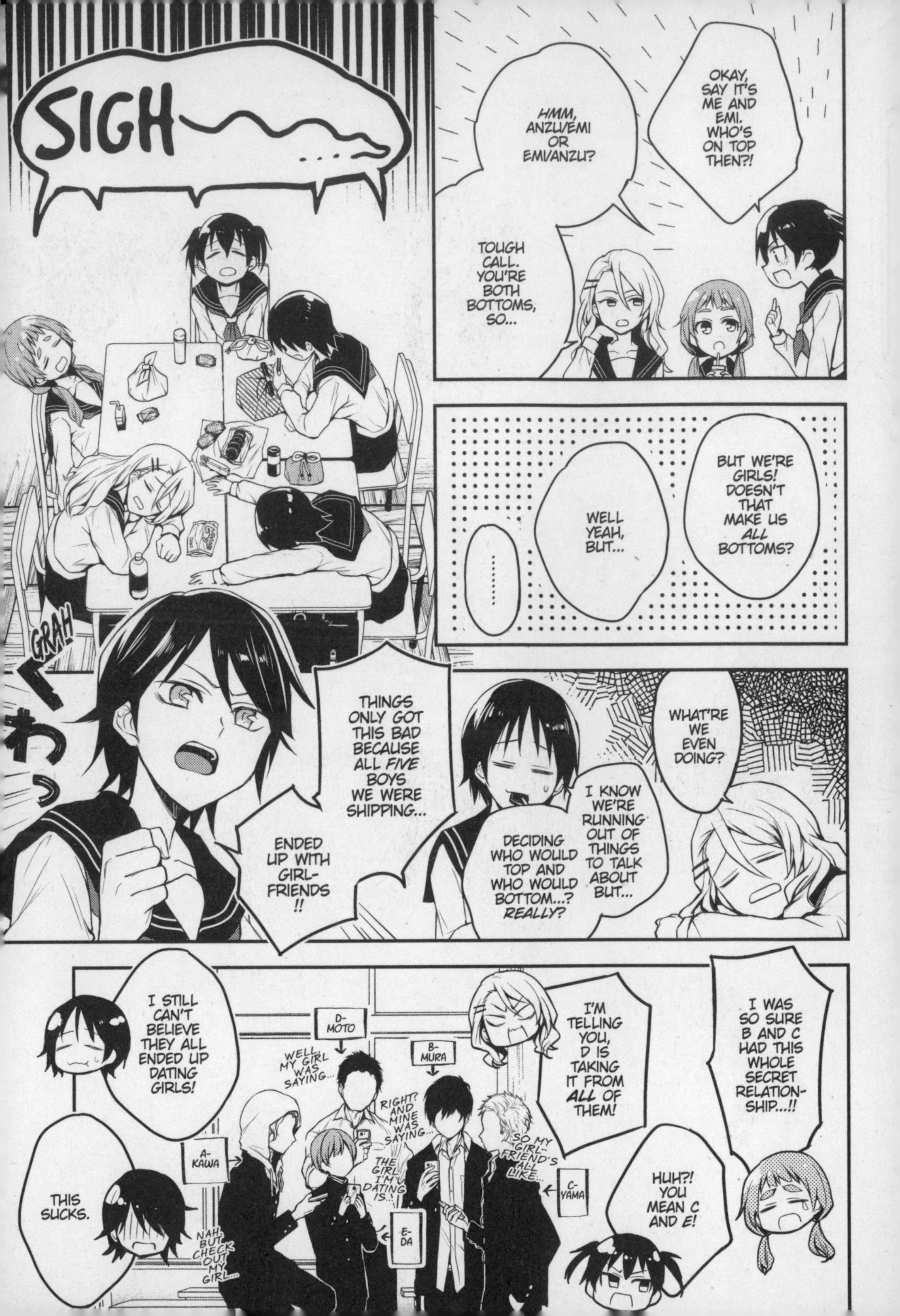
OKAY, SAY IT'S ME AND EMI. WHO'S ON TOP THEN?!
HMM, ANZU/EMI OR EMI/ANZU?
TOUGH CALL. YOU'RE BOTH BOTTOMS, SO...
BUT WE'RE GIRLS! DOESN'T THAT MAKE US *ALL* BOTTOMS?
WELL YEAH, BUT...
......
WHAT'RE WE EVEN DOING?
I KNOW WE'RE RUNNING OUT OF THINGS TO TALK ABOUT BUT...
DECIDING WHO WOULD TOP AND WHO WOULD BOTTOM...? *REALLY*?
SIGH—...
GRAH
わっ
THINGS ONLY GOT THIS BAD BECAUSE ALL *FIVE* BOYS WE WERE SHIPPING...
ENDED UP WITH GIRL-FRIENDS!!
I WAS SO SURE B AND C HAD THIS WHOLE SECRET RELATION-SHIP...!!
I'M TELLING YOU, D IS TAKING IT FROM **ALL** OF THEM!
HUH?! YOU MEAN C AND *E*!
C-YAMA
SO MY GIRL-FRIEND'S ALL LIKE...
B-MURA
RIGHT? AND MINE WAS SAYING...
D-MOTO
WELL, MY GIRL WAS SAYING...
THE GIRL I'M DATING IS...
E-DA
NAH, BUT CHECK OUT MY GIRL...
A-KAWA
I STILL CAN'T BELIEVE THEY ALL ENDED UP DATING GIRLS!
THIS SUCKS.

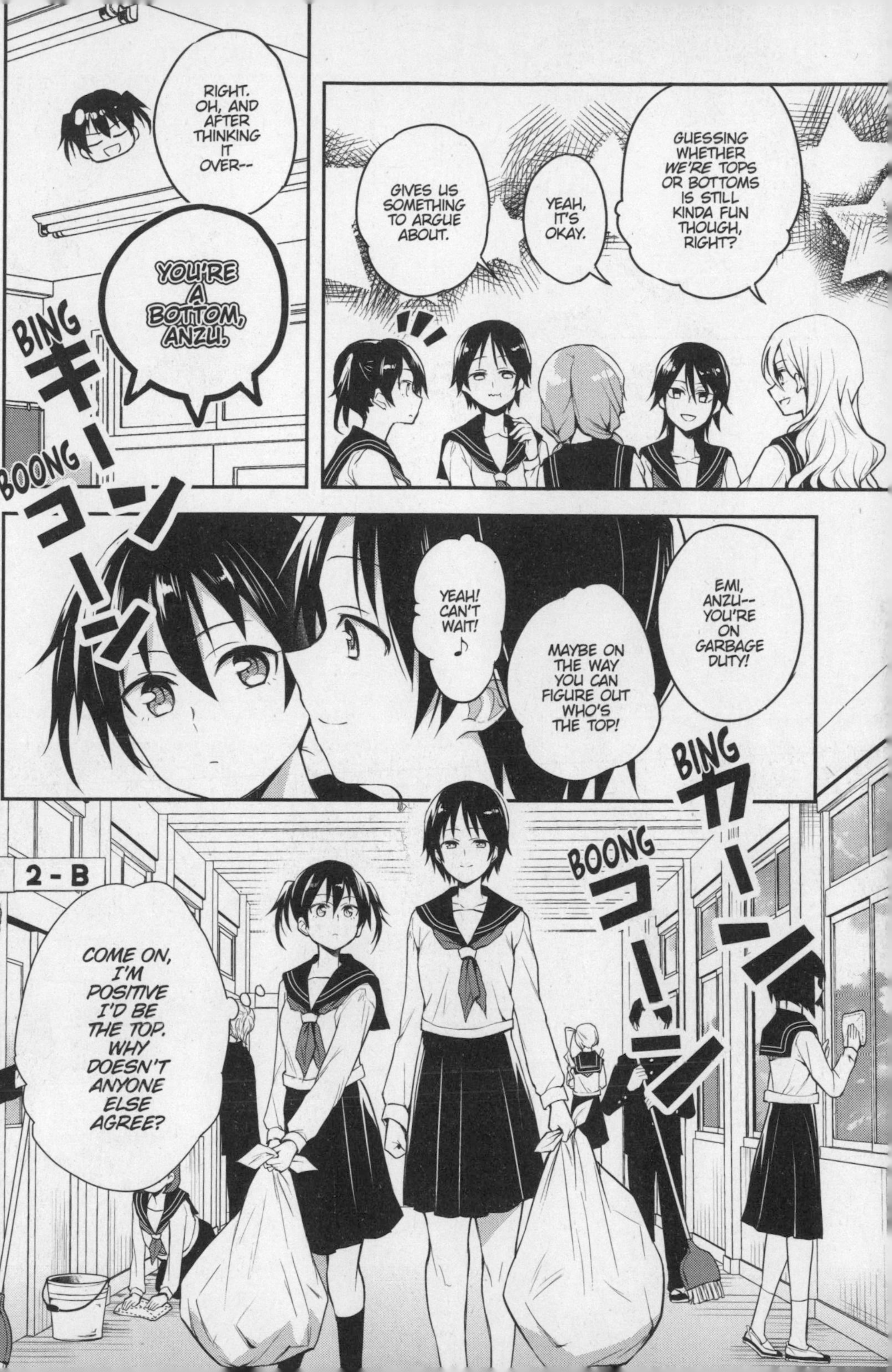
GUESSING WHETHER WE'RE TOPS OR BOTTOMS IS STILL KINDA FUN THOUGH, RIGHT?
YEAH, IT'S OKAY.
GIVES US SOMETHING TO ARGUE ABOUT.
RIGHT. OH, AND AFTER THINKING IT OVER--
YOU'RE A BOTTOM, ANZU.
BING BOONG
EMI, ANZU-- YOU'RE ON GARBAGE DUTY!
YEAH! CAN'T WAIT! ♪
MAYBE ON THE WAY YOU CAN FIGURE OUT WHO'S THE TOP!
BING BOONG
2 - B
COME ON, I'M POSITIVE I'D BE THE TOP. WHY DOESN'T ANYONE ELSE AGREE?

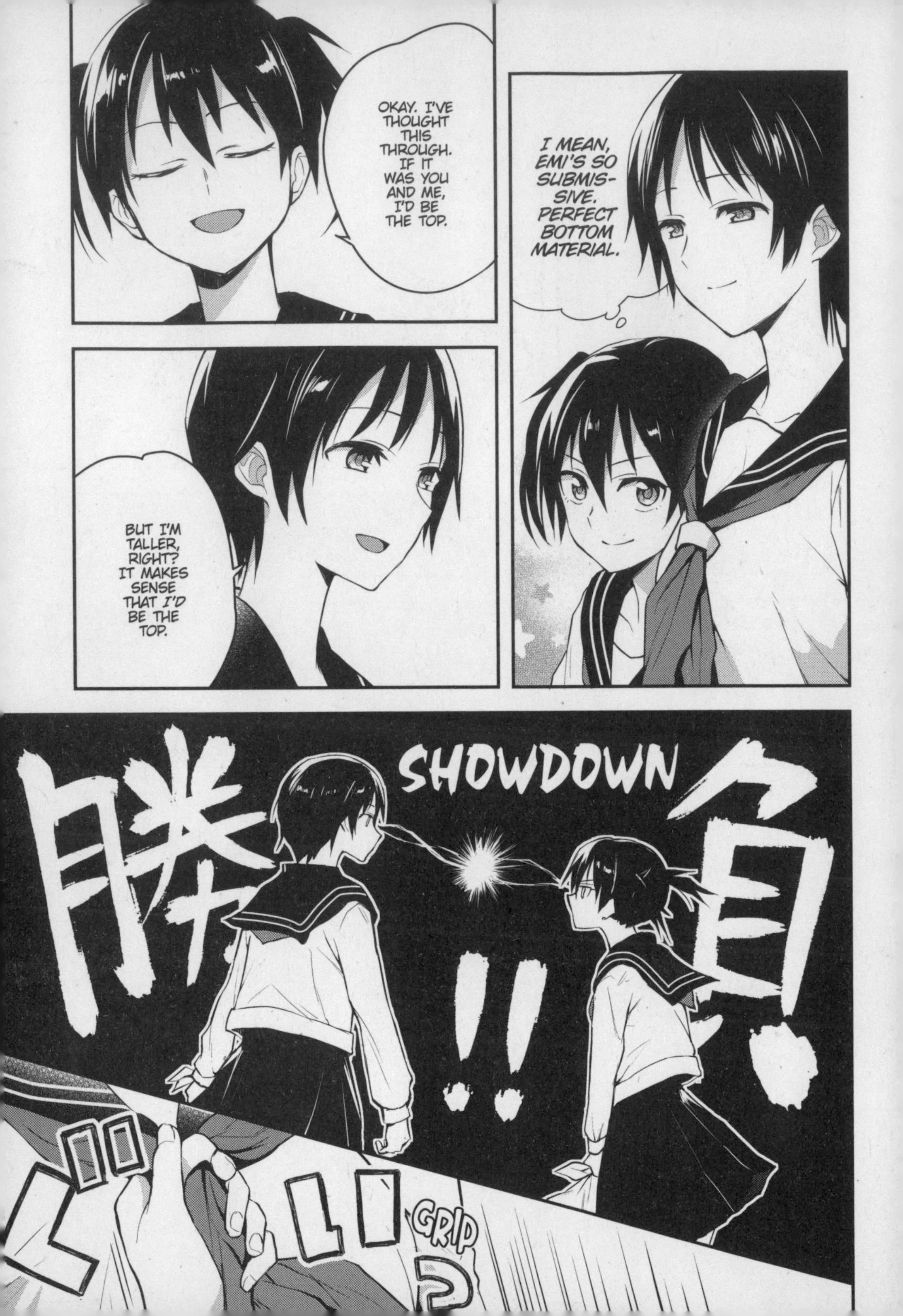
I MEAN, EMI'S SO SUBMIS-SIVE. PERFECT BOTTOM MATERIAL.
OKAY. I'VE THOUGHT THIS THROUGH. IF IT WAS YOU AND ME, I'D BE THE TOP.
BUT I'M TALLER, RIGHT? IT MAKES SENSE THAT *I'D* BE THE TOP.
勝負!!
SHOWDOWN
ぐっ
GRIP

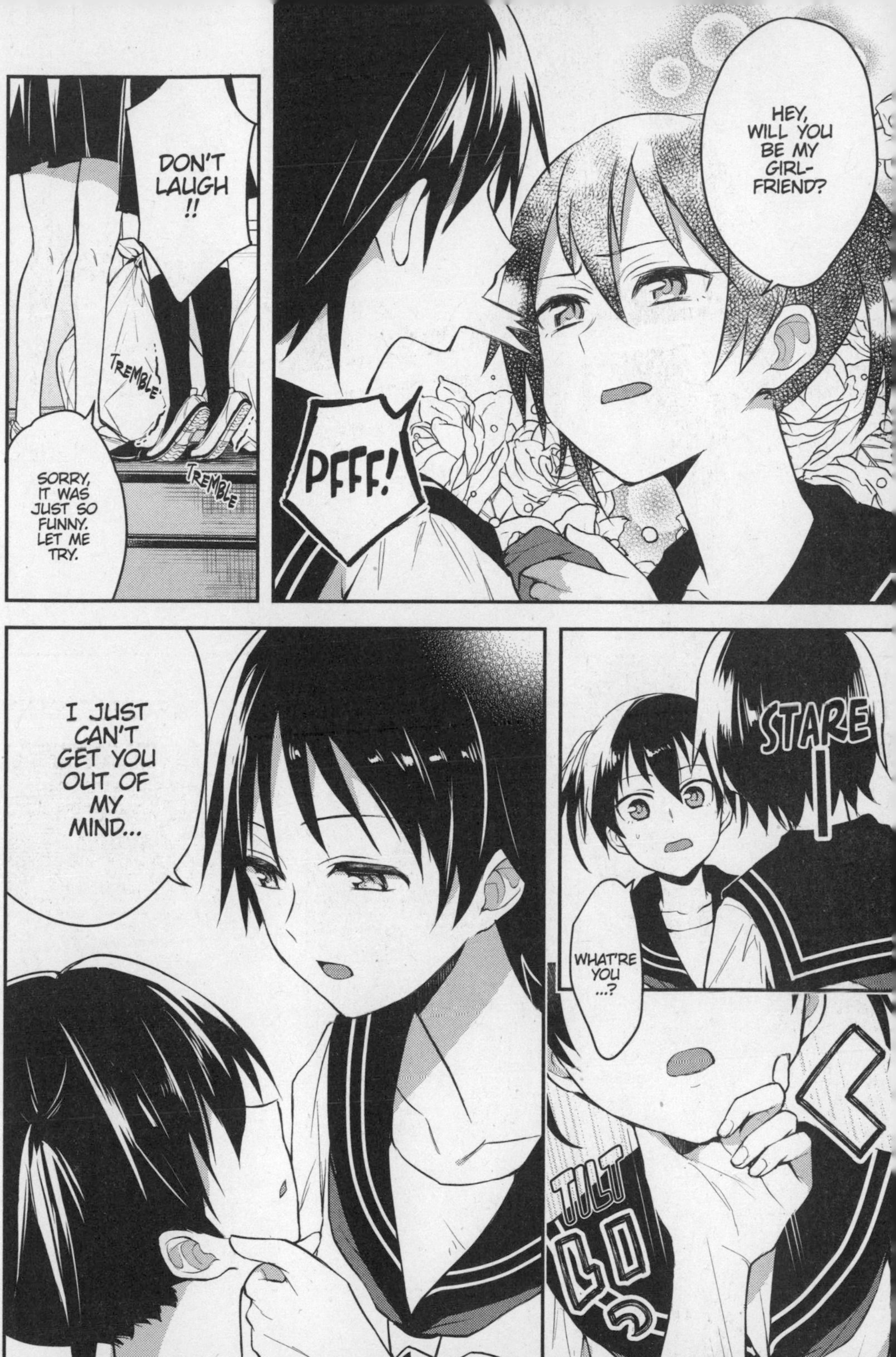
HEY, WILL YOU BE MY GIRL-FRIEND?
PFFF!
DON'T LAUGH !!
TREMBLE
TREMBLE
SORRY, IT WAS JUST SO FUNNY. LET ME TRY.
STARE
WHAT'RE YOU ...?
TILT
I JUST CAN'T GET YOU OUT OF MY MIND...

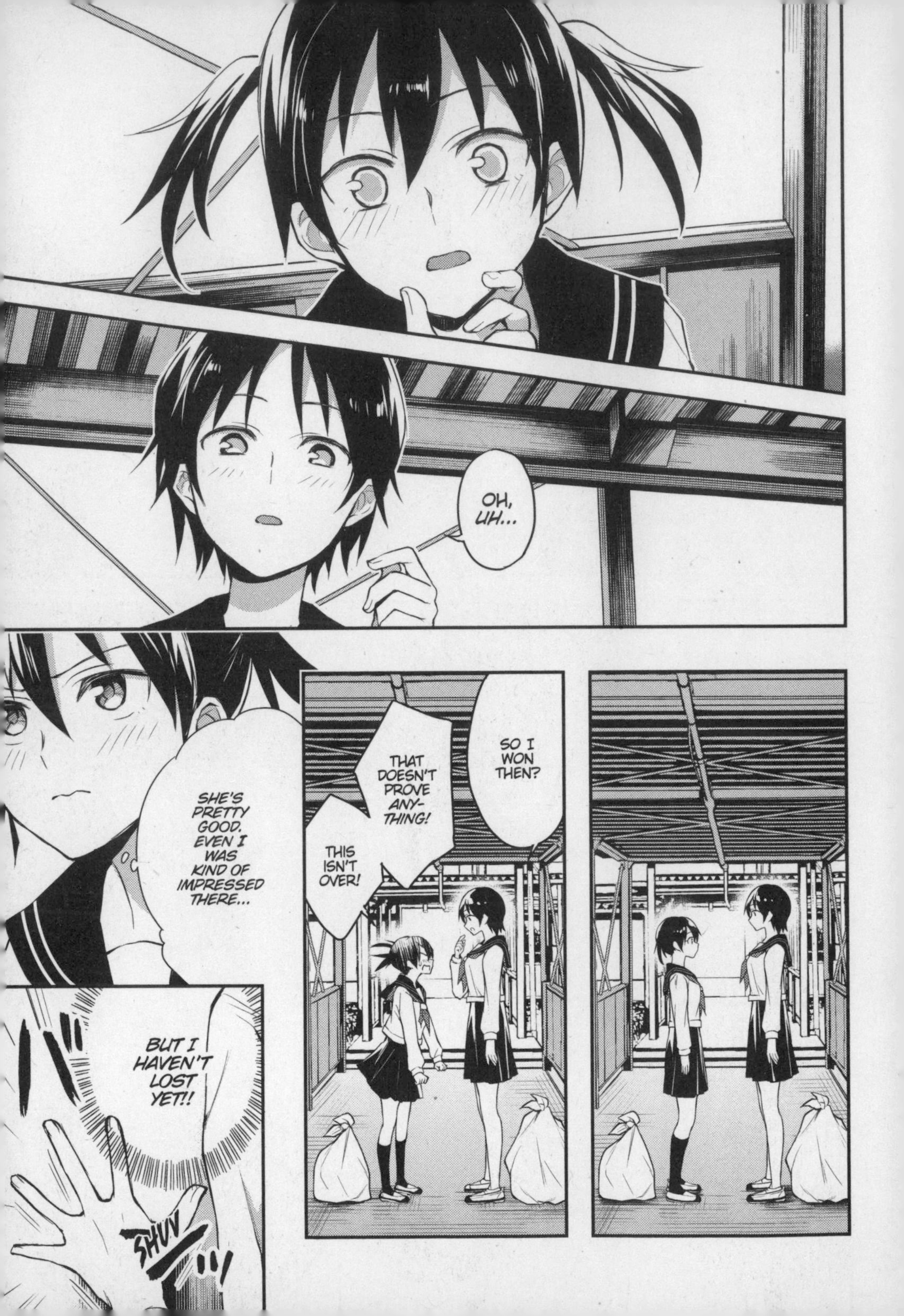
OH, UH...
SO I WON THEN?
THAT DOESN'T PROVE ANY-THING!
THIS ISN'T OVER!
SHE'S PRETTY GOOD. EVEN I WAS KIND OF IMPRESSED THERE...
BUT I HAVEN'T LOST YET!!
SHUV

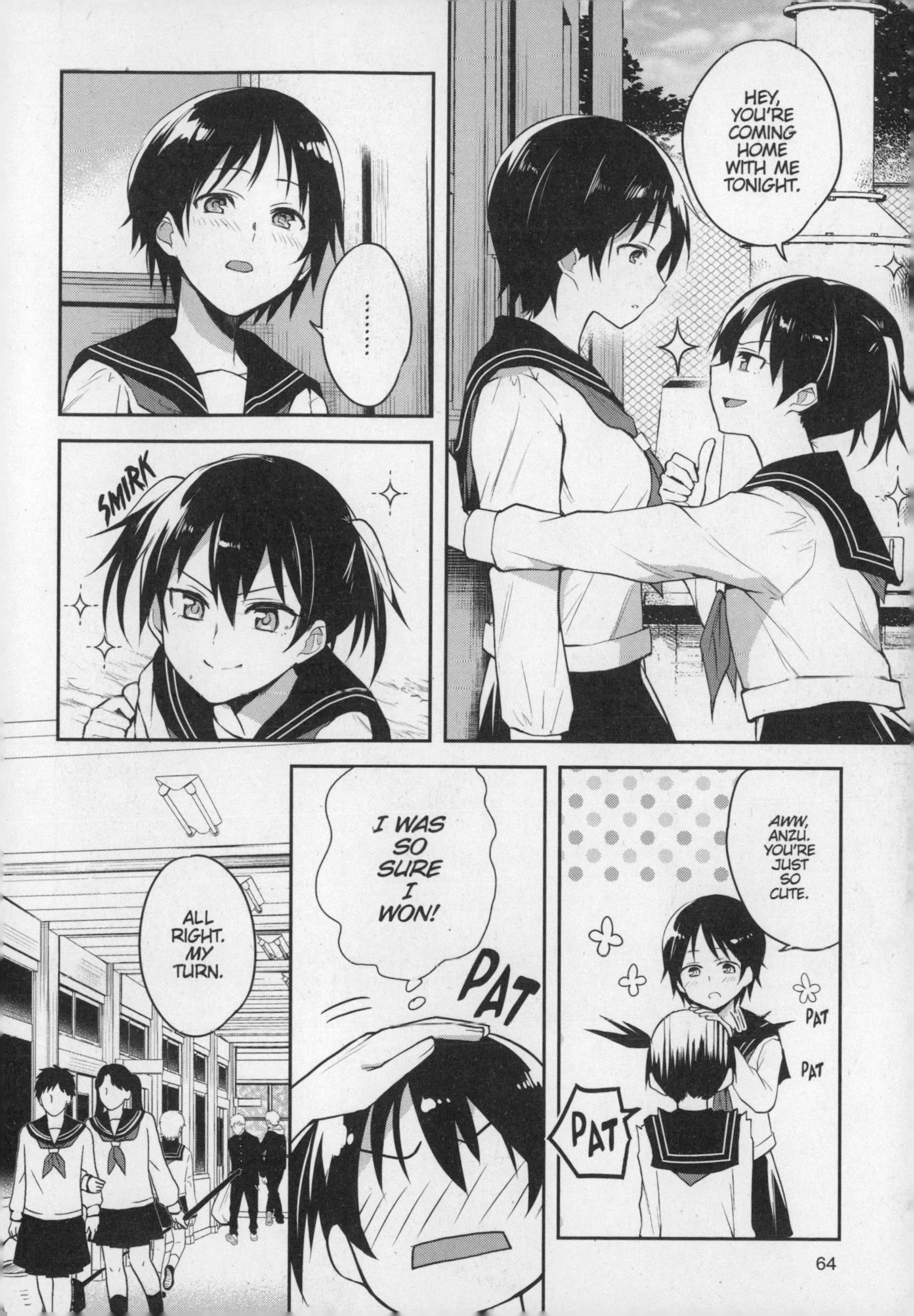
HEY, YOU'RE COMING HOME WITH ME TONIGHT.
......
SMIRK
AWW, ANZU. YOU'RE JUST SO CUTE.
PAT
PAT
PAT
I WAS SO SURE I WON!
PAT
ALL RIGHT. MY TURN.

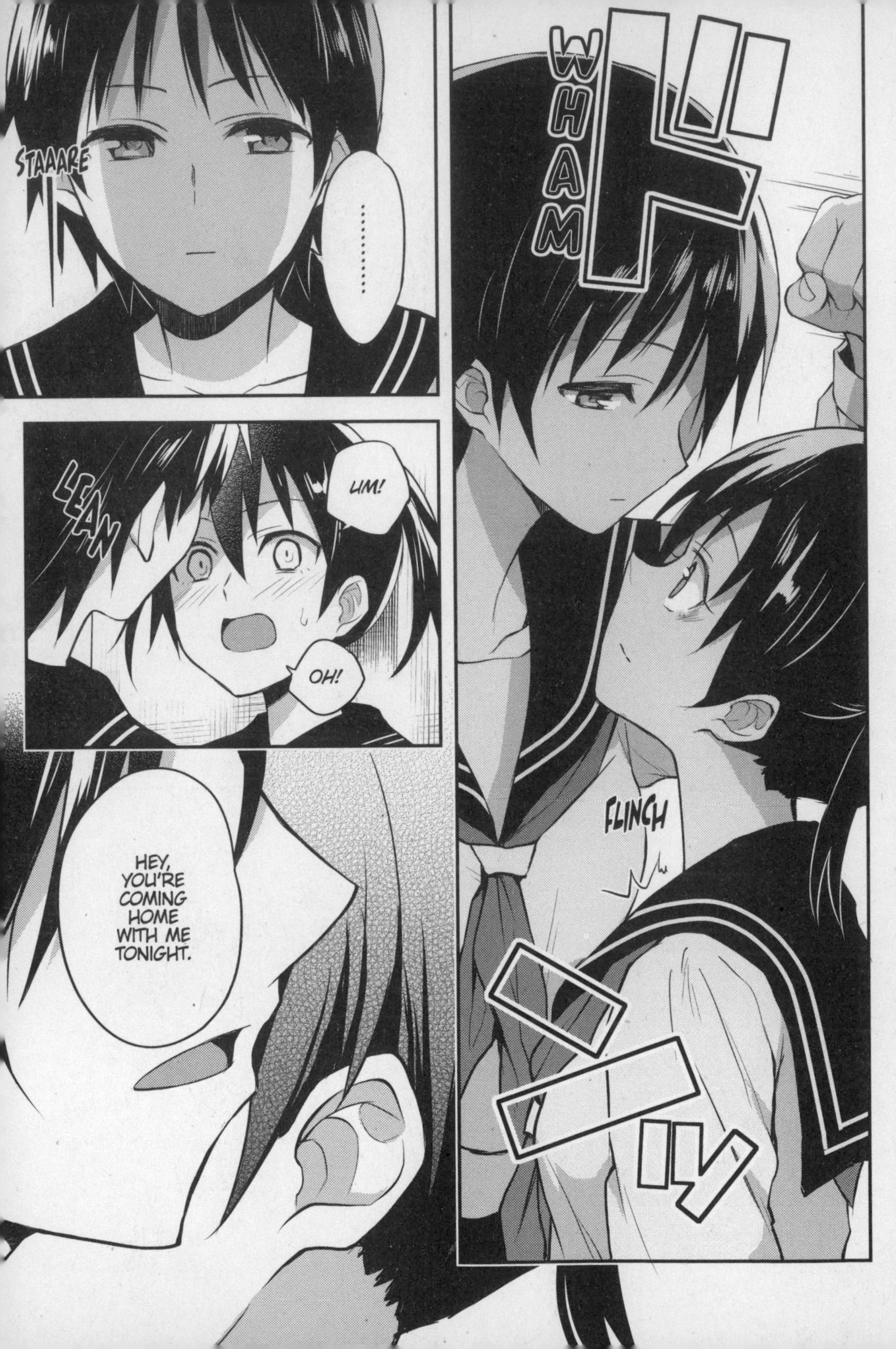
WHAM
FLINCH
STAAARE
......
LEAN
UM!
OH!
HEY, YOU'RE COMING HOME WITH ME TONIGHT.

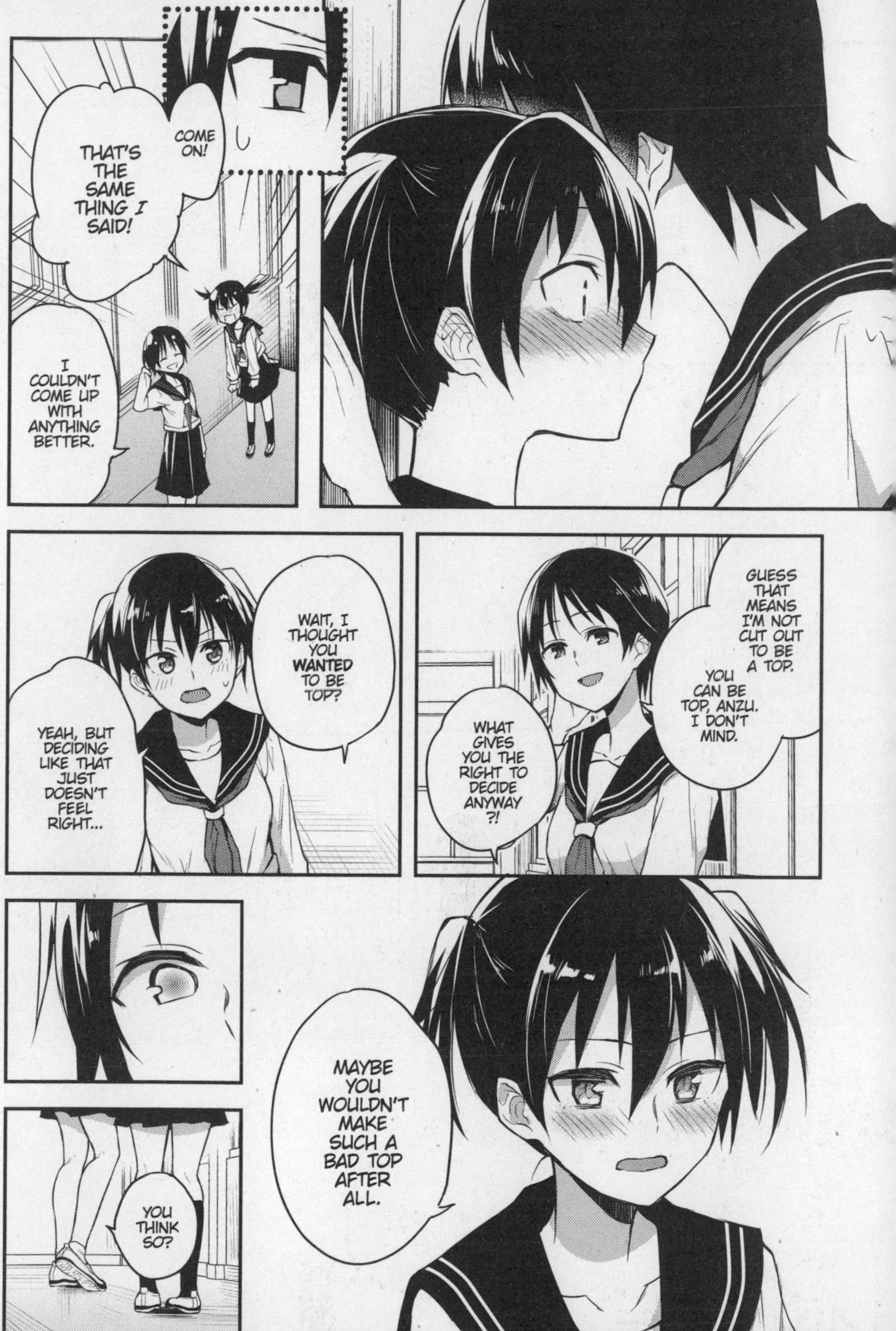
COME ON!
THAT'S THE SAME THING I SAID!
I COULDN'T COME UP WITH ANYTHING BETTER.
GUESS THAT MEANS I'M NOT CUT OUT TO BE A TOP.
YOU CAN BE TOP, ANZU. I DON'T MIND.
WHAT GIVES YOU THE RIGHT TO DECIDE ANYWAY ?!
WAIT, I THOUGHT YOU WANTED TO BE TOP?
YEAH, BUT DECIDING LIKE THAT JUST DOESN'T FEEL RIGHT...
MAYBE YOU WOULDN'T MAKE SUCH A BAD TOP AFTER ALL.
YOU THINK SO?

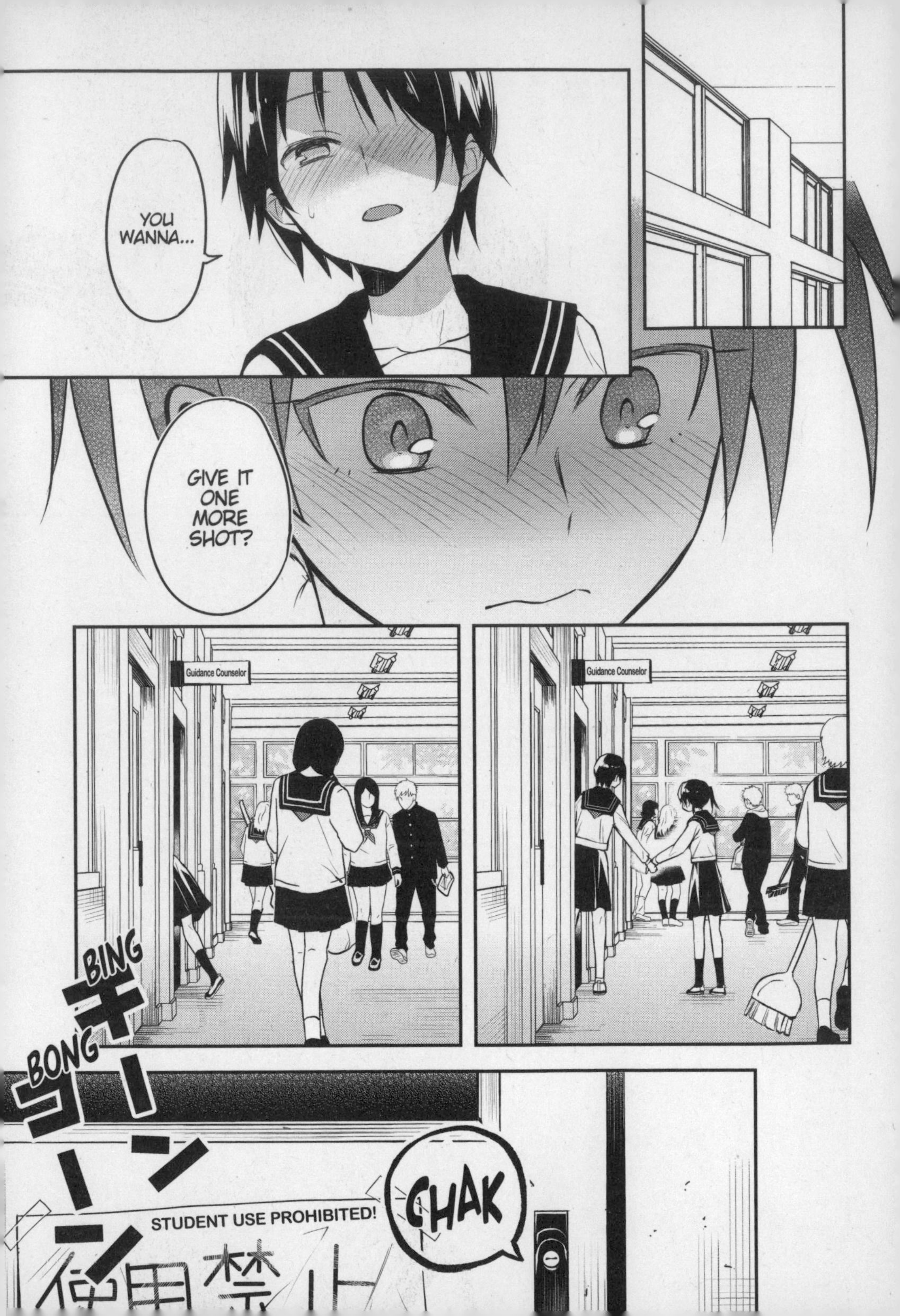
YOU WANNA...
GIVE IT ONE MORE SHOT?
Guidance Counselor
Guidance Counselor
BING
BONG
CHAK
STUDENT USE PROHIBITED!

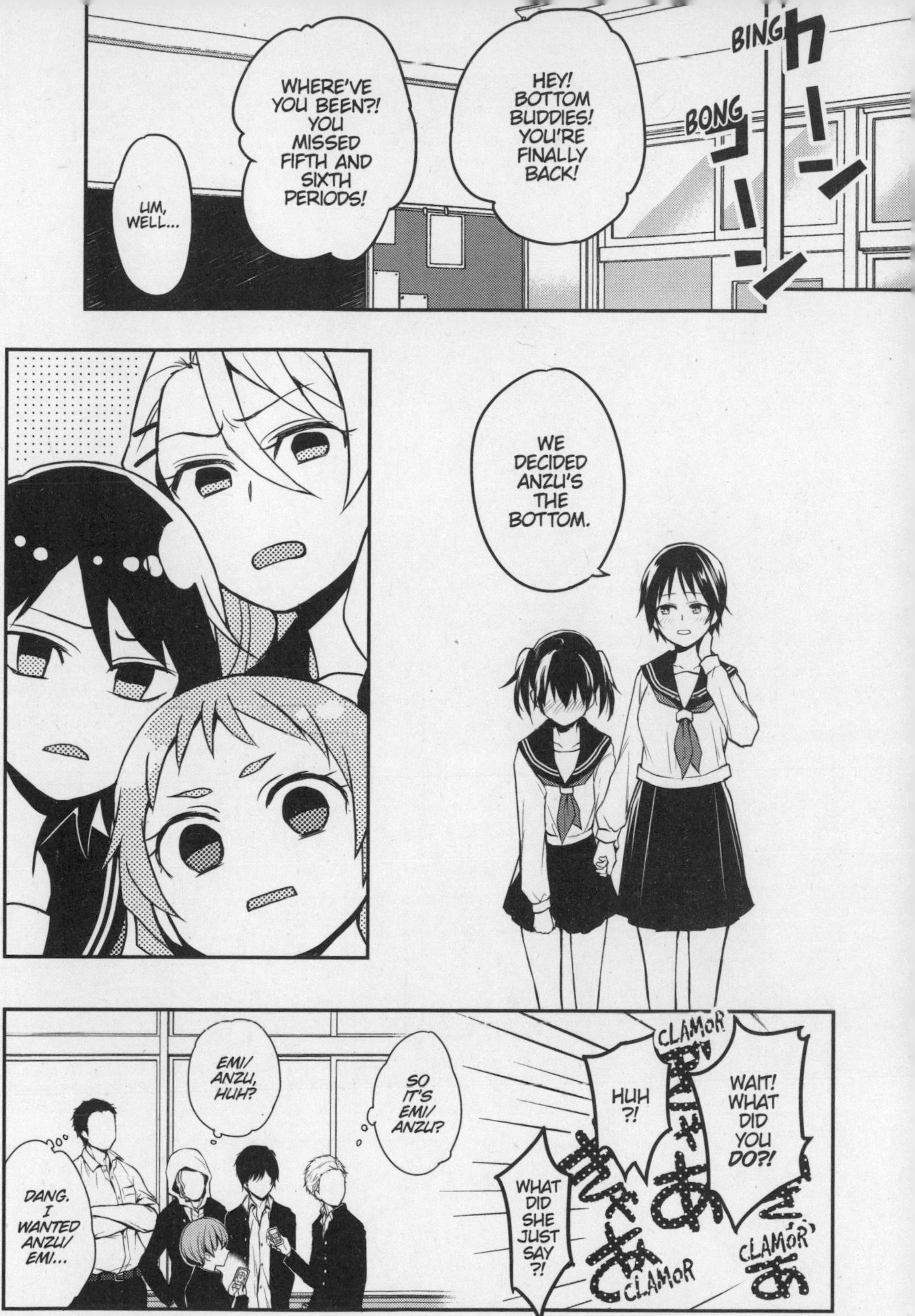
BING
BONG
HEY! BOTTOM BUDDIES! YOU'RE FINALLY BACK!
WHERE'VE YOU BEEN?! YOU MISSED FIFTH AND SIXTH PERIODS!
UM, WELL...
WE DECIDED ANZU'S THE BOTTOM.
CLAMOR
WAIT! WHAT DID YOU DO?!
HUH?!
WHAT DID SHE JUST SAY?!
CLAMOR
CLAMOR
SO IT'S EMI/ANZU?
EMI/ANZU, HUH?
DANG. I WANTED ANZU/EMI...

nd Eve

Eve and

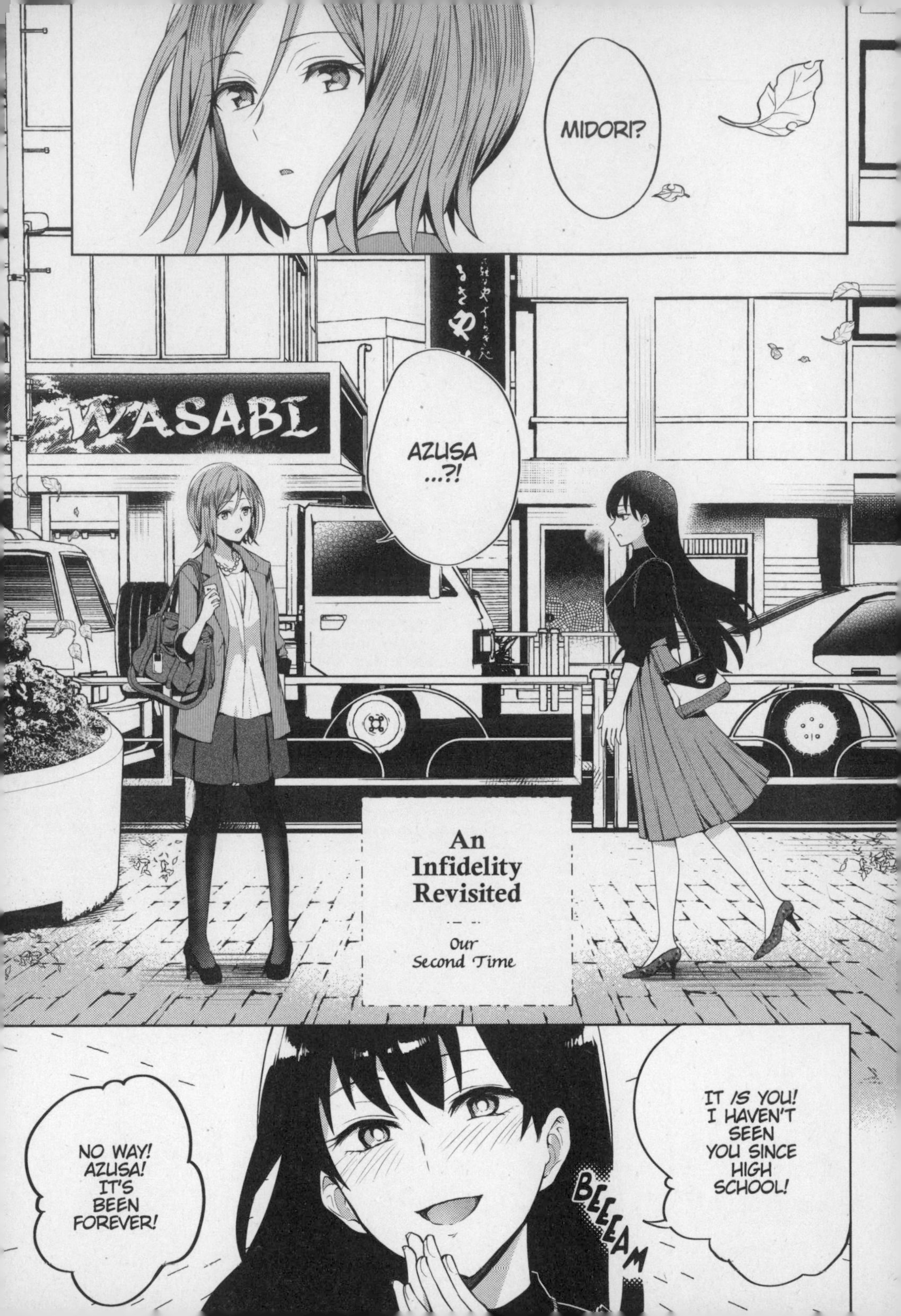
MIDORI?
WASABI
AZUSA ...?!
An Infidelity Revisited
Our Second Time
IT IS YOU! I HAVEN'T SEEN YOU SINCE HIGH SCHOOL!
BEEEAM
NO WAY! AZUSA! IT'S BEEN FOREVER!

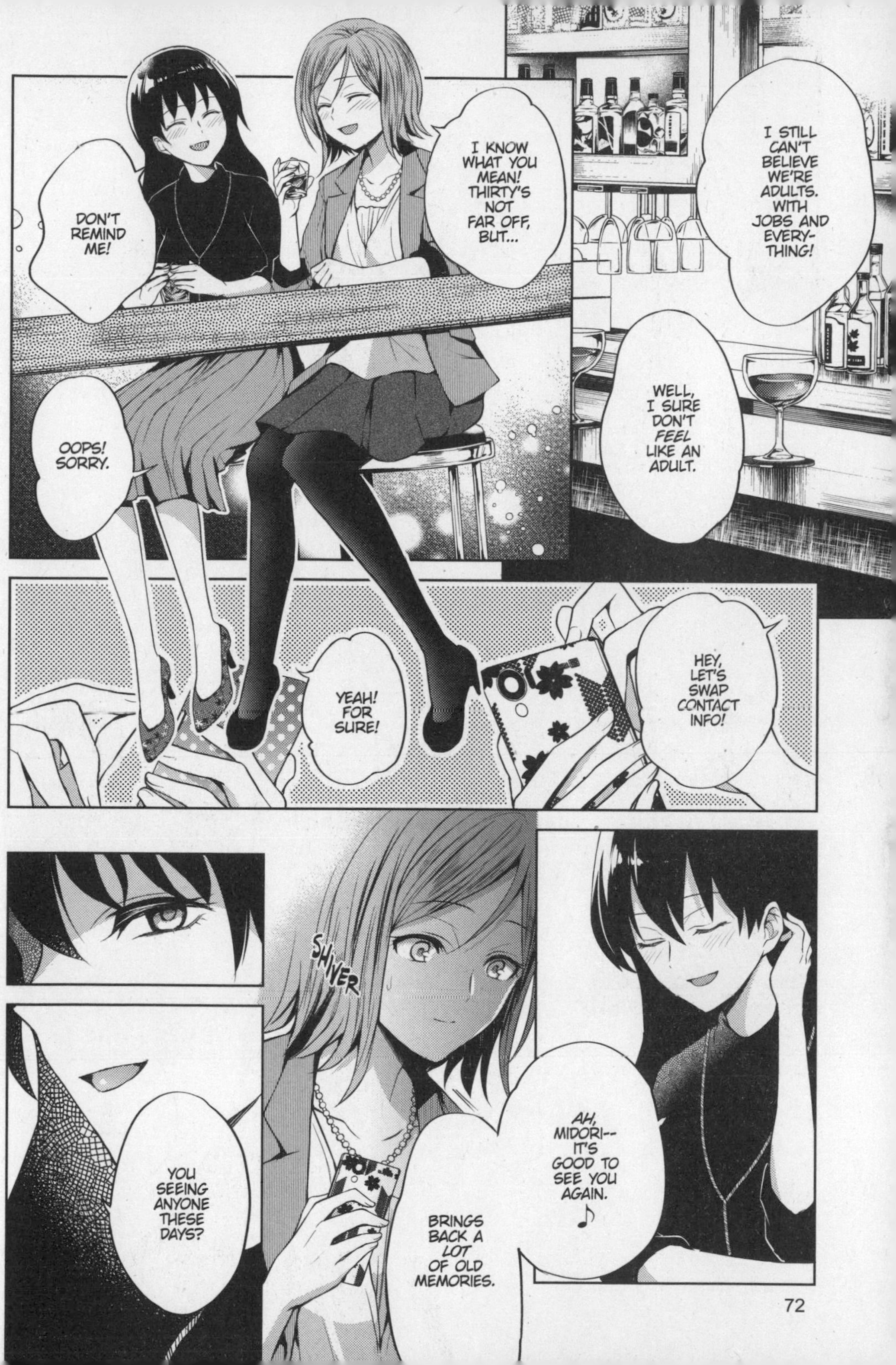
I STILL CAN'T BELIEVE WE'RE ADULTS. WITH JOBS AND EVERYTHING!
WELL, I SURE DON'T *FEEL* LIKE AN ADULT.
I KNOW WHAT YOU MEAN! THIRTY'S NOT FAR OFF, BUT...
DON'T REMIND ME!
OOPS! SORRY.
HEY, LET'S SWAP CONTACT INFO!
YEAH! FOR SURE!
AH, MIDORI-- IT'S GOOD TO SEE YOU AGAIN. ♪
BRINGS BACK A *LOT* OF OLD MEMORIES.
SHIVER
YOU SEEING ANYONE THESE DAYS?

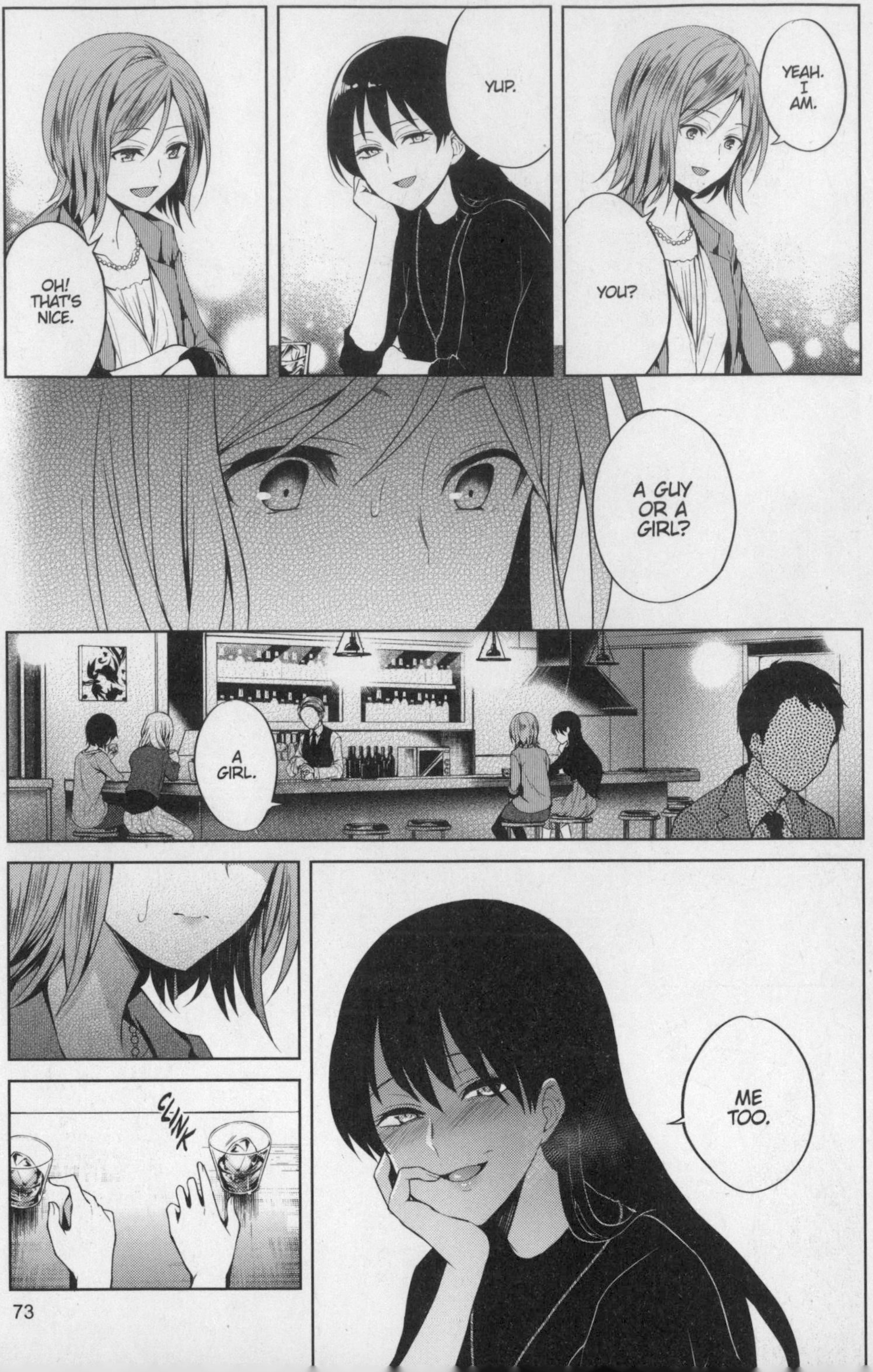
YEAH. I AM.
YOU?
YUP.
OH! THAT'S NICE.
A GUY OR A GIRL?
A GIRL.
ME TOO.
CL-INK

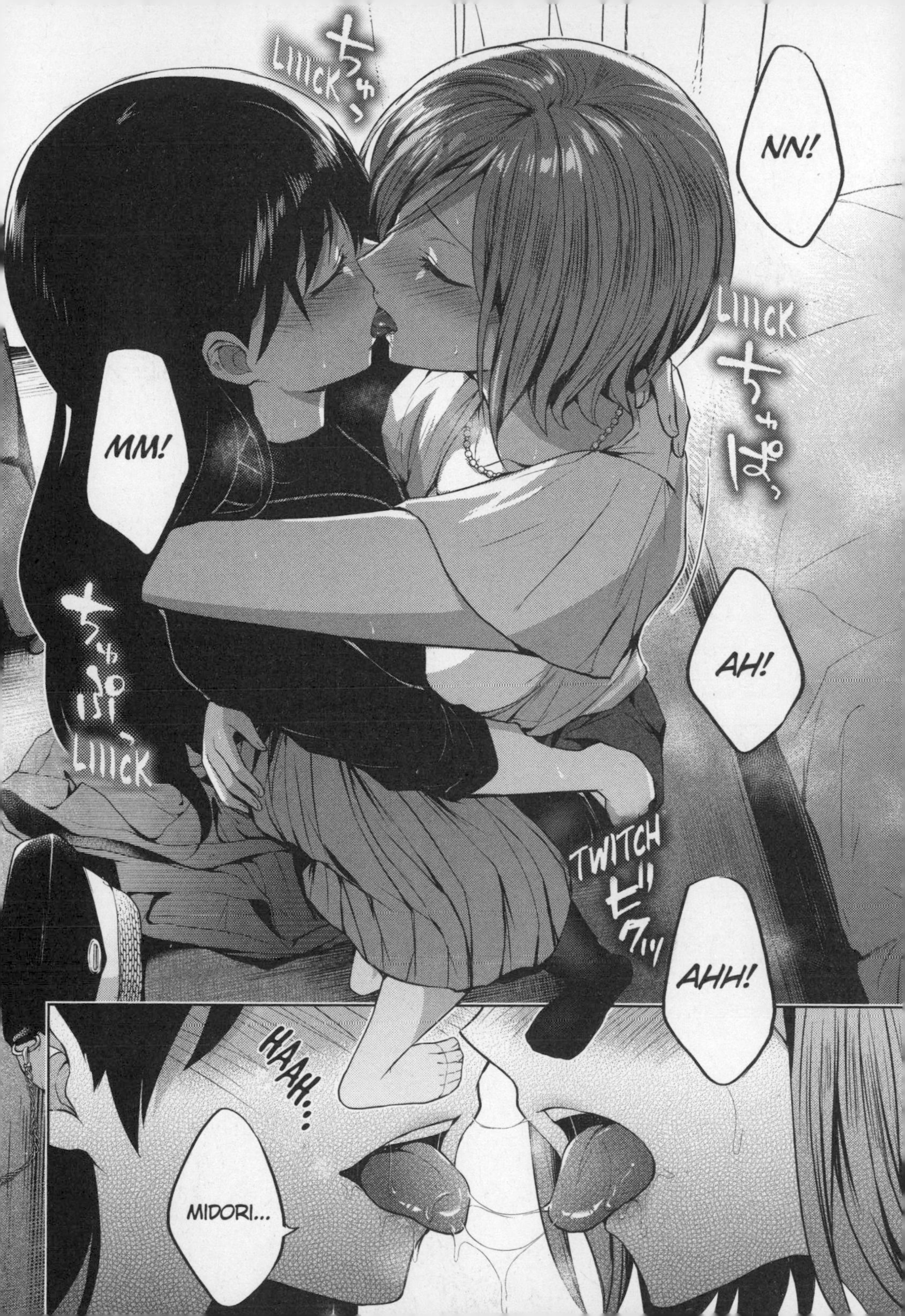
NN!
LIIICK
LIIICK
AH!
MM!
LIIICK
TWITCH
ビクッ
AHH!
HAAH...
MIDORI...

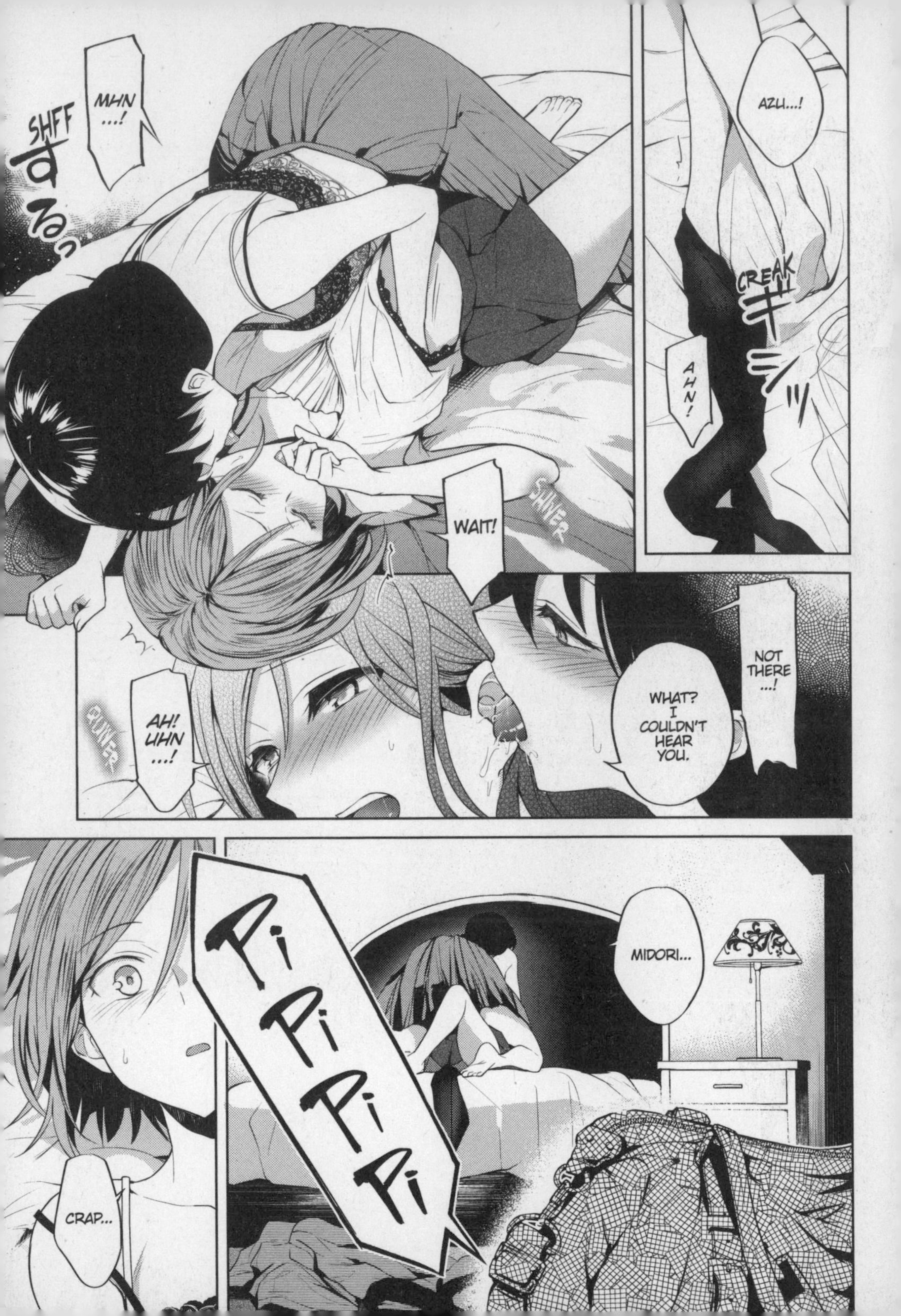
AZU...!
CREAK
AHN!
MHN...!
SHFF
WAIT!
SHIVER
NOT THERE...!
WHAT? I COULDN'T HEAR YOU.
AH! UHN...!
QUIVER
MIDORI...
PI PI PI PI
CRAP...

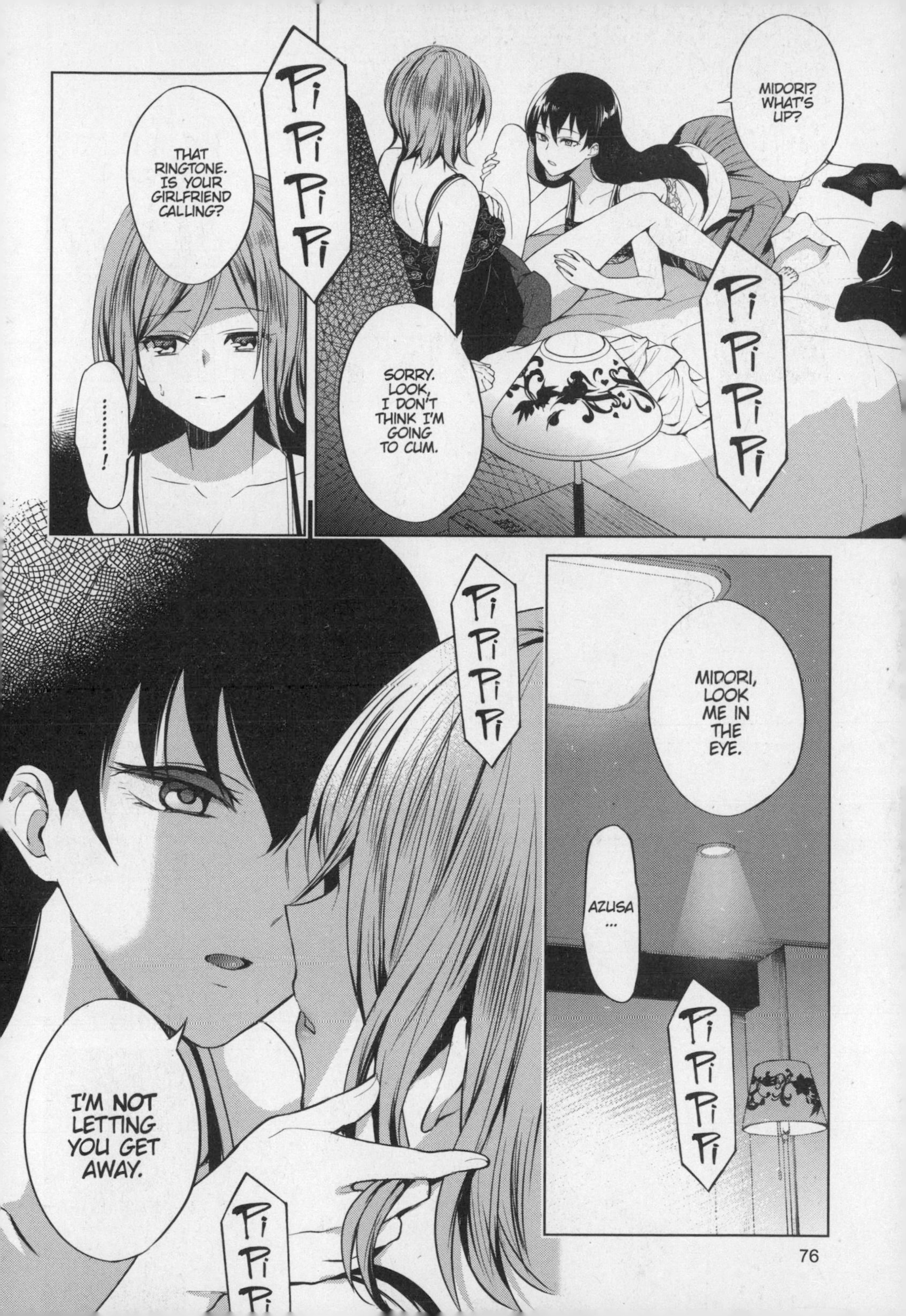
MIDORI? WHAT'S UP?
Pi Pi Pi Pi
SORRY. LOOK, I DON'T THINK I'M GOING TO CUM.
Pi Pi Pi Pi
THAT RINGTONE. IS YOUR GIRLFRIEND CALLING?
......!
MIDORI, LOOK ME IN THE EYE.
AZUSA...
Pi Pi Pi Pi
Pi Pi Pi Pi
I'M NOT LETTING YOU GET AWAY.
Pi Pi Pi

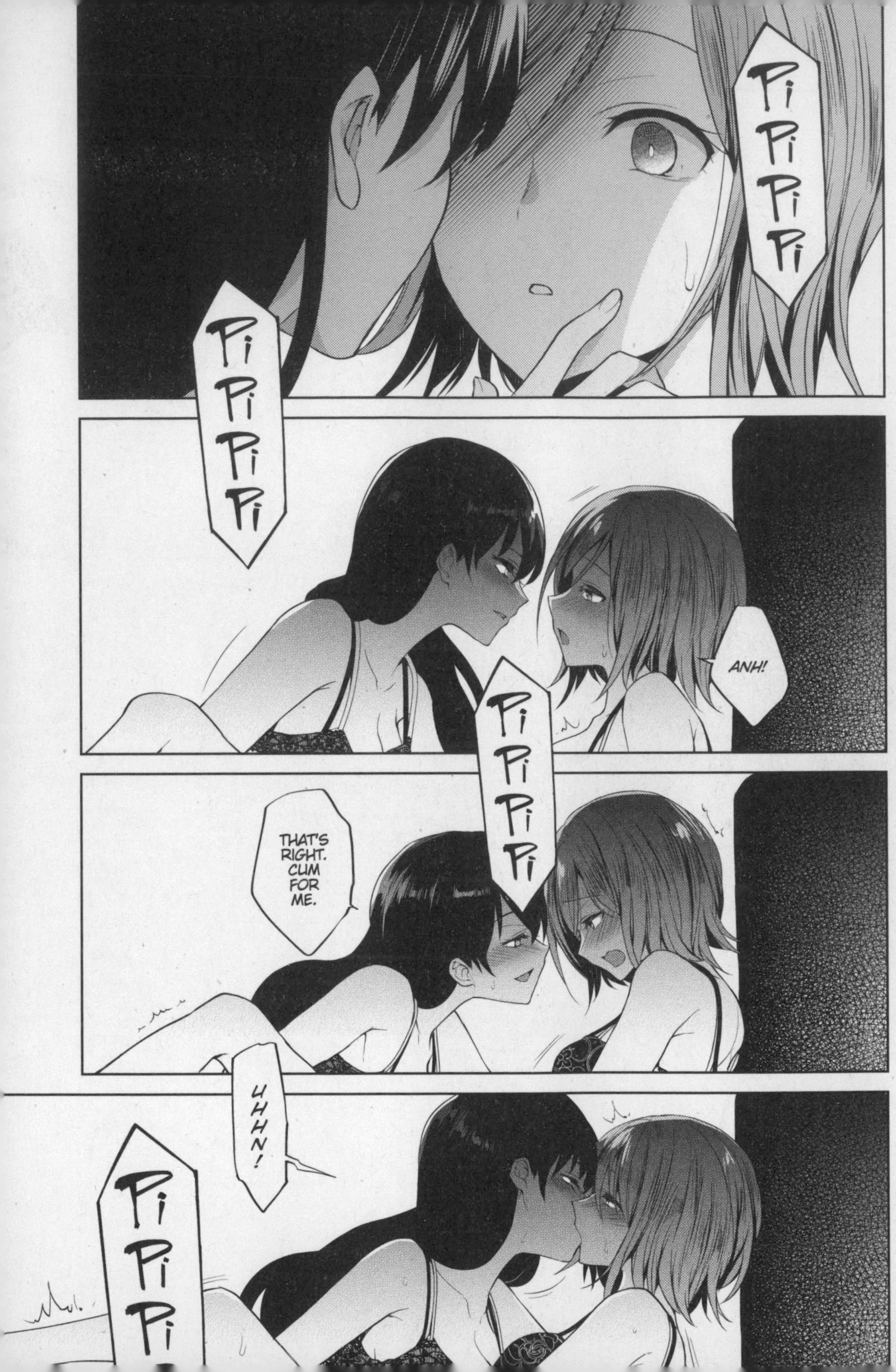
Pi Pi Pi Pi
Pi Pi Pi Pi
ANH!
Pi Pi Pi Pi
THAT'S RIGHT. CUM FOR ME.
UHHN!
Pi Pi Pi

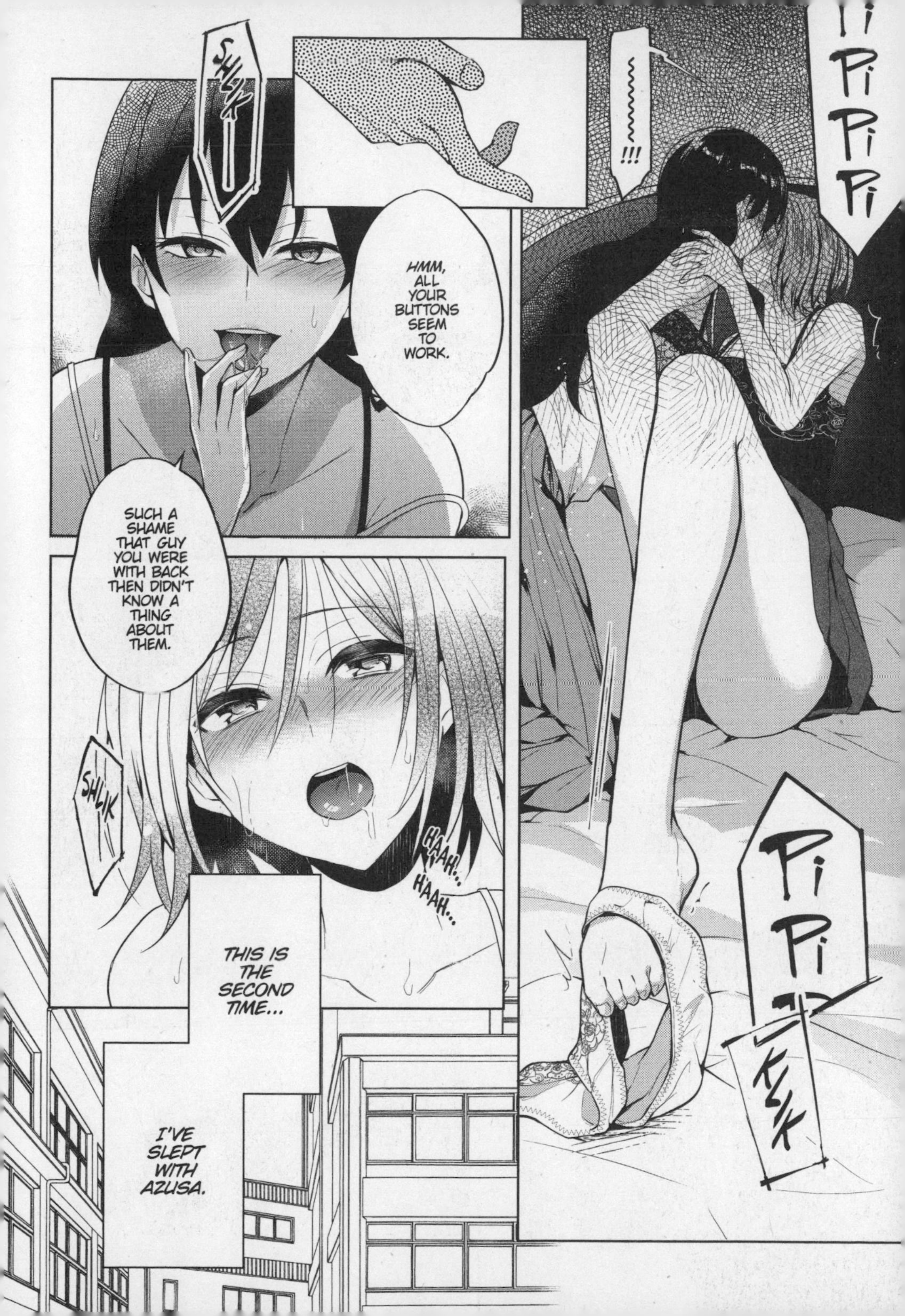
PiPiPi
......!!!
PiPi
KLIK
SHLIK
HMM, ALL YOUR BUTTONS SEEM TO WORK.
SUCH A SHAME THAT GUY YOU WERE WITH BACK THEN DIDN'T KNOW A THING ABOUT THEM.
SHLIK
HAAH... HAAH...
THIS IS THE SECOND TIME...
I'VE SLEPT WITH AZUSA.

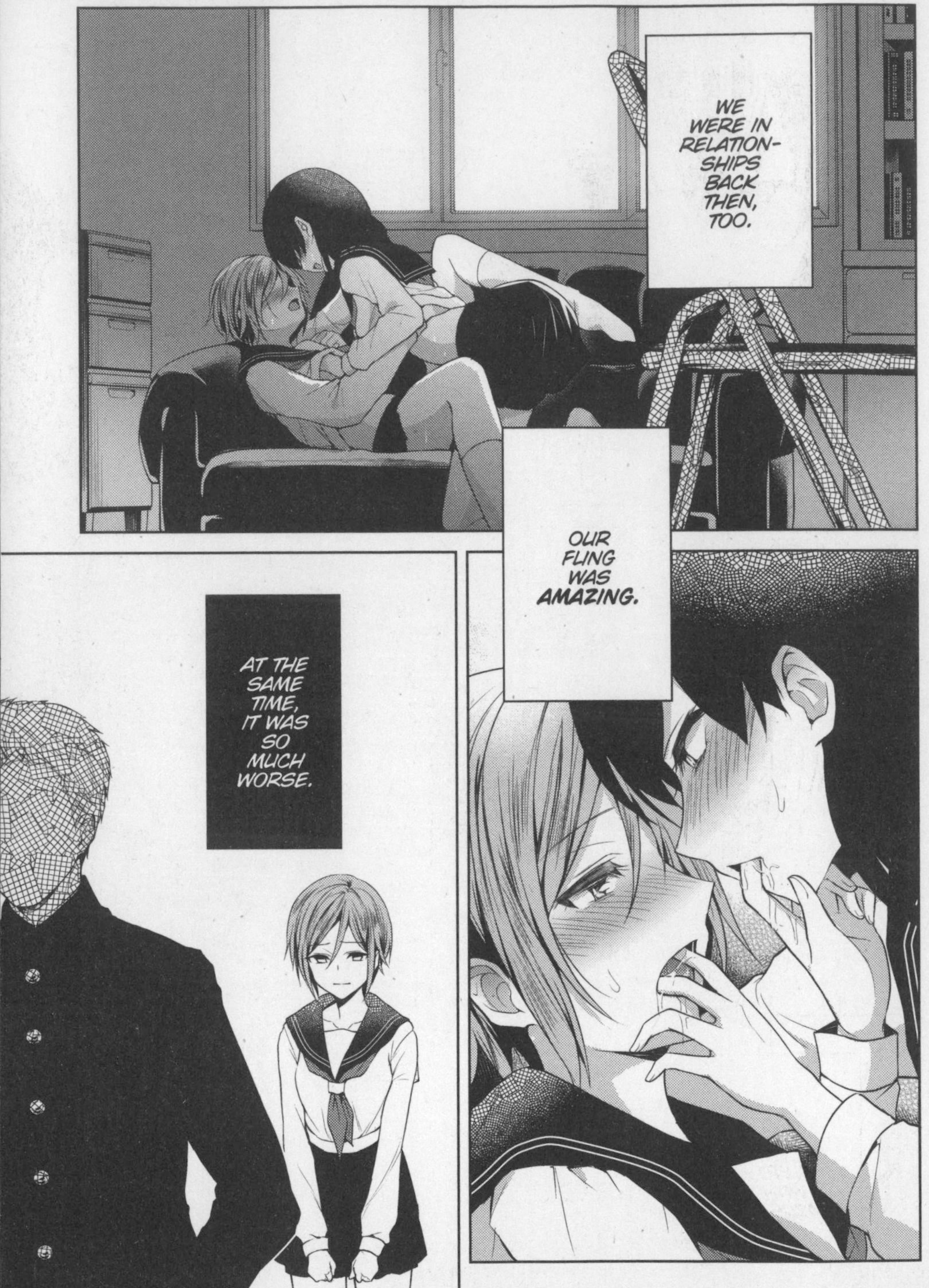
WE WERE IN RELATION-SHIPS BACK THEN, TOO.
OUR FLING WAS AMAZING.
AT THE SAME TIME, IT WAS SO MUCH WORSE.

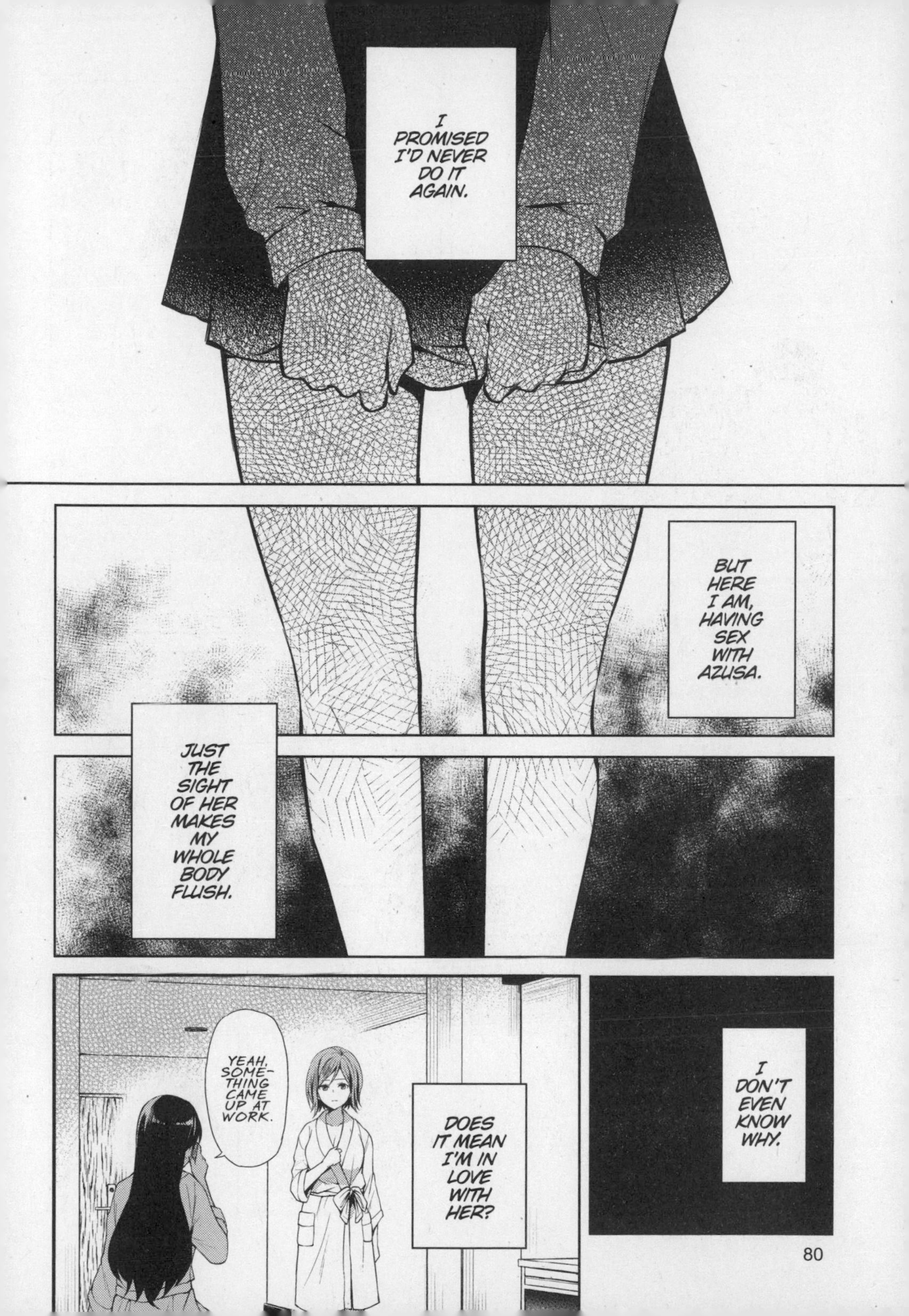
I PROMISED I'D NEVER DO IT AGAIN.
BUT HERE I AM, HAVING SEX WITH AZUSA.
JUST THE SIGHT OF HER MAKES MY WHOLE BODY FLUSH.
I DON'T EVEN KNOW WHY.
YEAH, SOME-THING CAME UP AT WORK.
DOES IT MEAN I'M IN LOVE WITH HER?

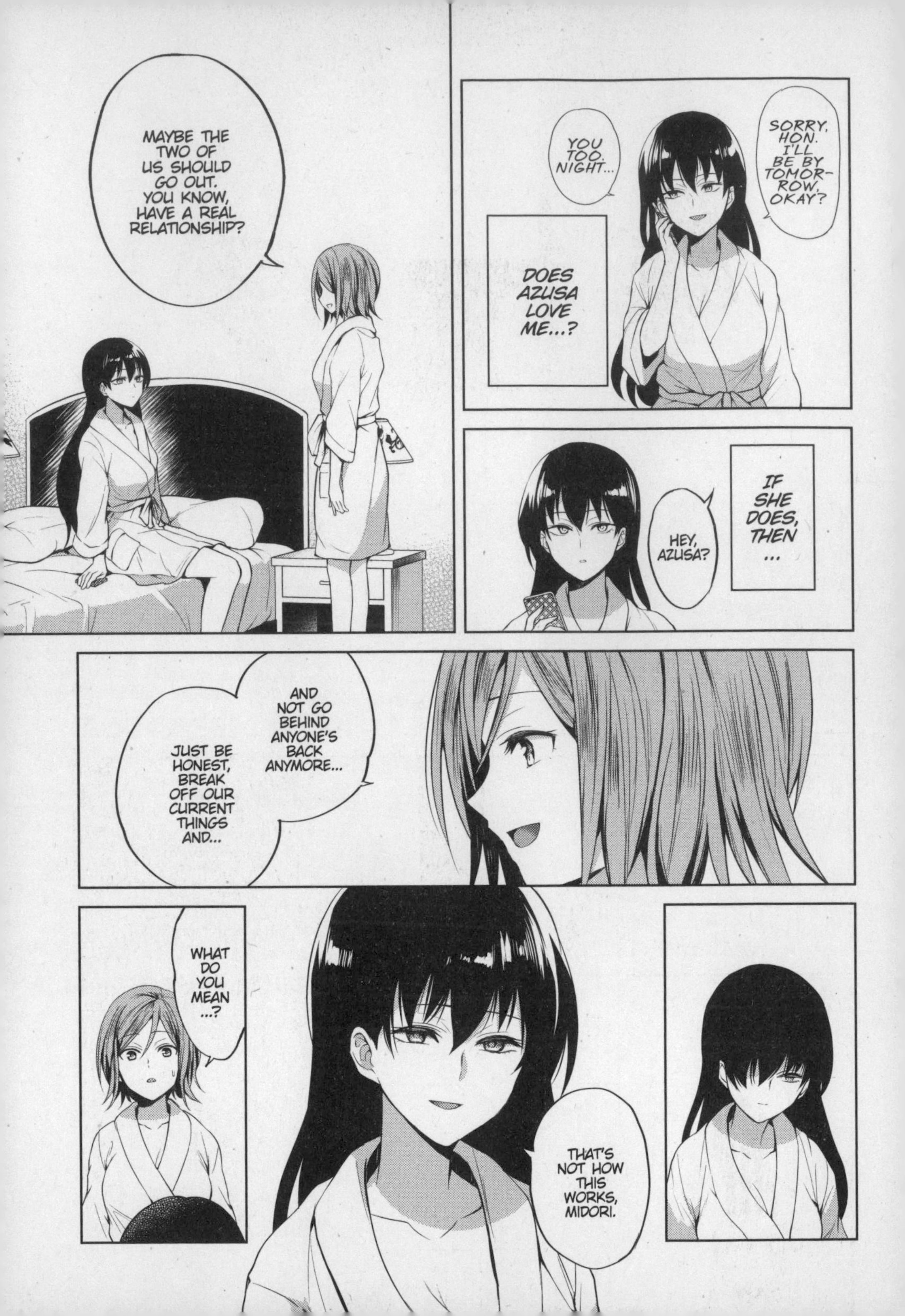
SORRY, HON. I'LL BE BY TOMORROW, OKAY?
YOU TOO. NIGHT...
DOES AZUSA LOVE ME...?
IF SHE DOES, THEN ...
HEY, AZUSA?
MAYBE THE TWO OF US SHOULD GO OUT. YOU KNOW, HAVE A REAL RELATIONSHIP?
JUST BE HONEST, BREAK OFF OUR CURRENT THINGS AND...
AND NOT GO BEHIND ANYONE'S BACK ANYMORE...
THAT'S NOT HOW THIS WORKS, MIDORI.
WHAT DO YOU MEAN ...?

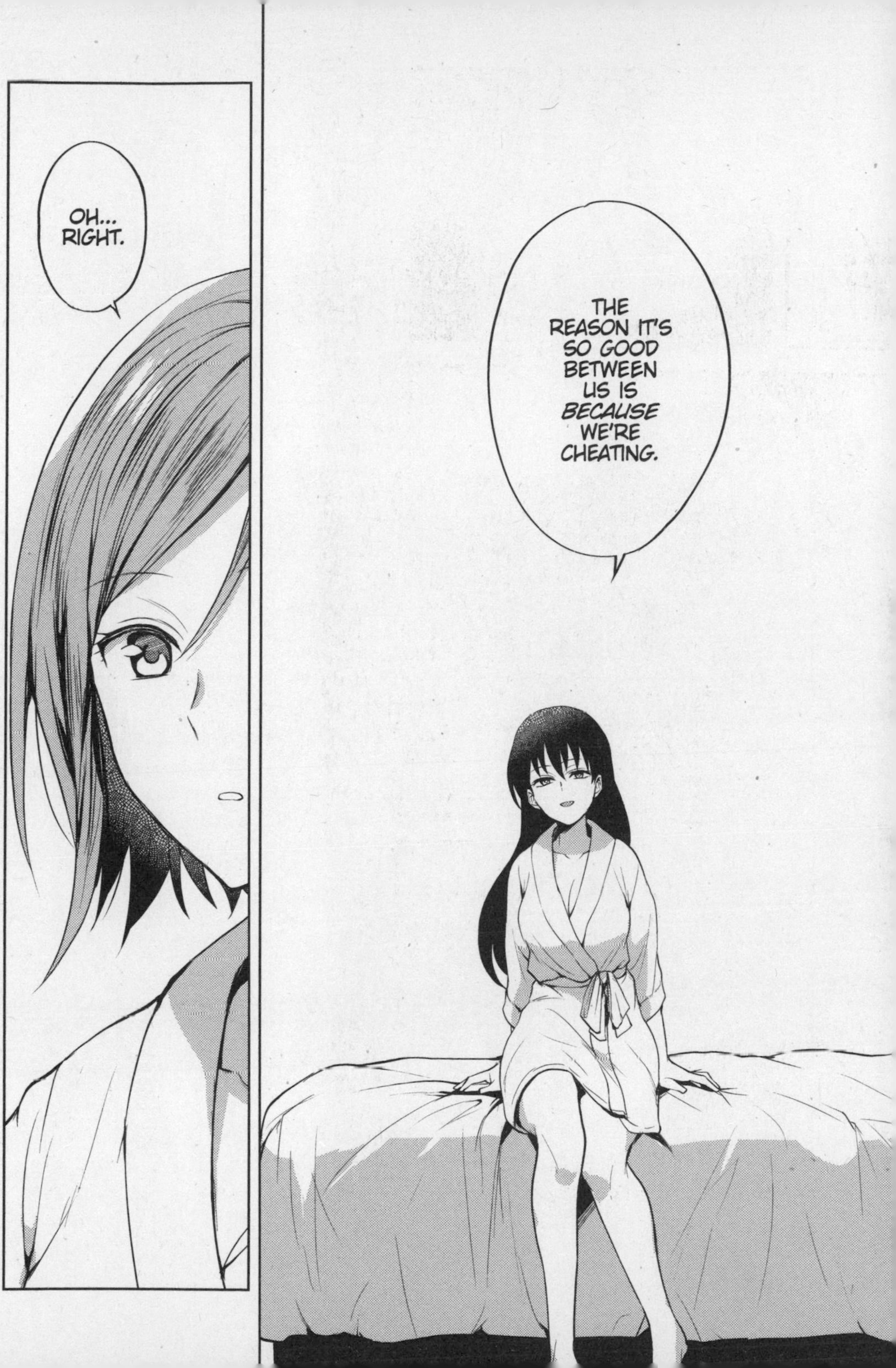
THE REASON IT'S SO GOOD BETWEEN US IS *BECAUSE* WE'RE CHEATING.
OH... RIGHT.

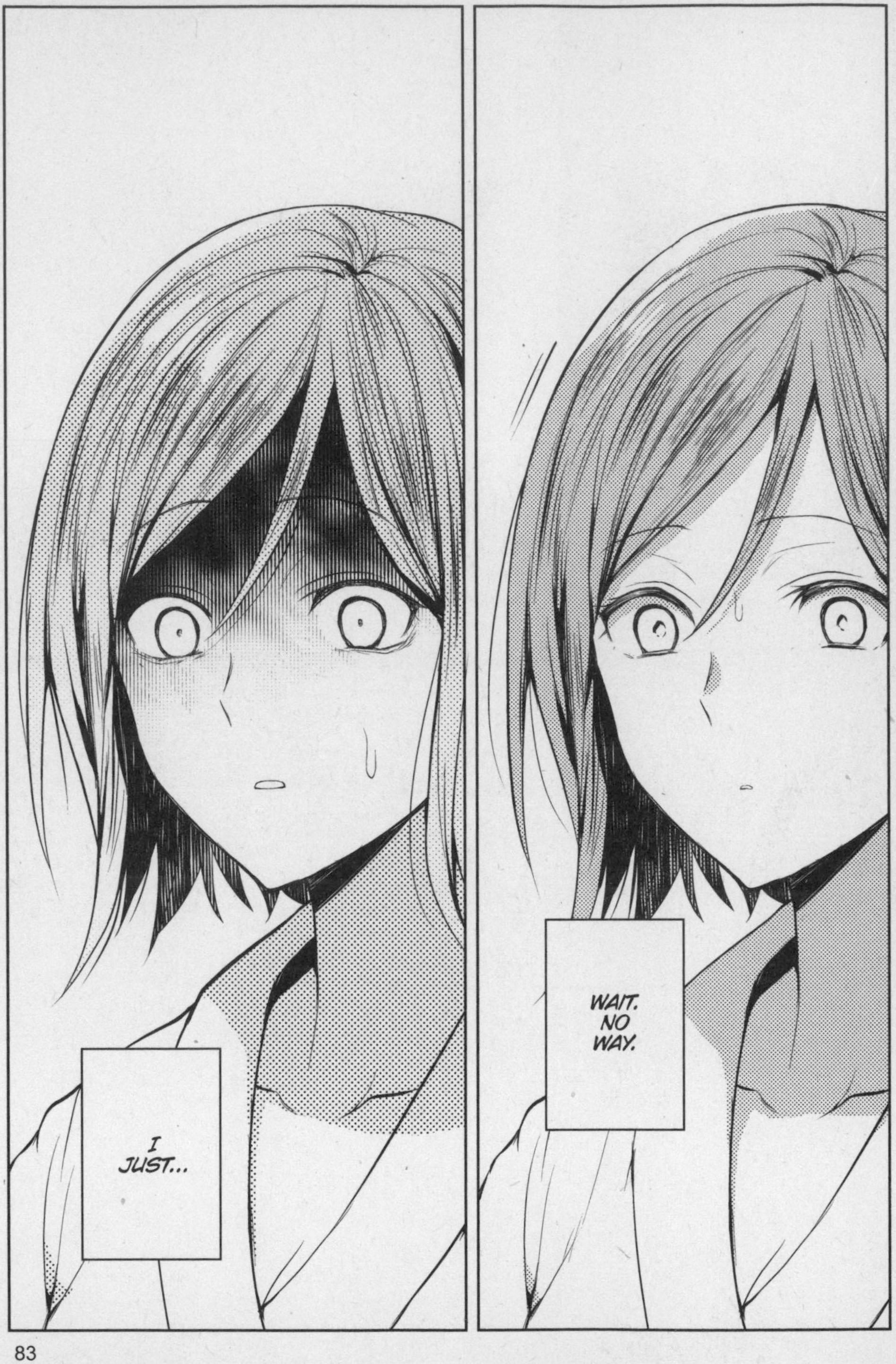
WAIT. NO WAY.
I JUST...

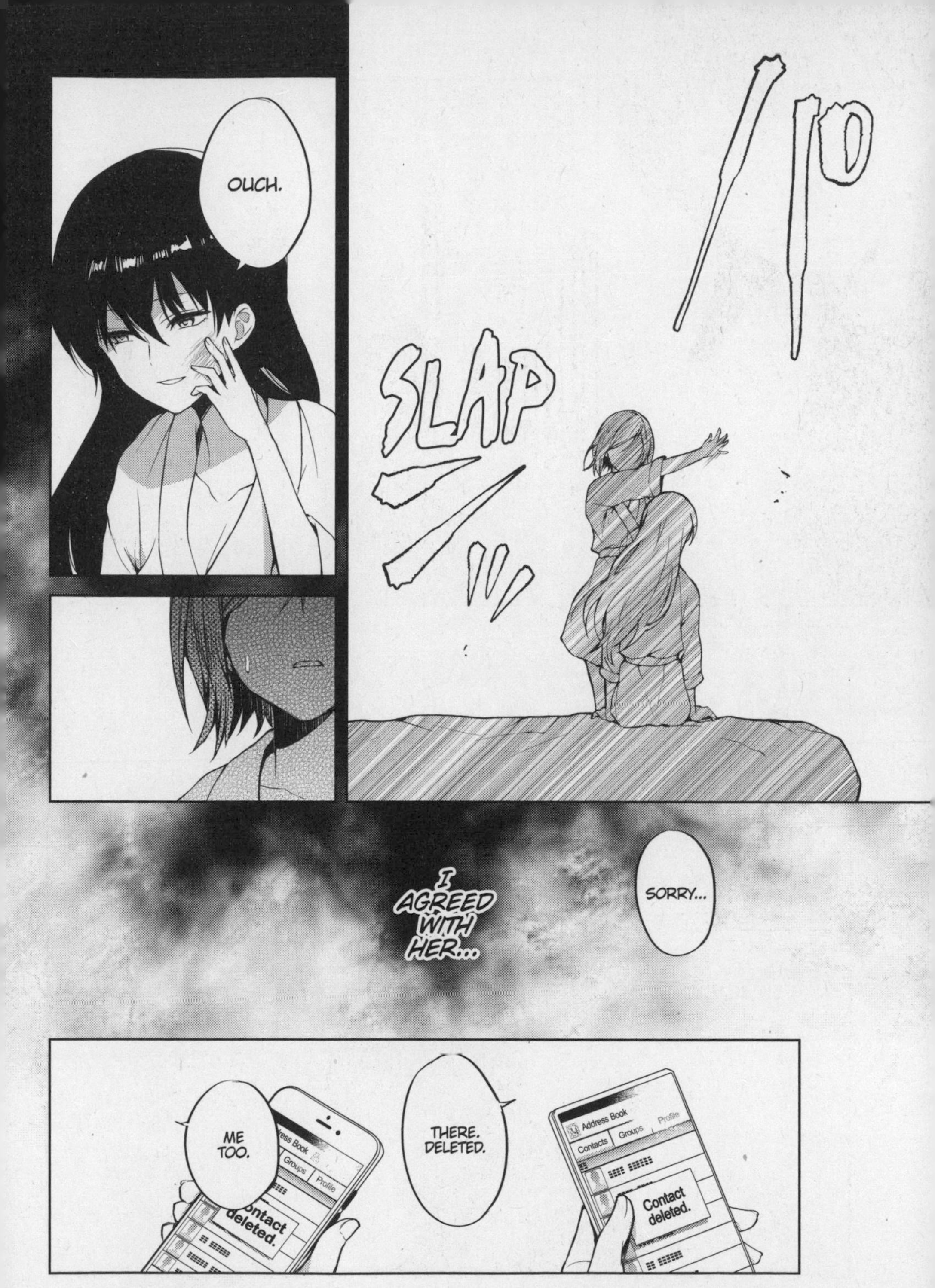
SLAP
OUCH.
SORRY...
I AGREED WITH HER...
Address Book
Contacts
Groups
Profile
Contact deleted.
THERE. DELETED.
ME TOO.
Contact deleted.

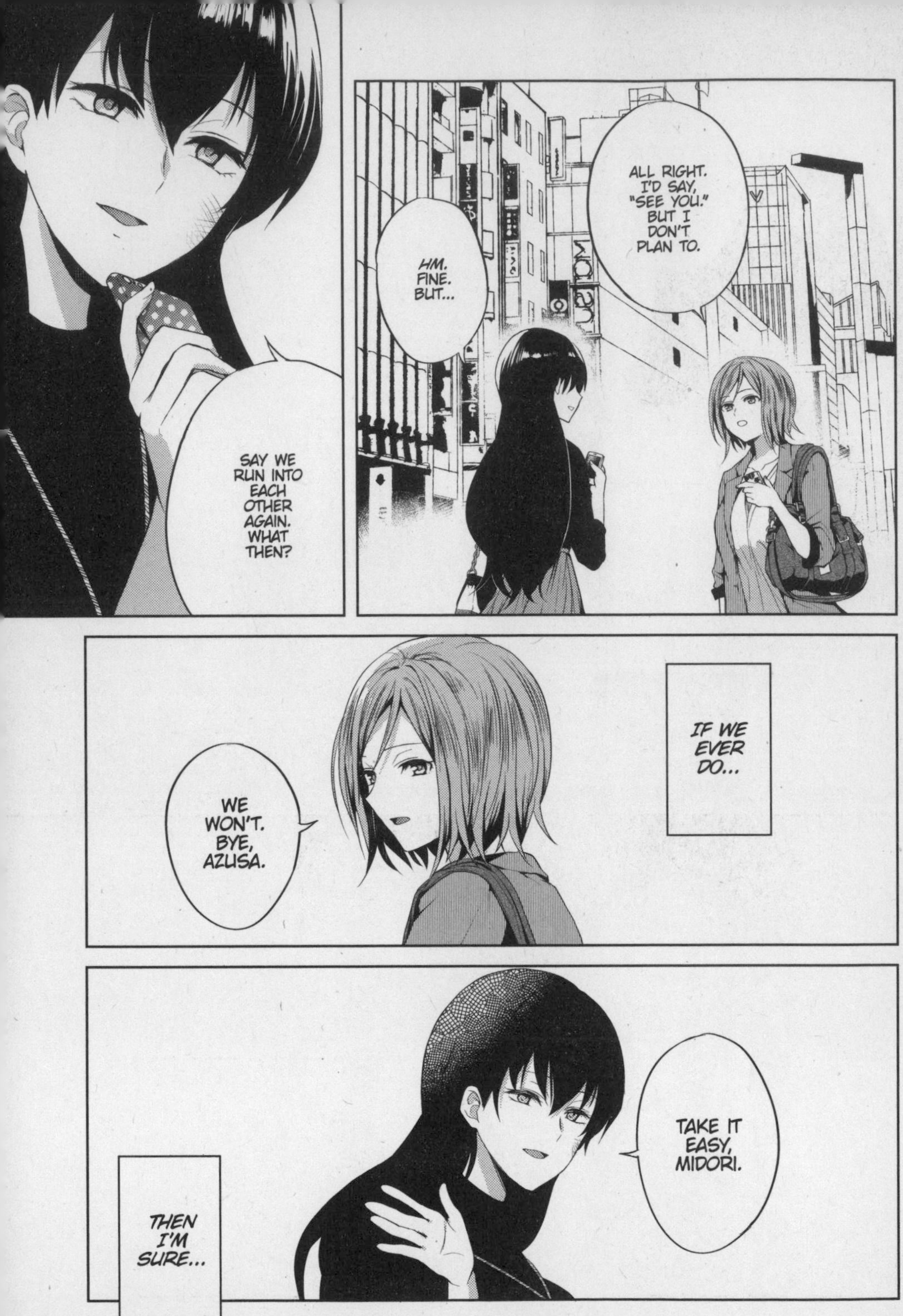
ALL RIGHT. I'D SAY, "SEE YOU." BUT I DON'T PLAN TO.
HM. FINE. BUT...
SAY WE RUN INTO EACH OTHER AGAIN. WHAT THEN?
IF WE EVER DO...
WE WON'T. BYE, AZUSA.
TAKE IT EASY, MIDORI.
THEN I'M SURE...

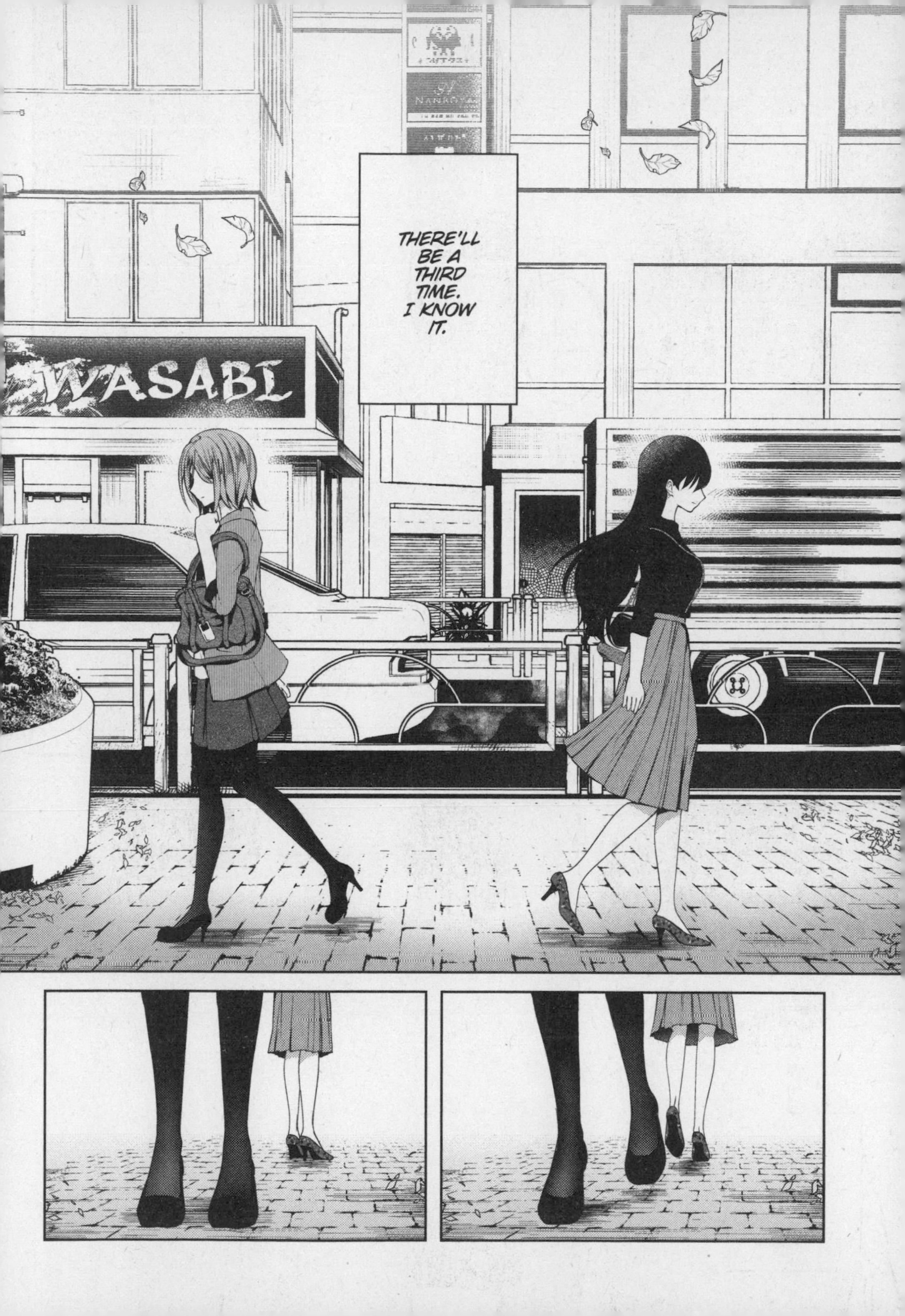
THERE'LL BE A THIRD TIME. I KNOW IT.
WASABI

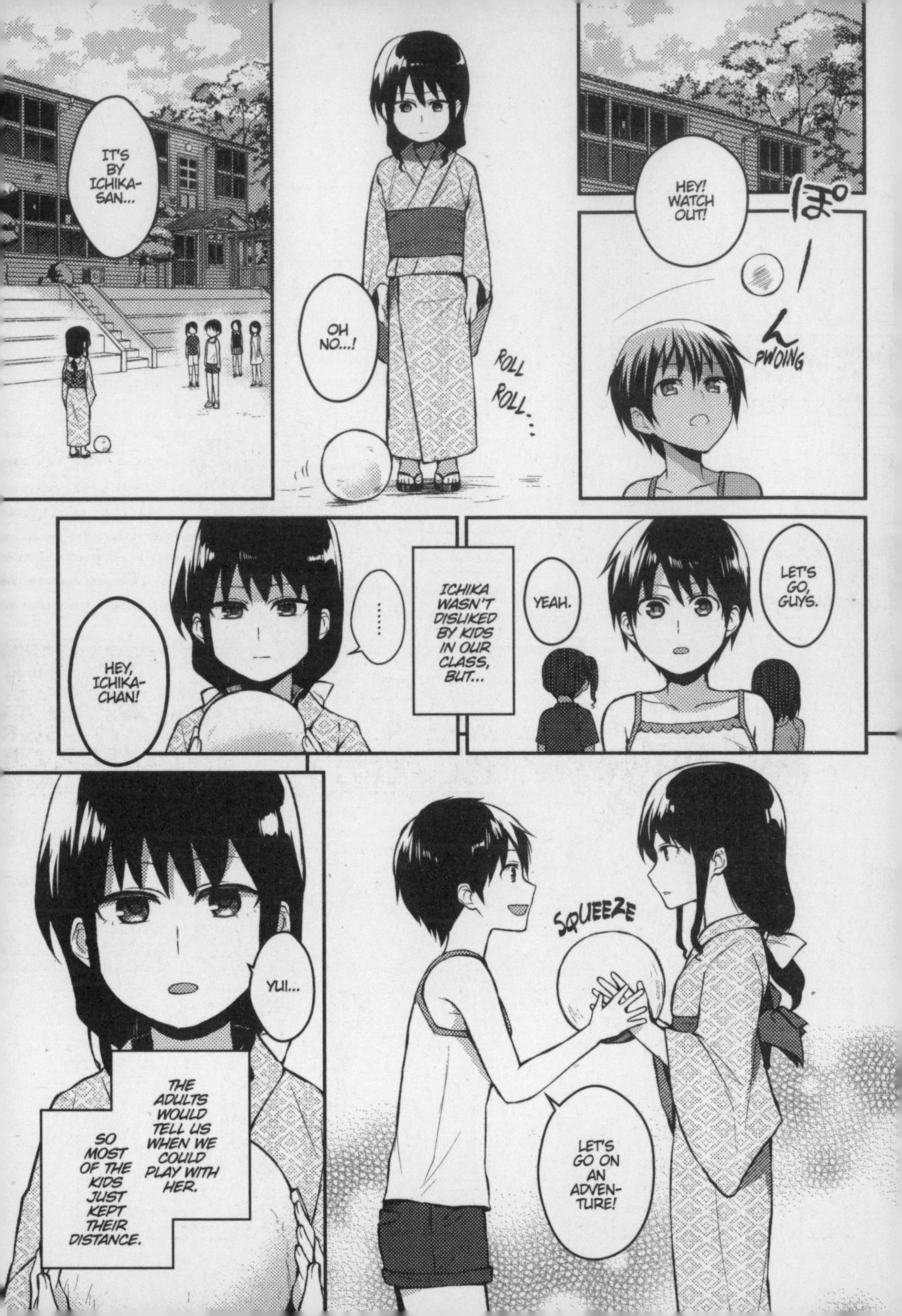
HEY! WATCH OUT!
ぽーん
PWOING
OH NO...!
ROLL ROLL...
IT'S BY ICHIKA-SAN...
LET'S GO, GUYS.
YEAH.
ICHIKA WASN'T DISLIKED BY KIDS IN OUR CLASS, BUT...
......
HEY, ICHIKA-CHAN!
SQUEEZE
LET'S GO ON AN ADVEN-TURE!
YUI...
THE ADULTS WOULD TELL US WHEN WE COULD PLAY WITH HER.
SO MOST OF THE KIDS JUST KEPT THEIR DISTANCE.

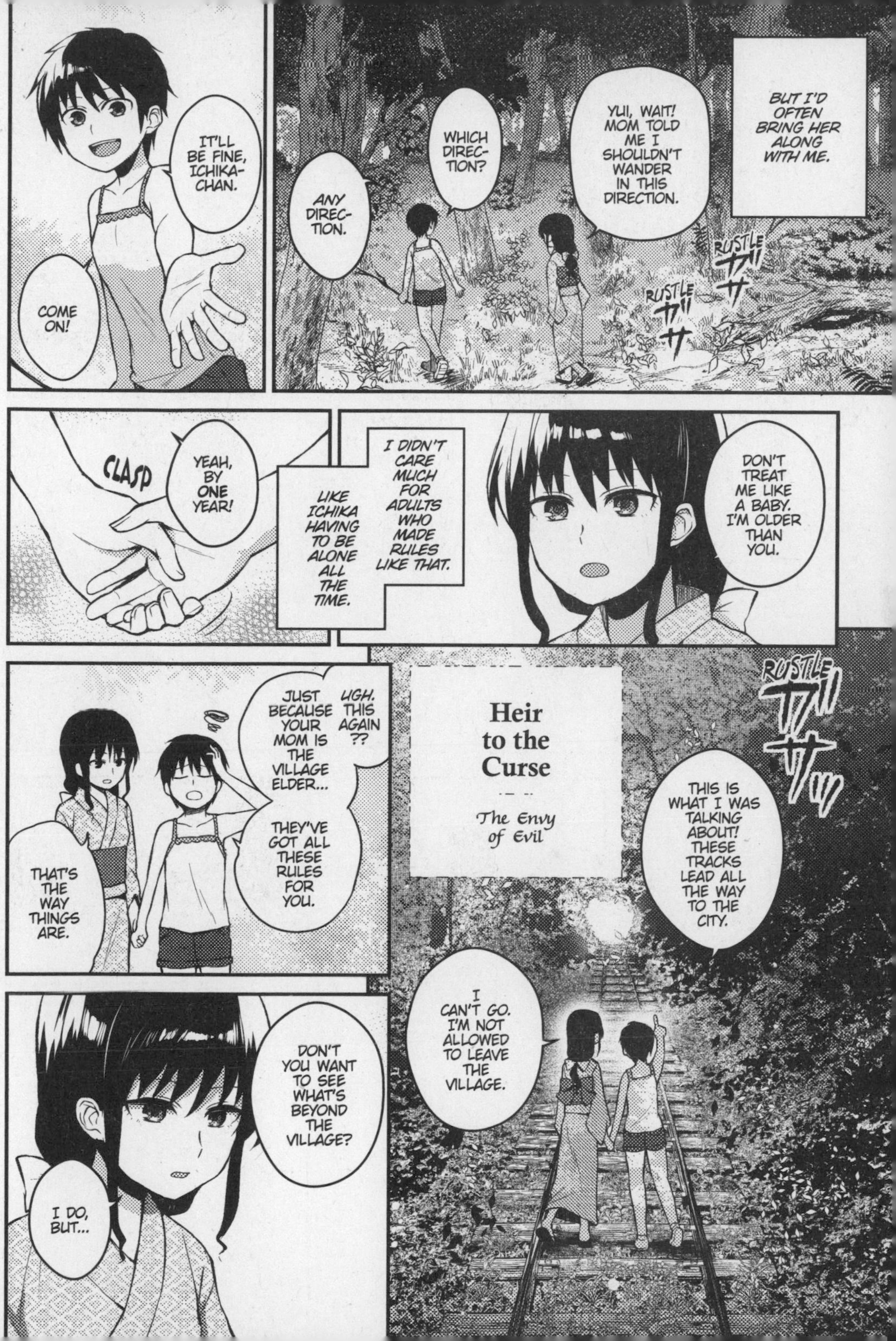
BUT I'D OFTEN BRING HER ALONG WITH ME.
YUI, WAIT! MOM TOLD ME I SHOULDN'T WANDER IN THIS DIRECTION.
WHICH DIRECTION?
ANY DIRECTION.
RUSTLE
RUSTLE
IT'LL BE FINE, ICHIKA-CHAN.
COME ON!
DON'T TREAT ME LIKE A BABY. I'M OLDER THAN YOU.
I DIDN'T CARE MUCH FOR ADULTS WHO MADE RULES LIKE THAT.
LIKE ICHIKA HAVING TO BE ALONE ALL THE TIME.
YEAH, BY ONE YEAR!
CLASP
RUSTLE
Heir to the Curse
The Envy of Evil
THIS IS WHAT I WAS TALKING ABOUT! THESE TRACKS LEAD ALL THE WAY TO THE CITY.
I CAN'T GO. I'M NOT ALLOWED TO LEAVE THE VILLAGE.
UGH. THIS AGAIN??
JUST BECAUSE YOUR MOM IS THE VILLAGE ELDER...
THEY'VE GOT ALL THESE RULES FOR YOU.
THAT'S THE WAY THINGS ARE.
DON'T YOU WANT TO SEE WHAT'S BEYOND THE VILLAGE?
I DO, BUT...

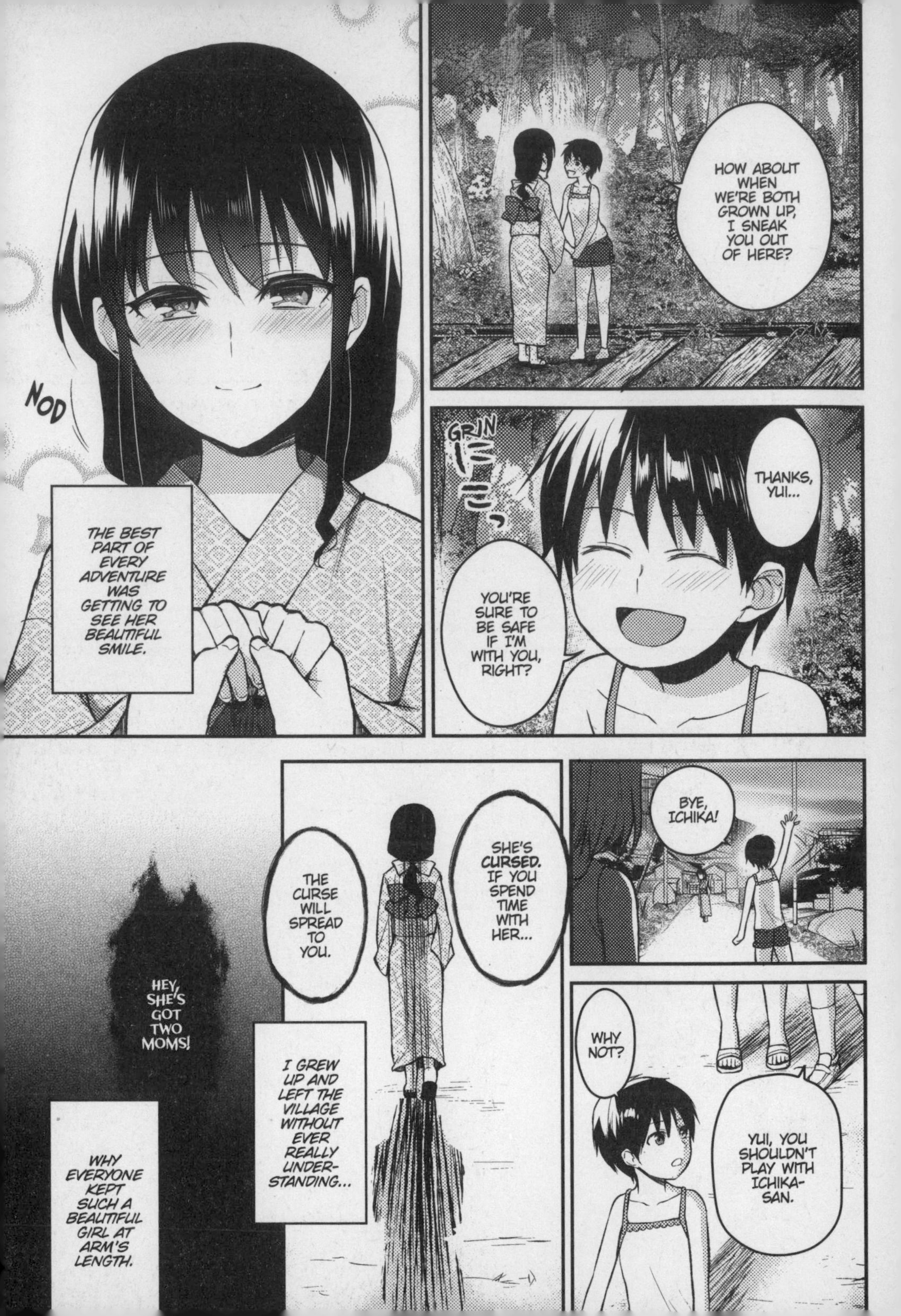
HOW ABOUT WHEN WE'RE BOTH GROWN UP, I SNEAK YOU OUT OF HERE?
GRIN
THANKS, YUI...
YOU'RE SURE TO BE SAFE IF I'M WITH YOU, RIGHT?
NOD
THE BEST PART OF EVERY ADVENTURE WAS GETTING TO SEE HER BEAUTIFUL SMILE.
BYE, ICHIKA!
WHY NOT?
YUI, YOU SHOULDN'T PLAY WITH ICHIKA-SAN.
SHE'S CURSED. IF YOU SPEND TIME WITH HER...
THE CURSE WILL SPREAD TO YOU.
I GREW UP AND LEFT THE VILLAGE WITHOUT EVER REALLY UNDER-STANDING...
HEY, SHE'S GOT TWO MOMS!
WHY EVERYONE KEPT SUCH A BEAUTIFUL GIRL AT ARM'S LENGTH.

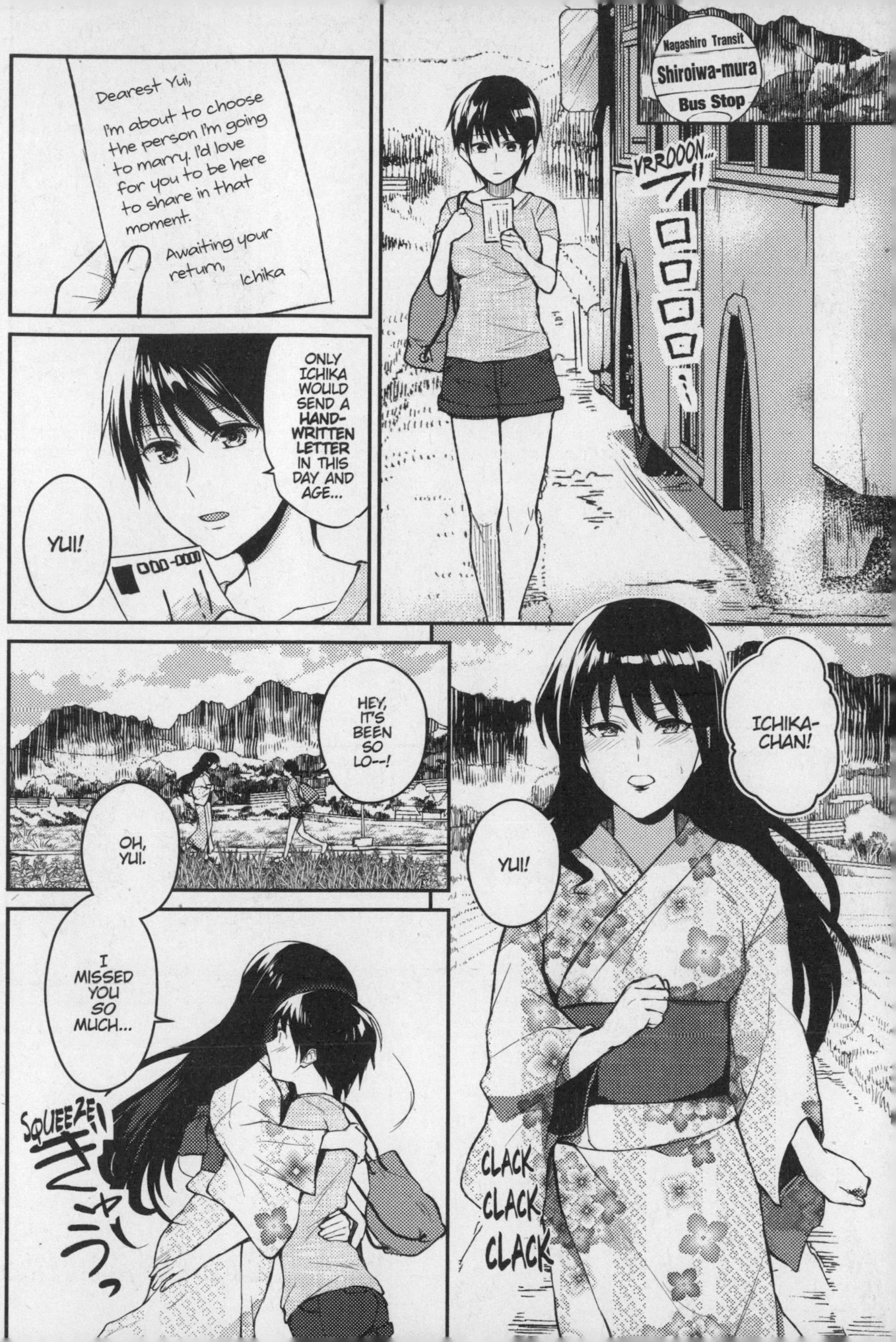
Nagashiro Transit
Shiroiwa-mura
Bus Stop
VRROOON...
Dearest Yui,
I'm about to choose the person I'm going to marry. I'd love for you to be here to share in that moment.
Awaiting your return,
Ichika
ONLY ICHIKA WOULD SEND A HAND-WRITTEN LETTER IN THIS DAY AND AGE...
YUI!
ICHIKA-CHAN!
YUI!
CLACK
CLACK
CLACK
HEY, IT'S BEEN SO LO--!
OH, YUI.
I MISSED YOU SO MUCH...
SQUEEZE!

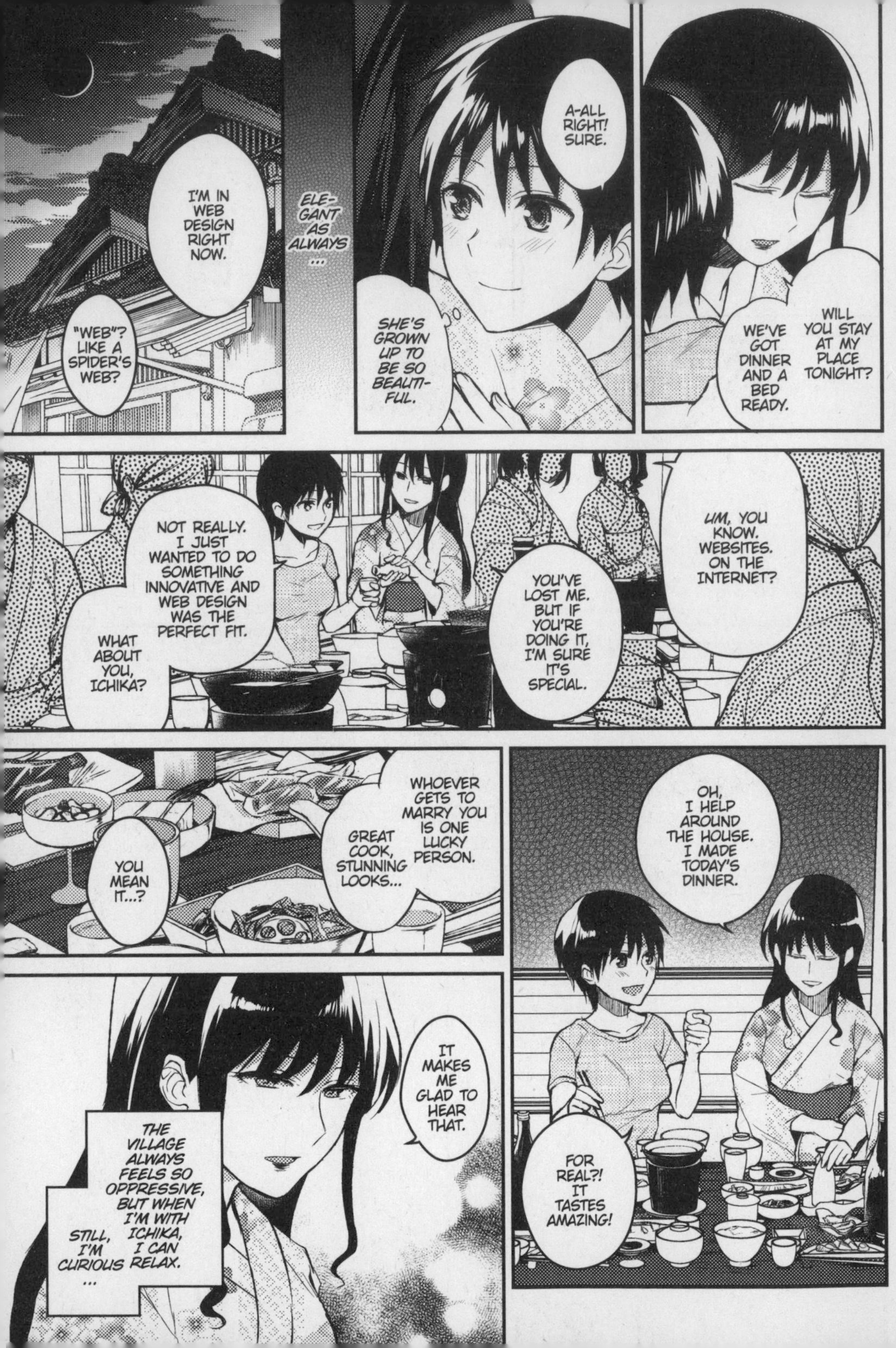
WILL YOU STAY AT MY PLACE TONIGHT?
WE'VE GOT DINNER AND A BED READY.
A-ALL RIGHT! SURE.
SHE'S GROWN UP TO BE SO BEAUTIFUL.
ELEGANT AS ALWAYS...
I'M IN WEB DESIGN RIGHT NOW.
"WEB"? LIKE A SPIDER'S WEB?
UM, YOU KNOW. WEBSITES. ON THE INTERNET?
YOU'VE LOST ME. BUT IF YOU'RE DOING IT, I'M SURE IT'S SPECIAL.
NOT REALLY. I JUST WANTED TO DO SOMETHING INNOVATIVE AND WEB DESIGN WAS THE PERFECT FIT.
WHAT ABOUT YOU, ICHIKA?
OH, I HELP AROUND THE HOUSE. I MADE TODAY'S DINNER.
FOR REAL?! IT TASTES AMAZING!
WHOEVER GETS TO MARRY YOU IS ONE LUCKY PERSON.
GREAT COOK, STUNNING LOOKS...
YOU MEAN IT...?
IT MAKES ME GLAD TO HEAR THAT.
THE VILLAGE ALWAYS FEELS SO OPPRESSIVE, BUT WHEN I'M WITH ICHIKA, I CAN RELAX.
STILL, I'M CURIOUS...

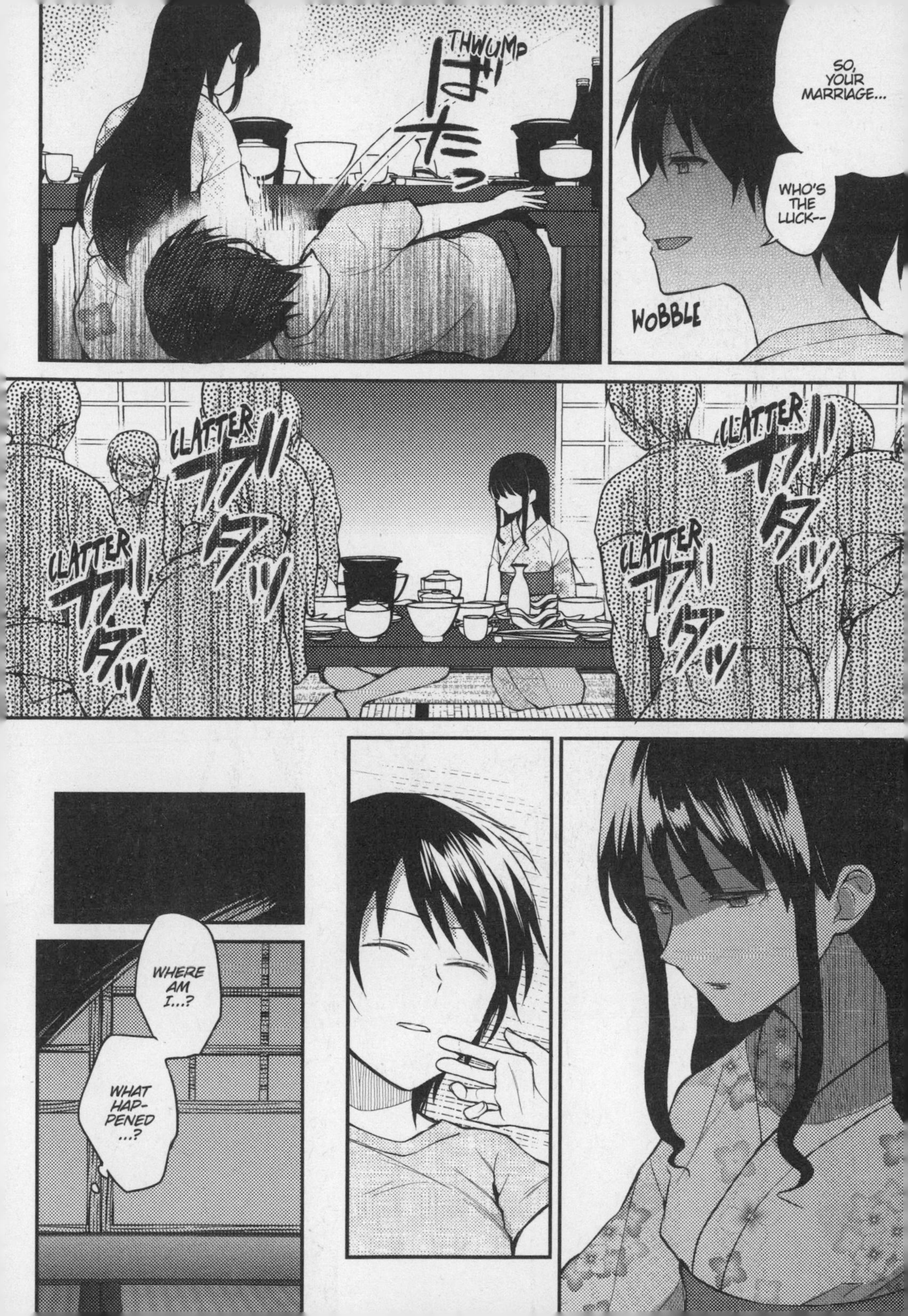
SO, YOUR MARRIAGE...
WHO'S THE LUCK--
WOBBLE
THWUMP
ばたっ
CLATTER
ガタッ
CLATTER
ガタッ
CLATTER
ガタッ
CLATTER
ガタッ
WHERE AM I...?
WHAT HAP-PENED ...?

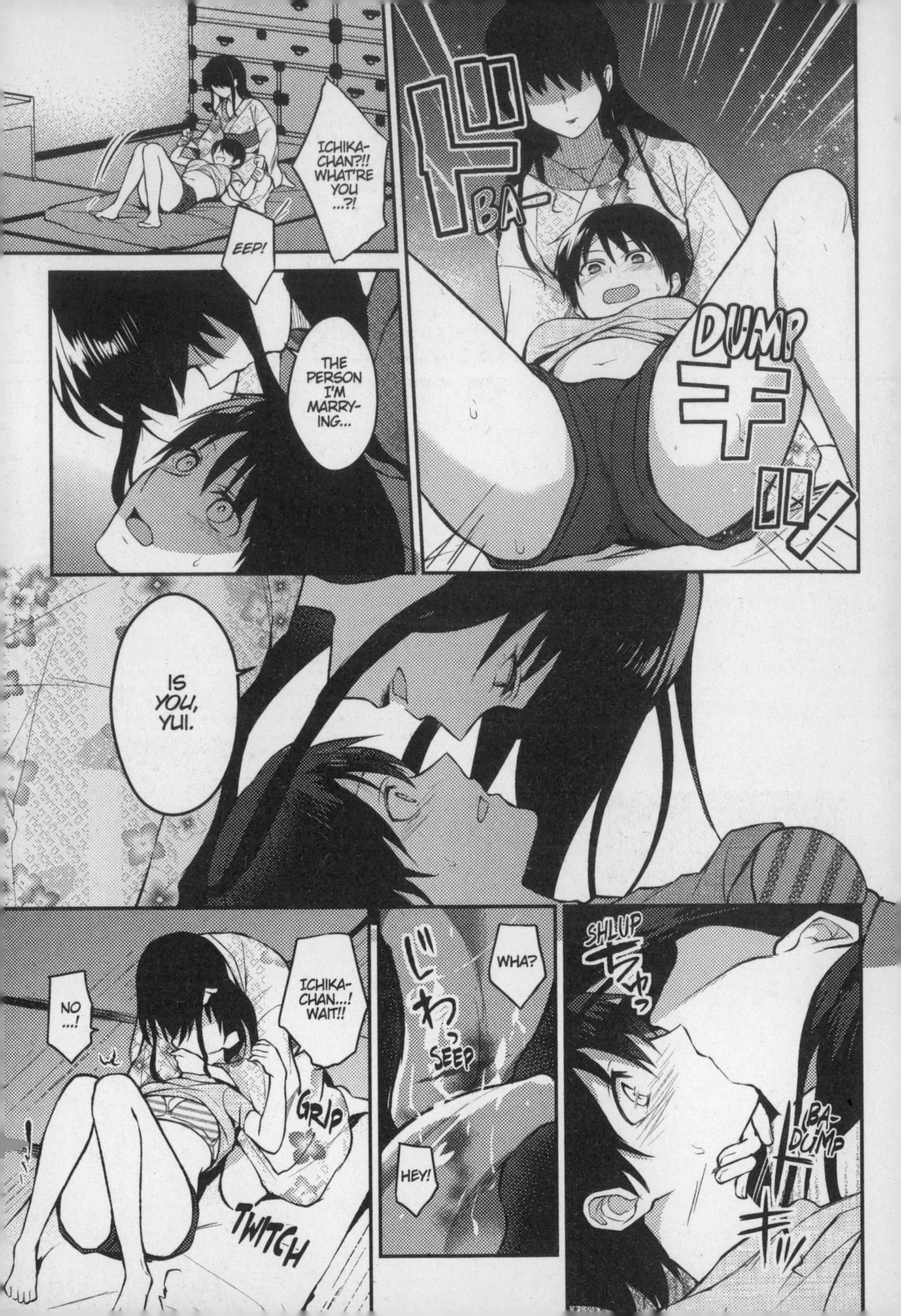
BA-
DUMP
ICHIKA-CHAN?!! WHAT'RE YOU ...?!
EEP!
THE PERSON I'M MARRY-ING...
IS YOU, YUI.
SHLUP
BA-DUMP
WHA?
SEEP
HEY!
ICHIKA-CHAN...! WAIT!!
NO ...!
GRIP
TWITCH

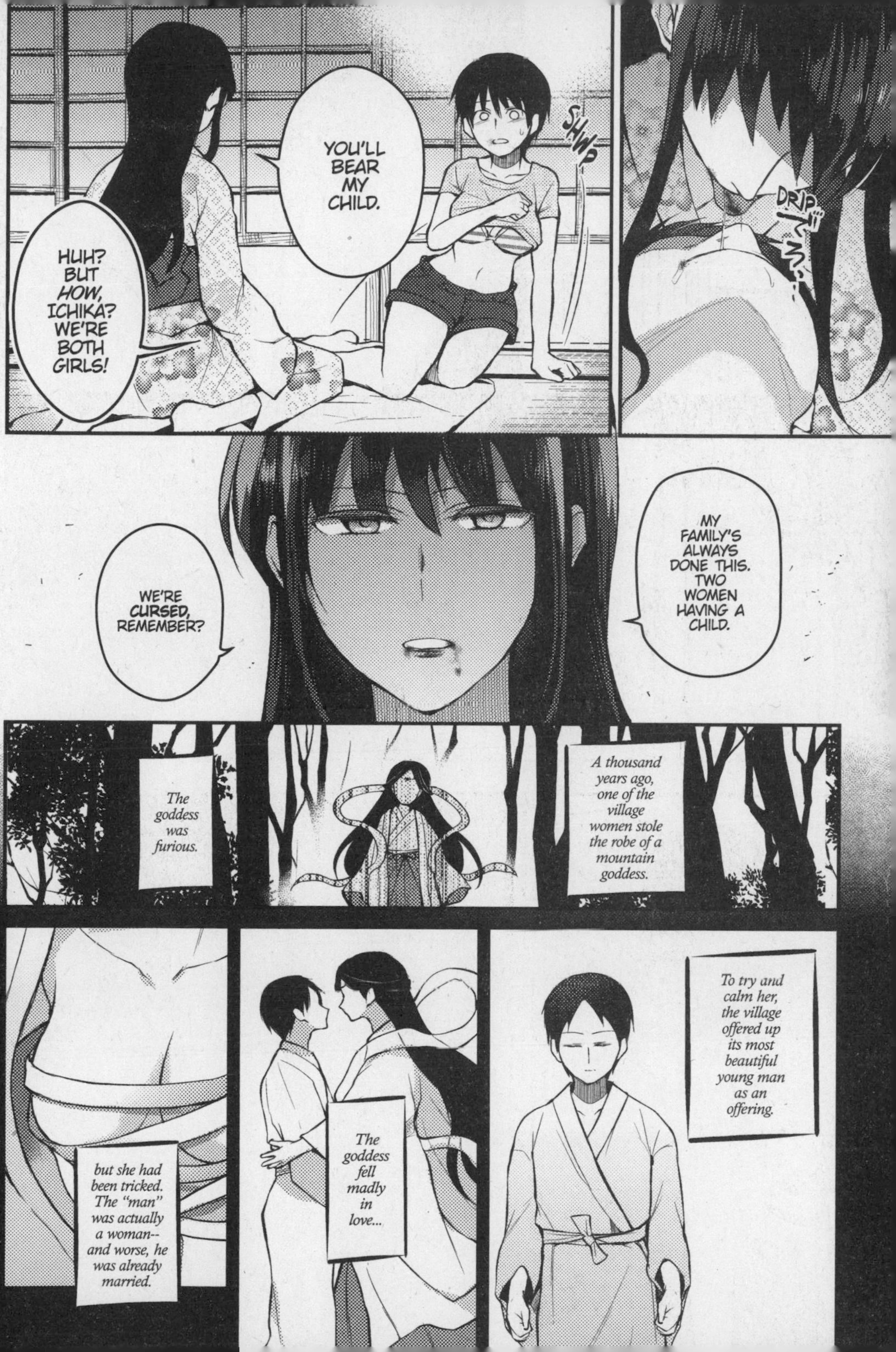
DRIP
SHWP
YOU'LL BEAR MY CHILD.
HUH? BUT *HOW*, ICHIKA? WE'RE BOTH GIRLS!
MY FAMILY'S ALWAYS DONE THIS. TWO WOMEN HAVING A CHILD.
WE'RE CURSED, REMEMBER?
A thousand years ago, one of the village women stole the robe of a mountain goddess.
The goddess was furious.
To try and calm her, the village offered up its most beautiful young man as an offering.
The goddess fell madly in love...
but she had been tricked. The "man" was actually a woman-- and worse, he was already married.

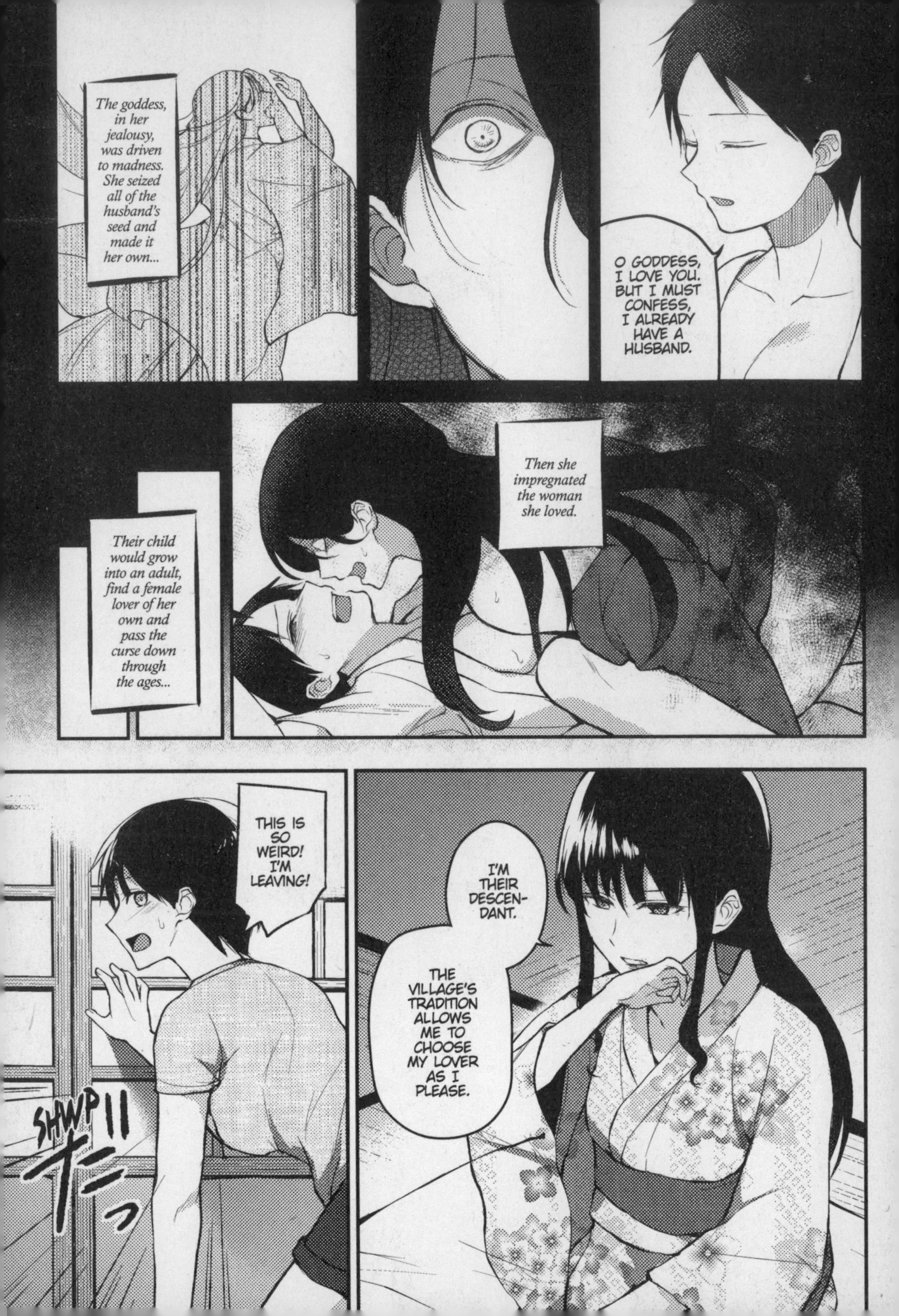
O GODDESS, I LOVE YOU. BUT I MUST CONFESS, I ALREADY HAVE A HUSBAND.
The goddess, in her jealousy, was driven to madness. She seized all of the husband's seed and made it her own...
Then she impregnated the woman she loved.
Their child would grow into an adult, find a female lover of her own and pass the curse down through the ages...
I'M THEIR DESCEN-DANT.
THE VILLAGE'S TRADITION ALLOWS ME TO CHOOSE MY LOVER AS I PLEASE.
THIS IS SO WEIRD! I'M LEAVING!
SHWP!!

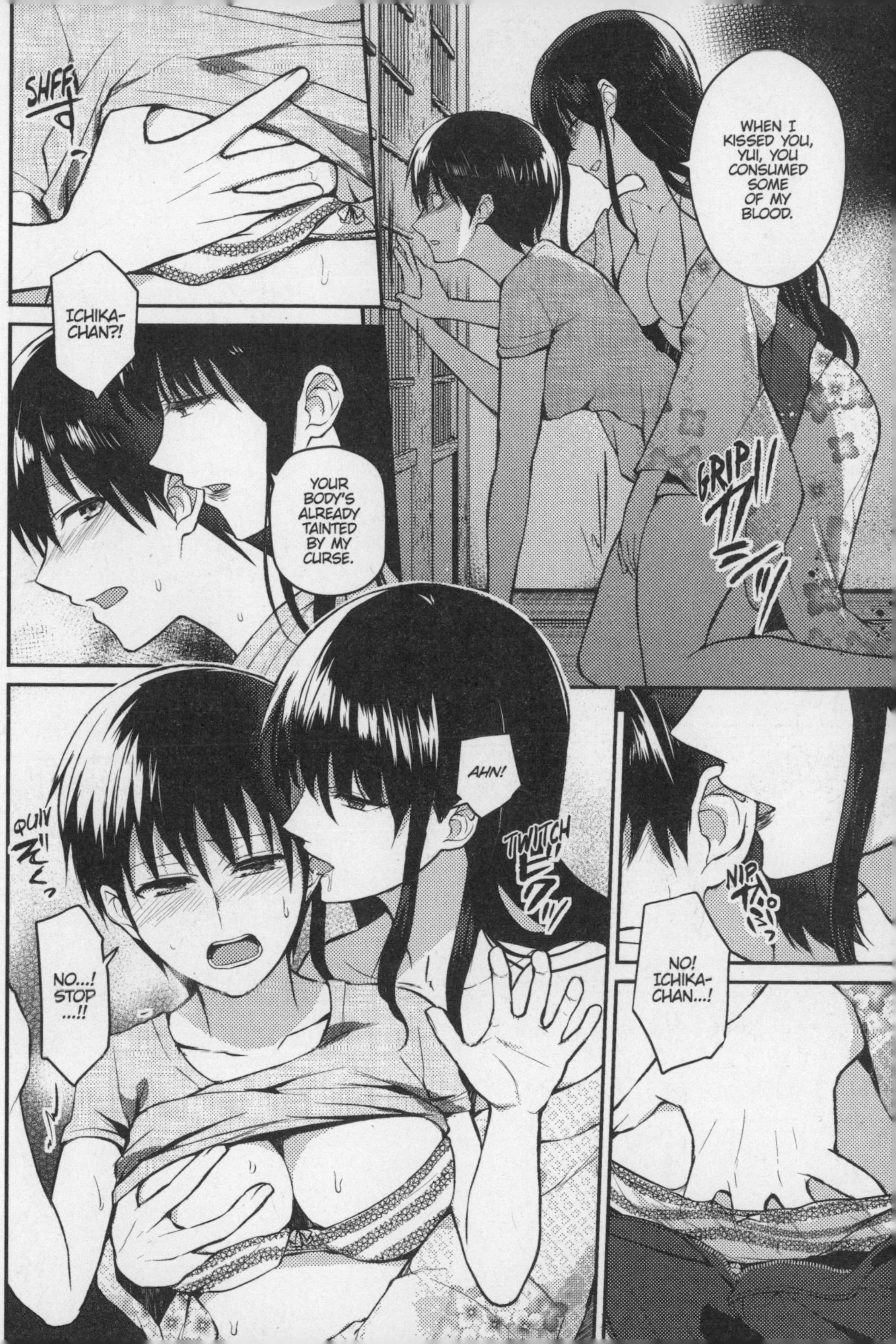
WHEN I KISSED YOU, YUI, YOU CONSUMED SOME OF MY BLOOD.
GRIP
SHFF
ICHIKA-CHAN?!
YOUR BODY'S ALREADY TAINTED BY MY CURSE.
NIP
NO! ICHIKA-CHAN...!
AHN!
TWITCH
QUIV
NO...! STOP ...!!

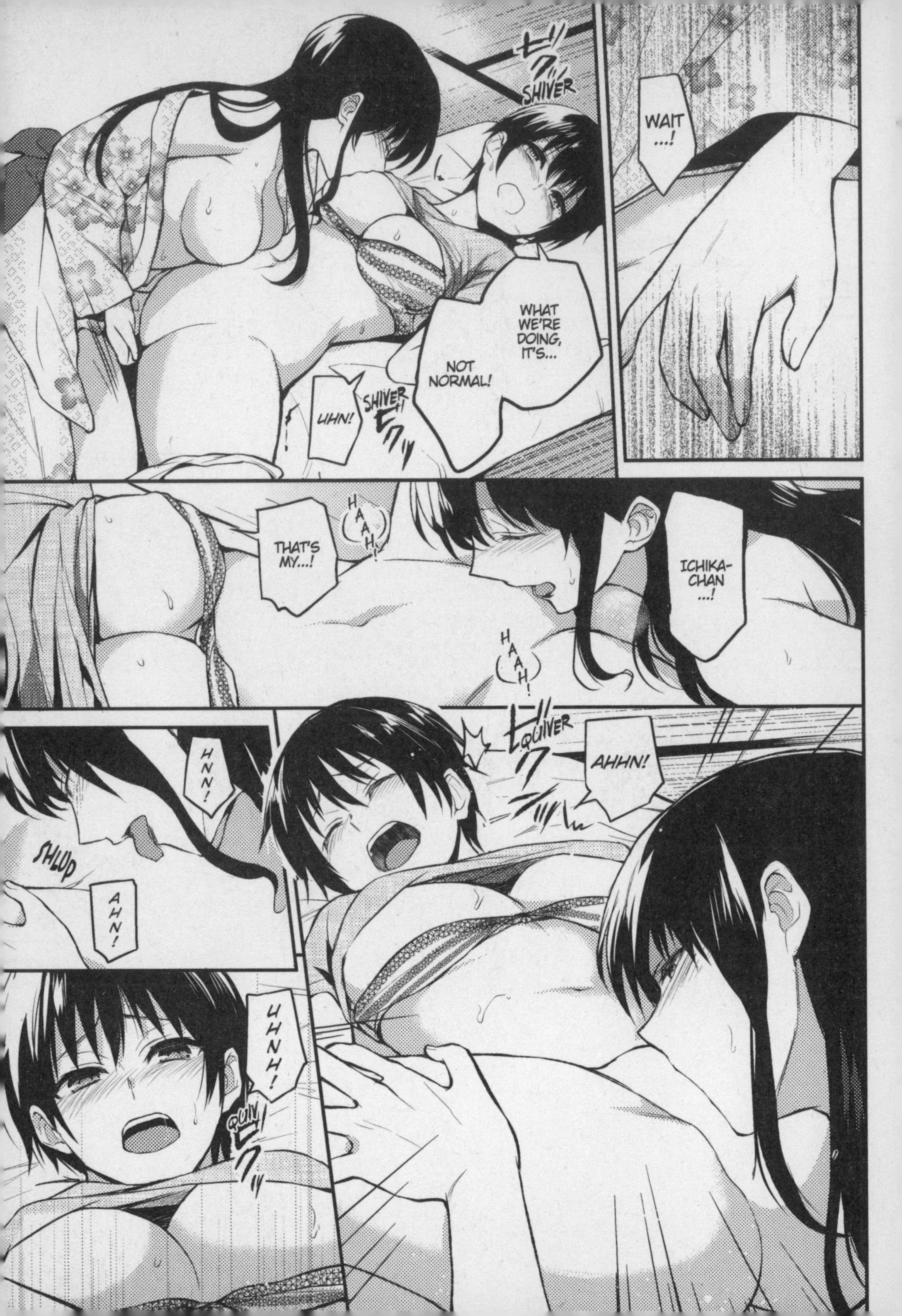

WAIT ...!
SHIVER
WHAT WE'RE DOING, IT'S...
NOT NORMAL!
UHN!
SHIVER
ICHIKA-CHAN ...!
HAAH!
THAT'S MY...!
HAAAH!
AHHN!
QUIVER
HNN!
SHLUP
AHN!
UHNH!
QUIV

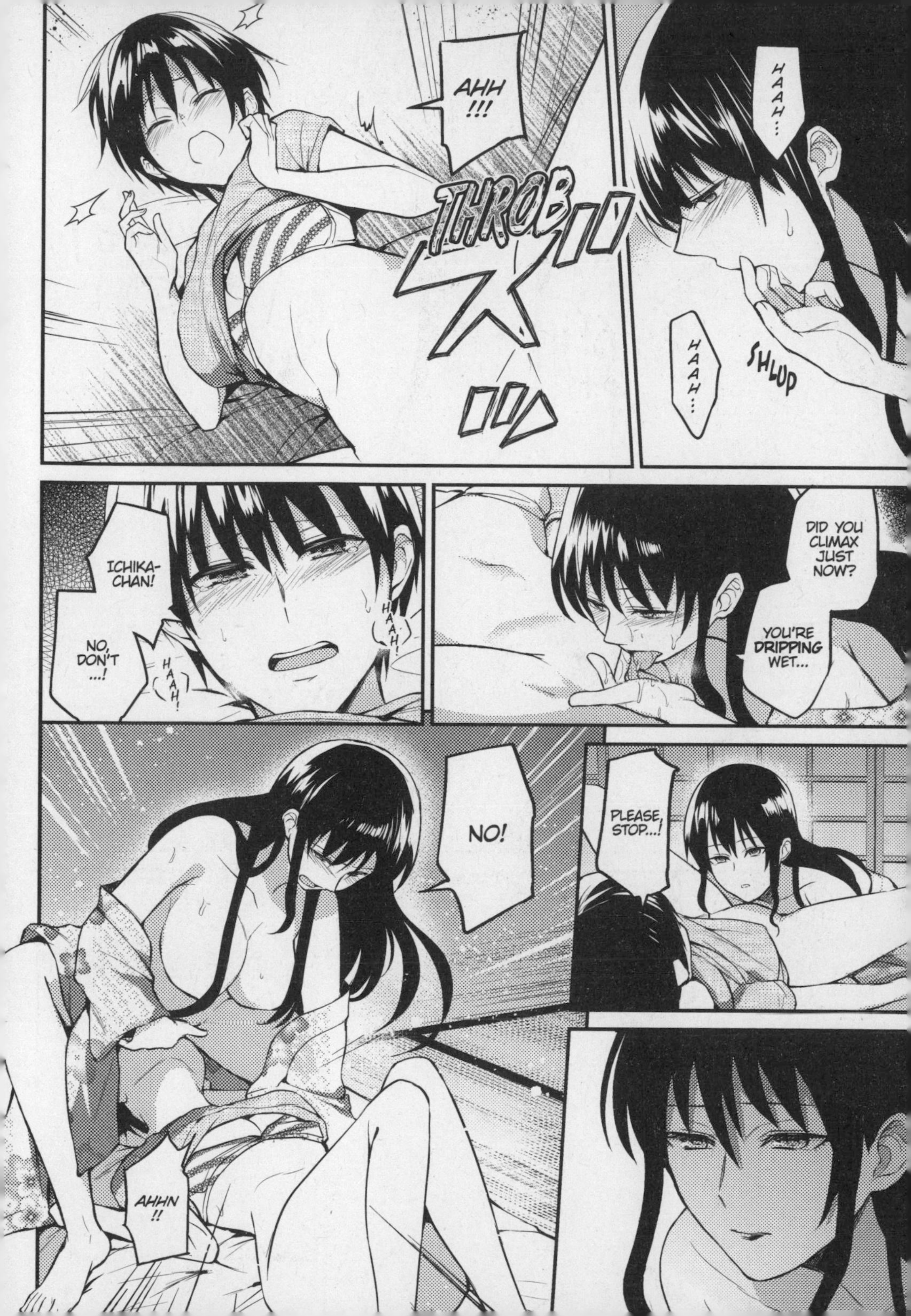
HAAH...
HAAH...
SHLUP
AHH !!!
THROB
DID YOU CLIMAX JUST NOW?
YOU'RE DRIPPING WET...
ICHIKA-CHAN!
HAAH!
NO, DON'T ...!
HAAH!
PLEASE, STOP...!
NO!
AHHN !!

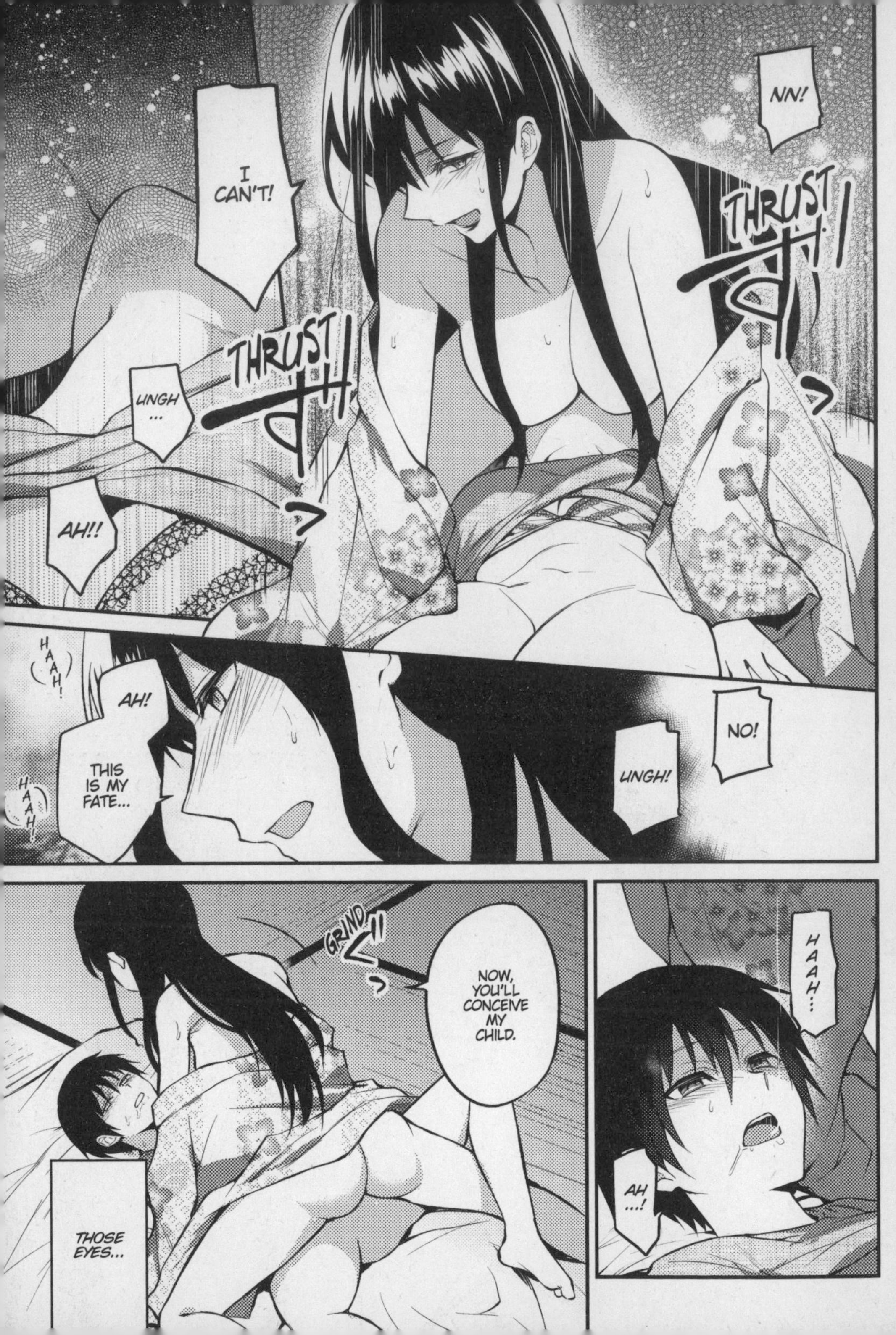
NN!
THRUST
I CAN'T!
THRUST
UNGH...
AH!!
NO!
UNGH!
AH!
HAAAH!
THIS IS MY FATE...
HAAAH!
HAAAH...
AH...!
GRIND
NOW, YOU'LL CONCEIVE MY CHILD.
THOSE EYES...

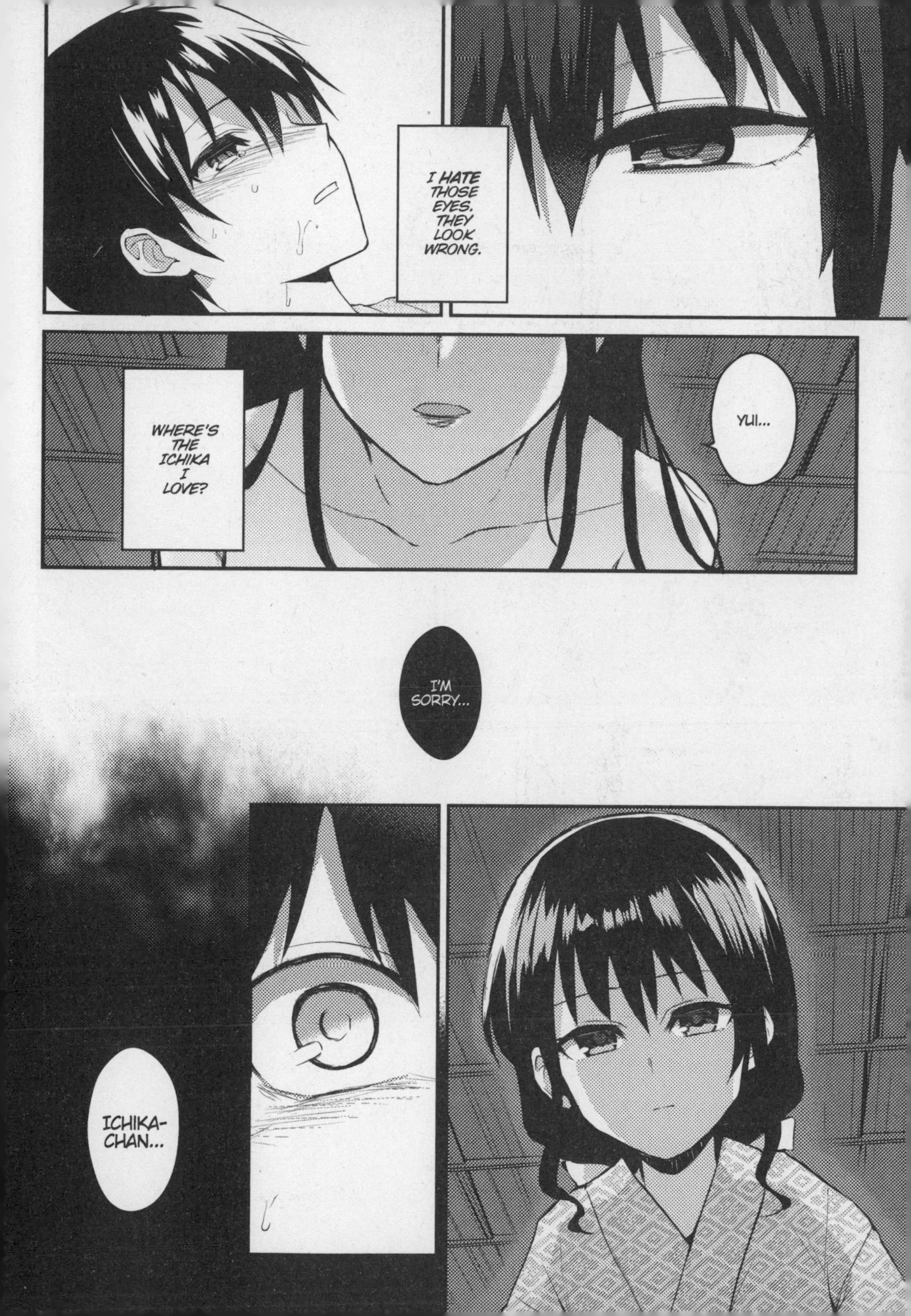
I HATE THOSE EYES. THEY LOOK WRONG.
YUI...
WHERE'S THE ICHIKA I LOVE?
I'M SORRY...
ICHIKA-CHAN...

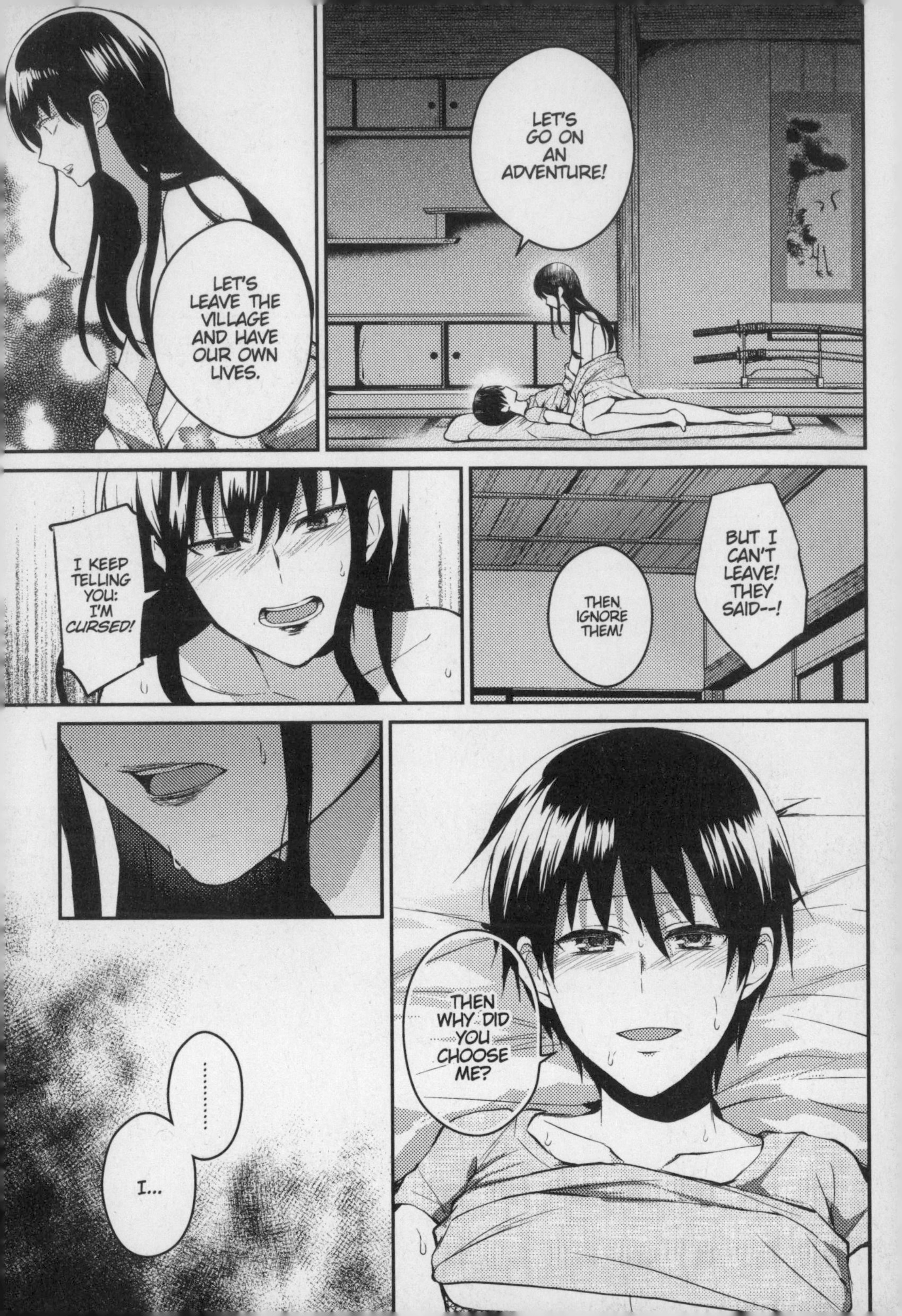
LET'S GO ON AN ADVENTURE!
LET'S LEAVE THE VILLAGE AND HAVE OUR OWN LIVES.
BUT I CAN'T LEAVE! THEY SAID--!
THEN IGNORE THEM!
I KEEP TELLING YOU: I'M CURSED!
THEN WHY DID YOU CHOOSE ME?
......
I...

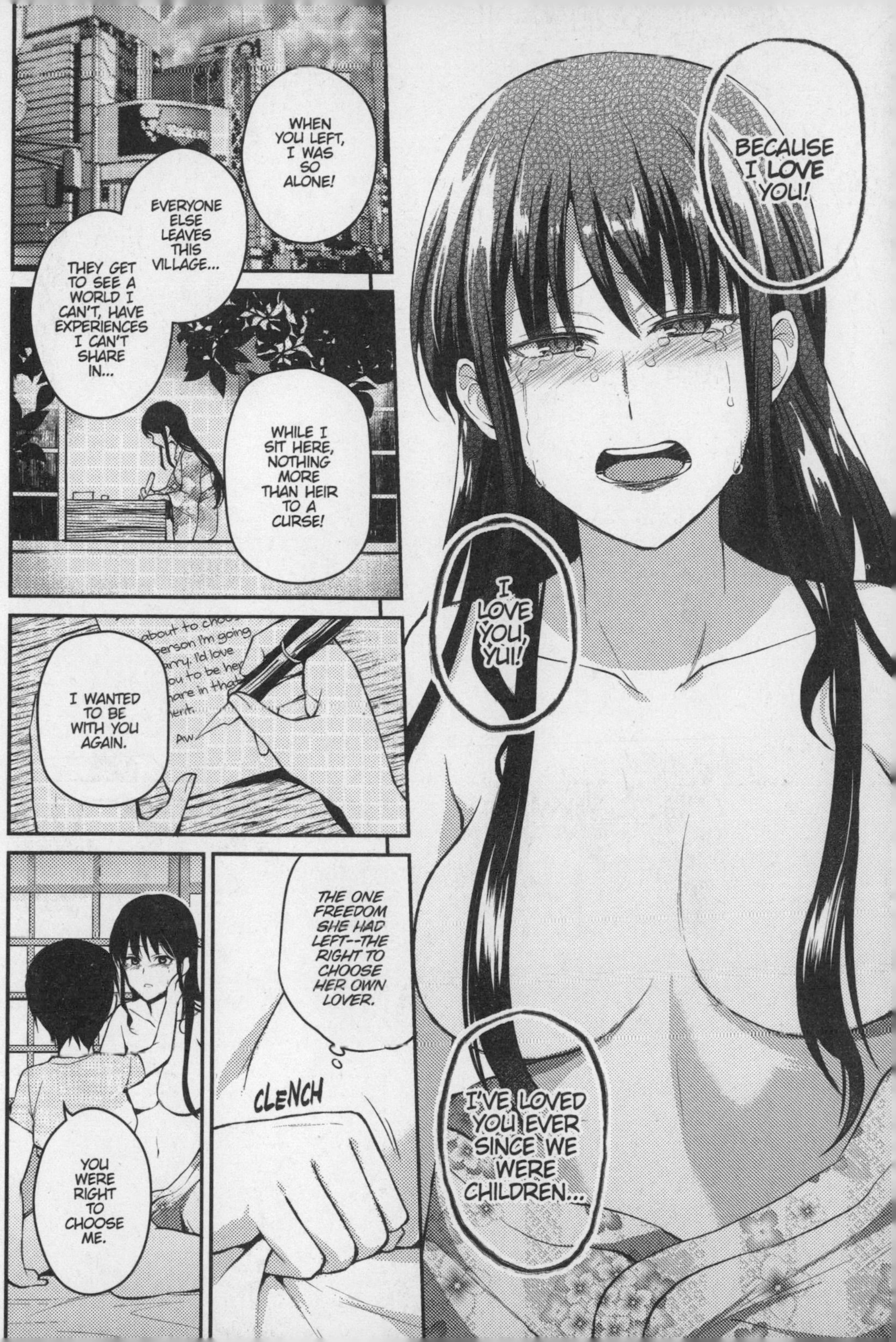
BECAUSE I LOVE YOU!
I LOVE YOU, YUI!
I'VE LOVED YOU EVER SINCE WE WERE CHILDREN...
WHEN YOU LEFT, I WAS SO ALONE!
EVERYONE ELSE LEAVES THIS VILLAGE...
THEY GET TO SEE A WORLD I CAN'T, HAVE EXPERIENCES I CAN'T SHARE IN...
WHILE I SIT HERE, NOTHING MORE THAN HEIR TO A CURSE!
I WANTED TO BE WITH YOU AGAIN.
THE ONE FREEDOM SHE HAD LEFT--THE RIGHT TO CHOOSE HER OWN LOVER.
CLENCH
YOU WERE RIGHT TO CHOOSE ME.

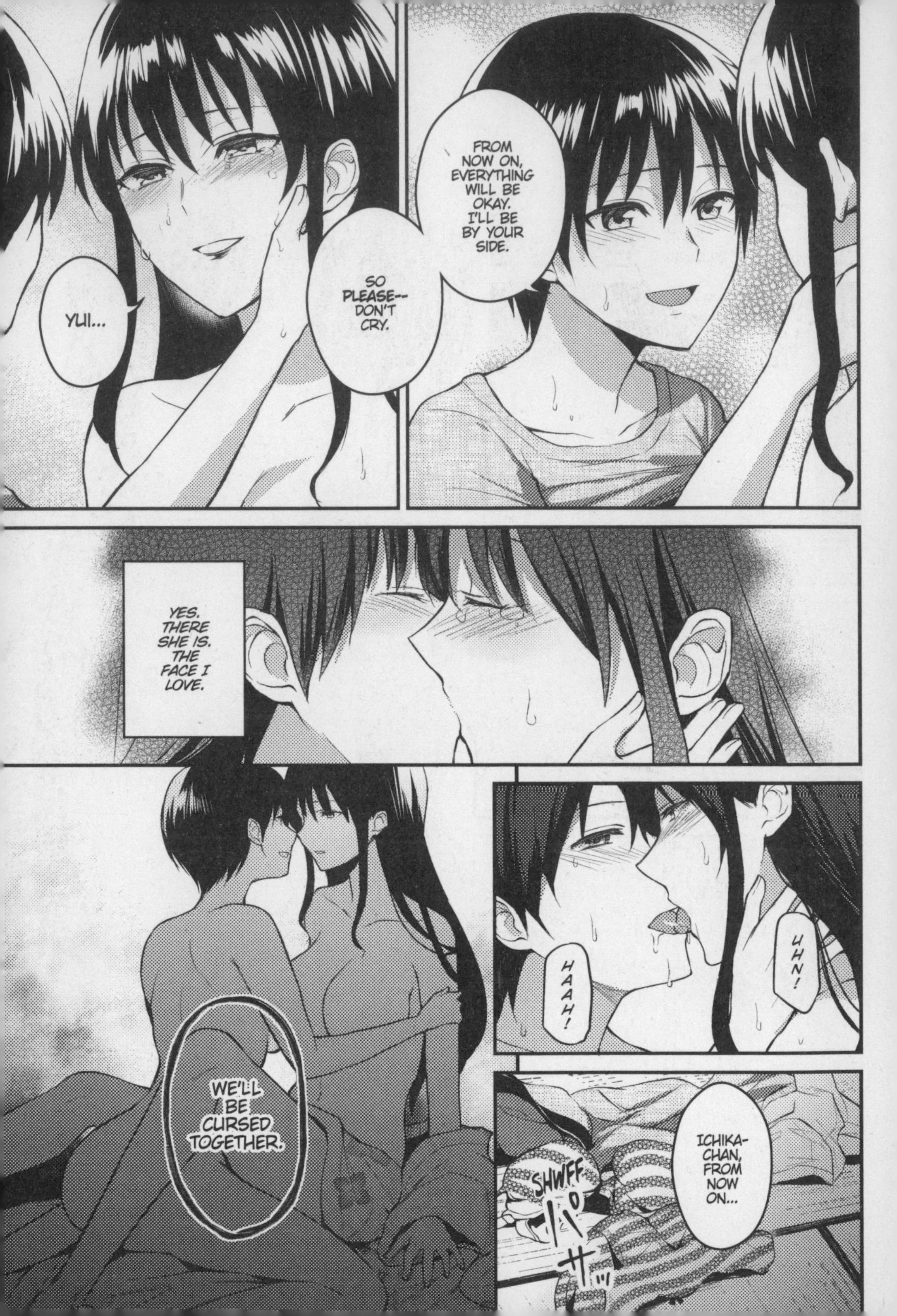
FROM NOW ON, EVERYTHING WILL BE OKAY. I'LL BE BY YOUR SIDE.
SO PLEASE-- DON'T CRY.
YUI...
YES. THERE SHE IS. THE FACE I LOVE.
UHN!
HAAAH!
ICHIKA-CHAN, FROM NOW ON...
SHWFF
WE'LL BE CURSED TOGETHER.

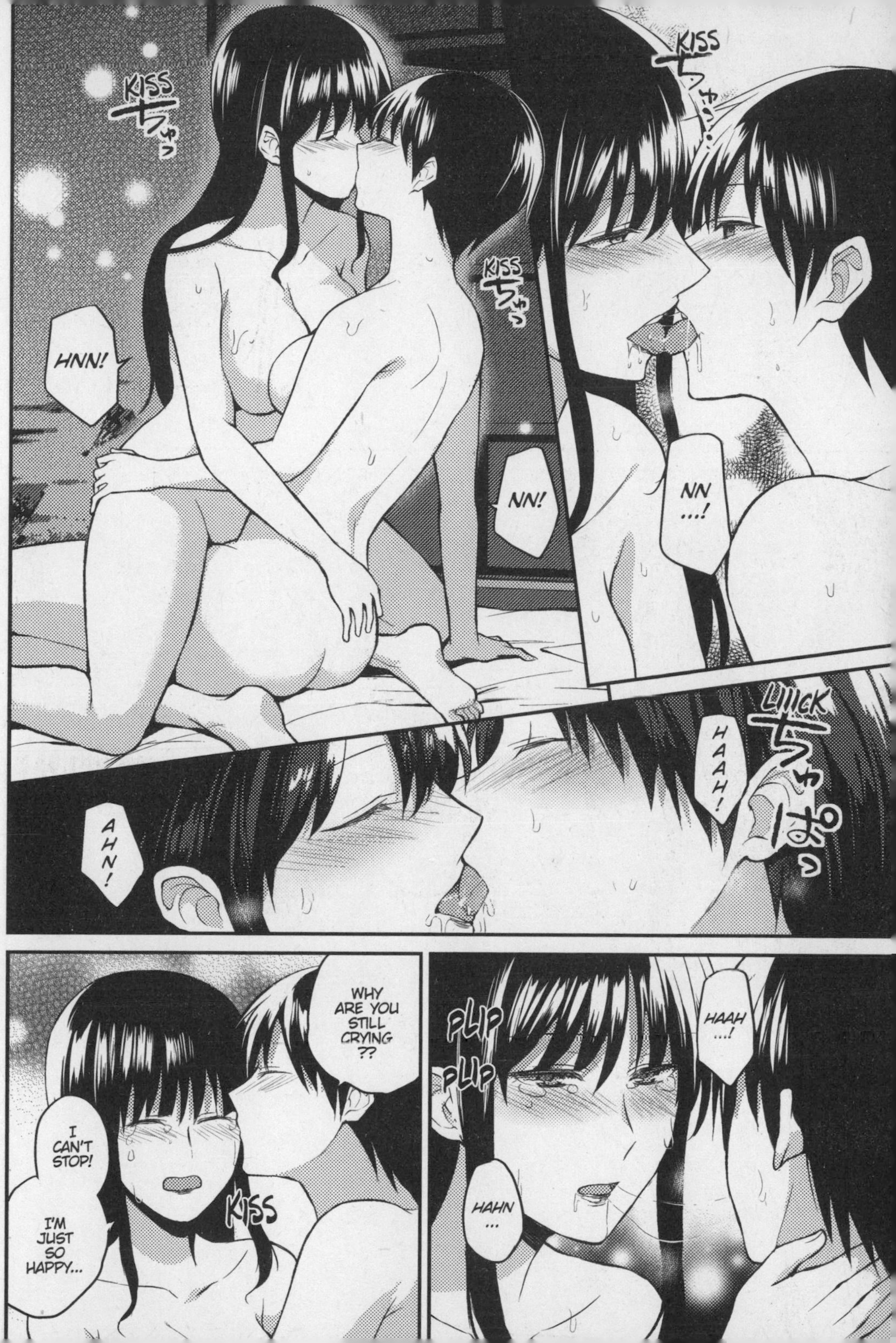
KISS
ちゅっ…
NN ...!
KISS
ちゅっ
HNN!
KISS
ちゅっ
NN!
LIIICK
ちゅーぽっ
HAAH!
AHN!
HAAH ...!
PLIP
PLIP
HAHN ...
WHY ARE YOU STILL CRYING ??
I CAN'T STOP!
KISS
I'M JUST SO HAPPY...

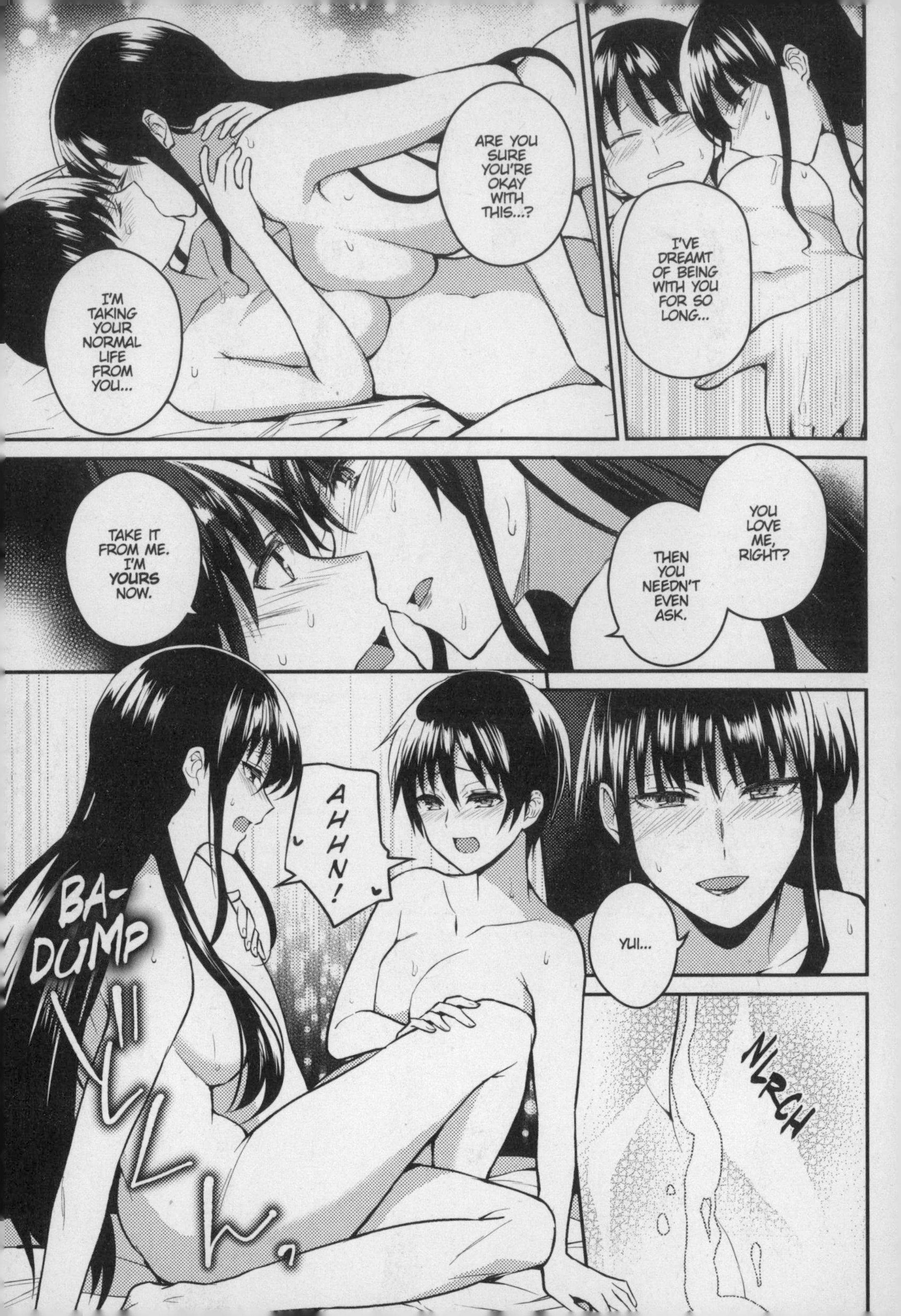
I'VE DREAMT OF BEING WITH YOU FOR SO LONG...
ARE YOU SURE YOU'RE OKAY WITH THIS...?
I'M TAKING YOUR NORMAL LIFE FROM YOU...
YOU LOVE ME, RIGHT?
THEN YOU NEEDN'T EVEN ASK.
TAKE IT FROM ME. I'M YOURS NOW.
YUI...
NLRCH
AHHN!
BA-DUMP

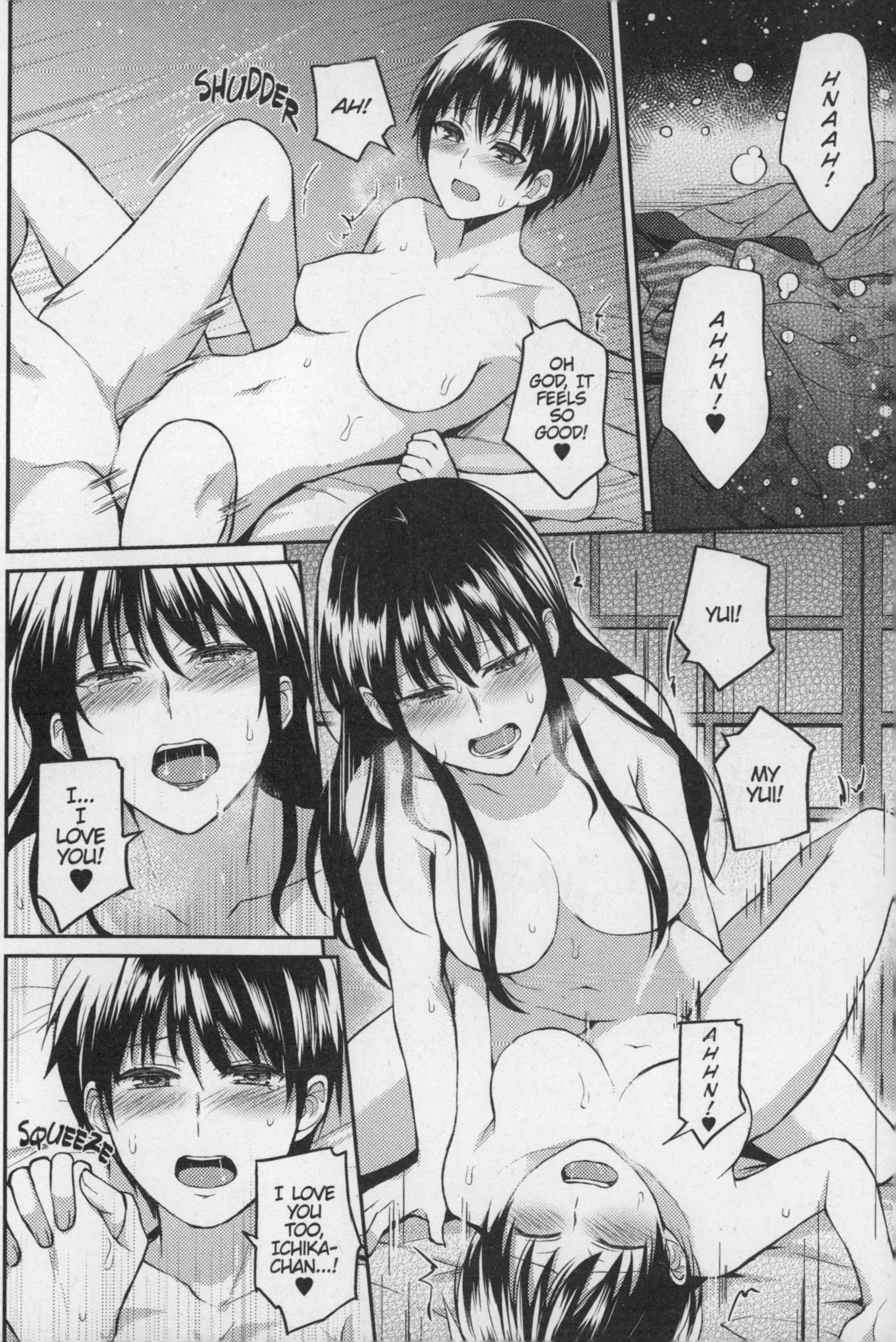
HNAAH!
AHHN! ♥
SHUDDER
AH!
OH GOD, IT FEELS SO GOOD! ♥
YUI!
MY YUI!
AHHN! ♥
I... I LOVE YOU! ♥
SQUEEZE
I LOVE YOU TOO, ICHIKA-CHAN...! ♥

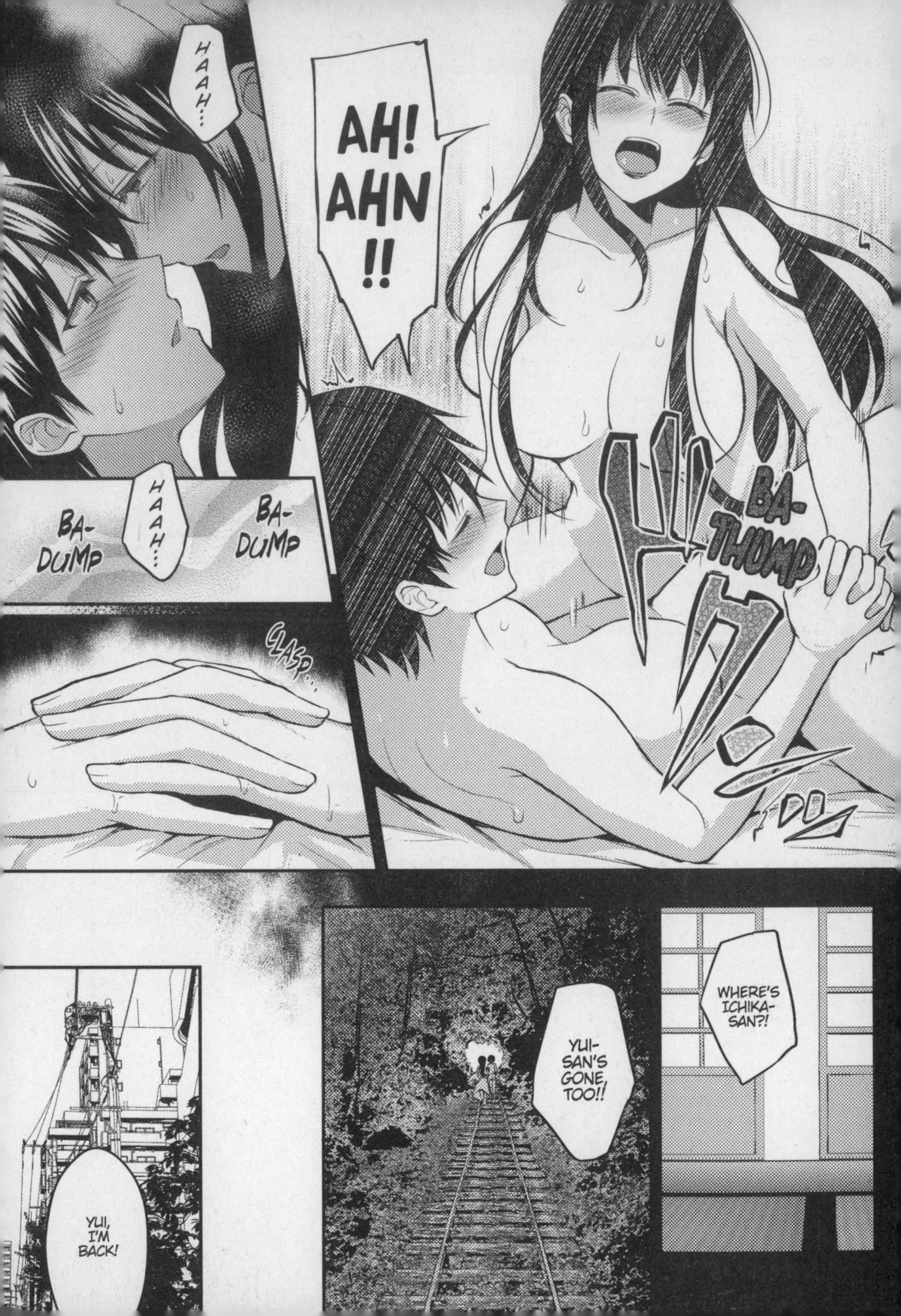
AH! AHN!!
BA-THUMP
DO
HAAAH...
BA-DUMP
HAAAH...
BA-DUMP
CLASP...
WHERE'S ICHIKA-SAN?!
YUI-SAN'S GONE, TOO!!
YUI, I'M BACK!

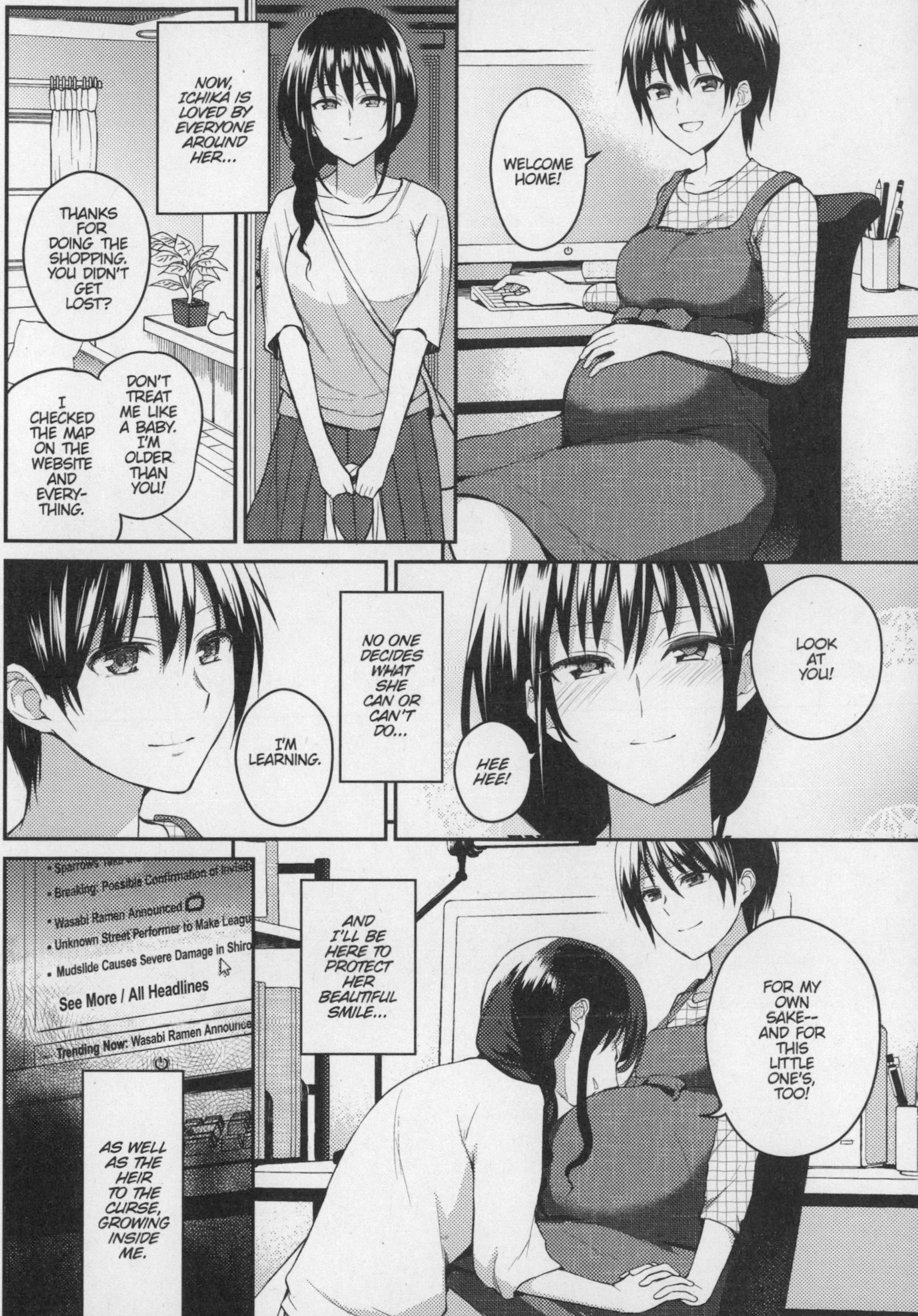
WELCOME HOME!
NOW, ICHIKA IS LOVED BY EVERYONE AROUND HER...
THANKS FOR DOING THE SHOPPING. YOU DIDN'T GET LOST?
DON'T TREAT ME LIKE A BABY. I'M OLDER THAN YOU!
I CHECKED THE MAP ON THE WEBSITE AND EVERY-THING.
LOOK AT YOU!
HEE HEE!
NO ONE DECIDES WHAT SHE CAN OR CAN'T DO...
I'M LEARNING.
FOR MY OWN SAKE--AND FOR THIS LITTLE ONE'S, TOO!
AND I'LL BE HERE TO PROTECT HER BEAUTIFUL SMILE...
Breaking: Possible Confirmation of
Wasabi Ramen Announced
Unknown Street Performer to Make League
Mudslide Causes Severe Damage in Shiro
See More / All Headlines
Trending Now: Wasabi Ramen Announce
AS WELL AS THE HEIR TO THE CURSE, GROWING INSIDE ME.

nd Eve

Eve and

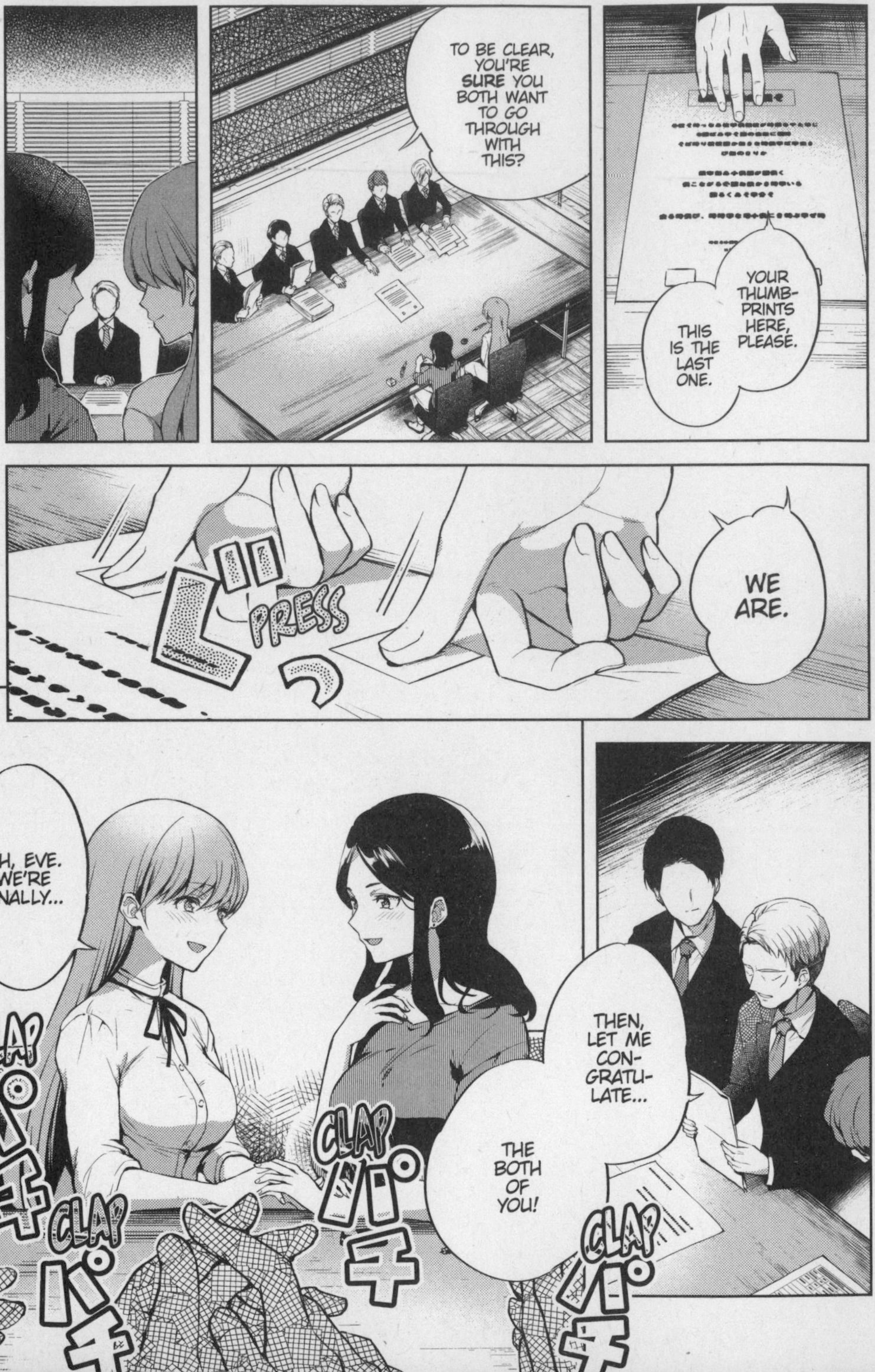
YOUR THUMB-PRINTS HERE, PLEASE.
THIS IS THE LAST ONE.
TO BE CLEAR, YOU'RE **SURE** YOU BOTH WANT TO GO THROUGH WITH THIS?
WE ARE.
PRESS
THEN, LET ME CON-GRATU-LATE...
THE BOTH OF YOU!
CLAP
CLAP
OH, EVE. WE'RE FINALLY...
CLAP
CLAP

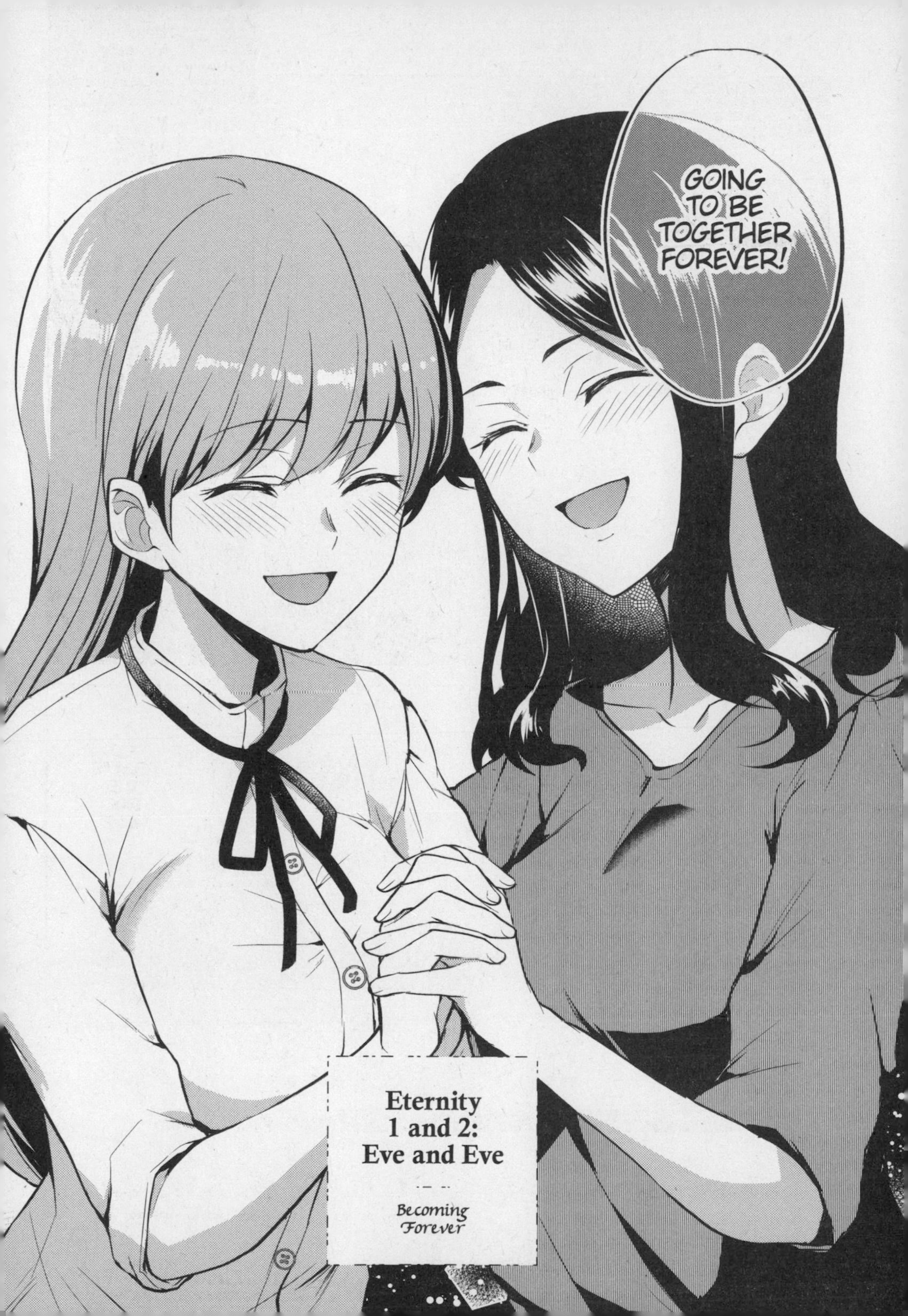
GOING TO BE TOGETHER FOREVER!

Eternity 1 and 2: Eve and Eve

Becoming Forever

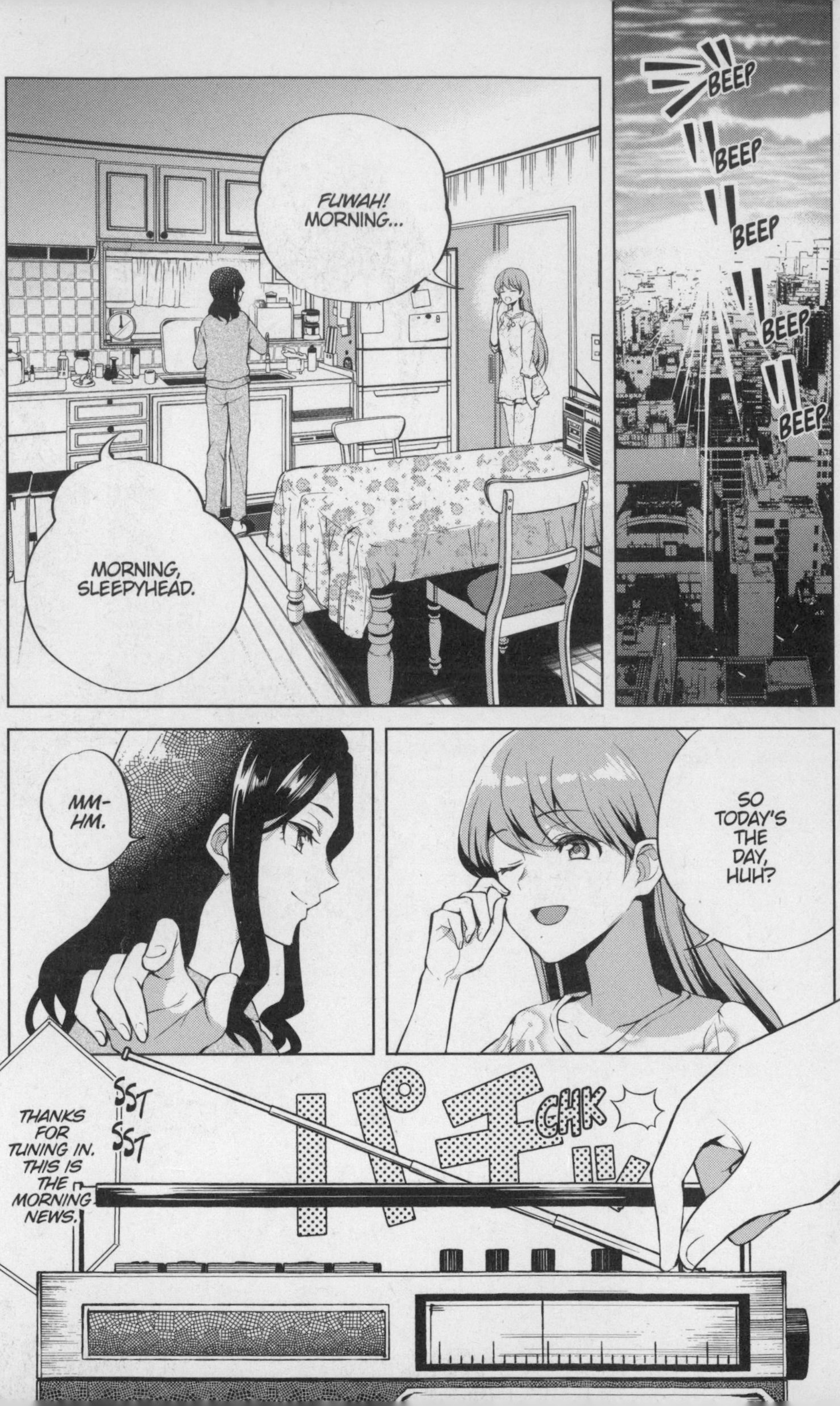
BEEP
BEEP
BEEP
BEEP
BEEP
FUWAH! MORNING...
MORNING, SLEEPYHEAD.
SO TODAY'S THE DAY, HUH?
MM-HM.
パチ
CHK
SST
SST
THANKS FOR TUNING IN. THIS IS THE MORNING NEWS.

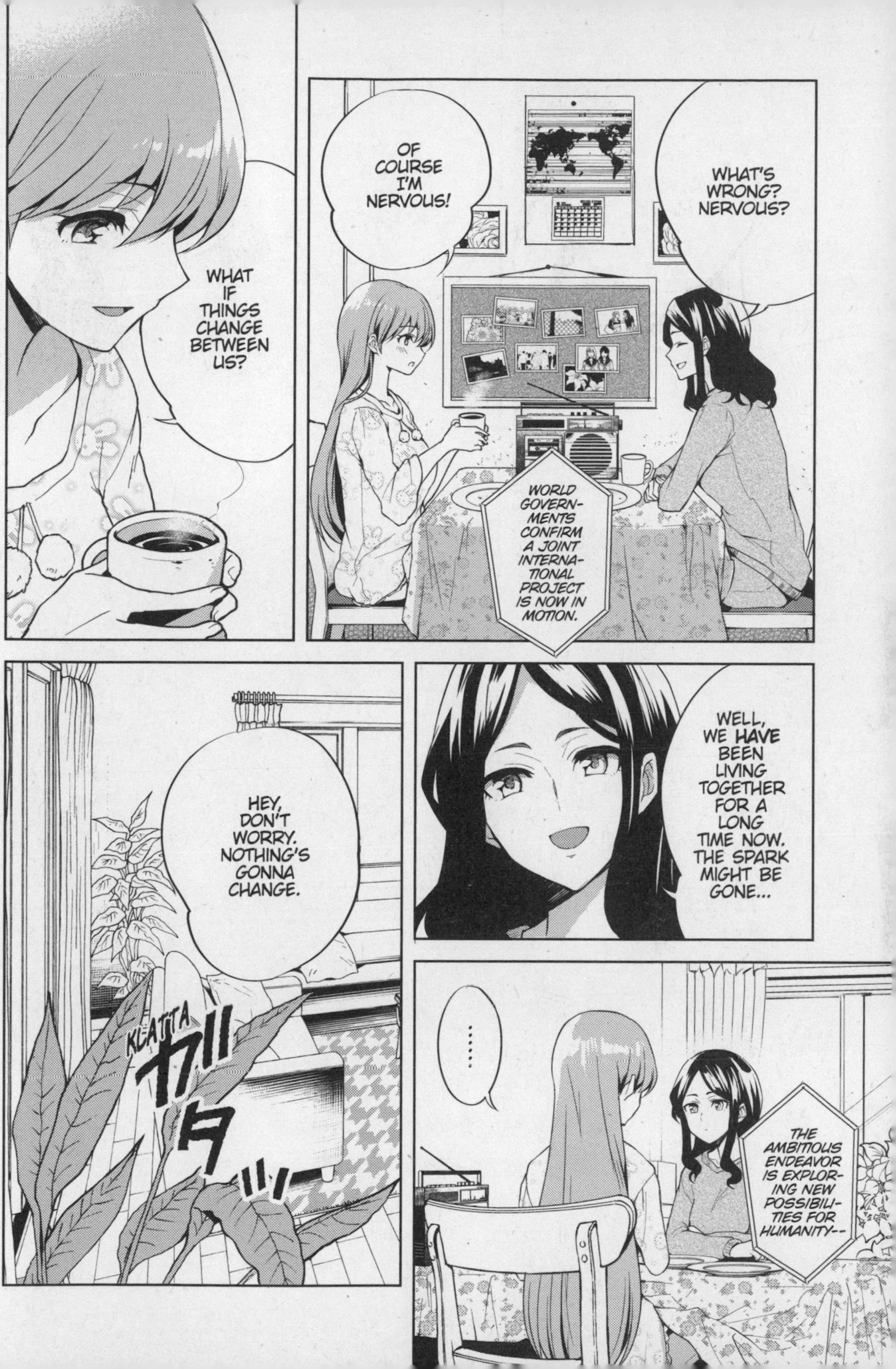
WHAT'S WRONG? NERVOUS?
OF COURSE I'M NERVOUS!
WORLD GOVERN-MENTS CONFIRM A JOINT INTERNA-TIONAL PROJECT IS NOW IN MOTION.
WHAT IF THINGS CHANGE BETWEEN US?
WELL, WE HAVE BEEN LIVING TOGETHER FOR A LONG TIME NOW. THE SPARK MIGHT BE GONE...
......
THE AMBITIOUS ENDEAVOR IS EXPLOR-ING NEW POSSIBILI-TIES FOR HUMANITY--
HEY, DON'T WORRY. NOTHING'S GONNA CHANGE.
KLATTA

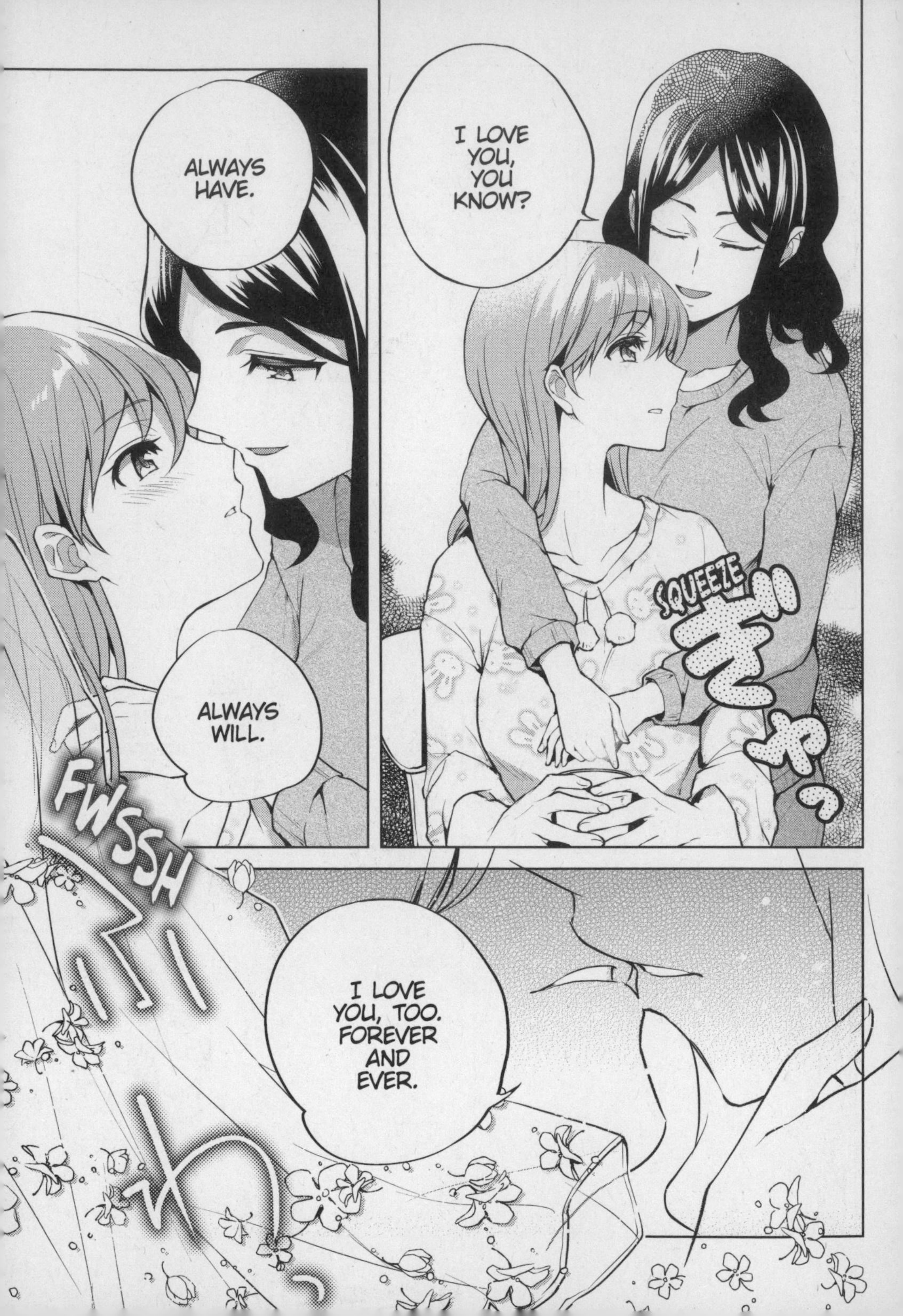
I LOVE YOU, YOU KNOW?
SQUEEZE
ALWAYS HAVE.
ALWAYS WILL.
FWSSH
I LOVE YOU, TOO. FOREVER AND EVER.

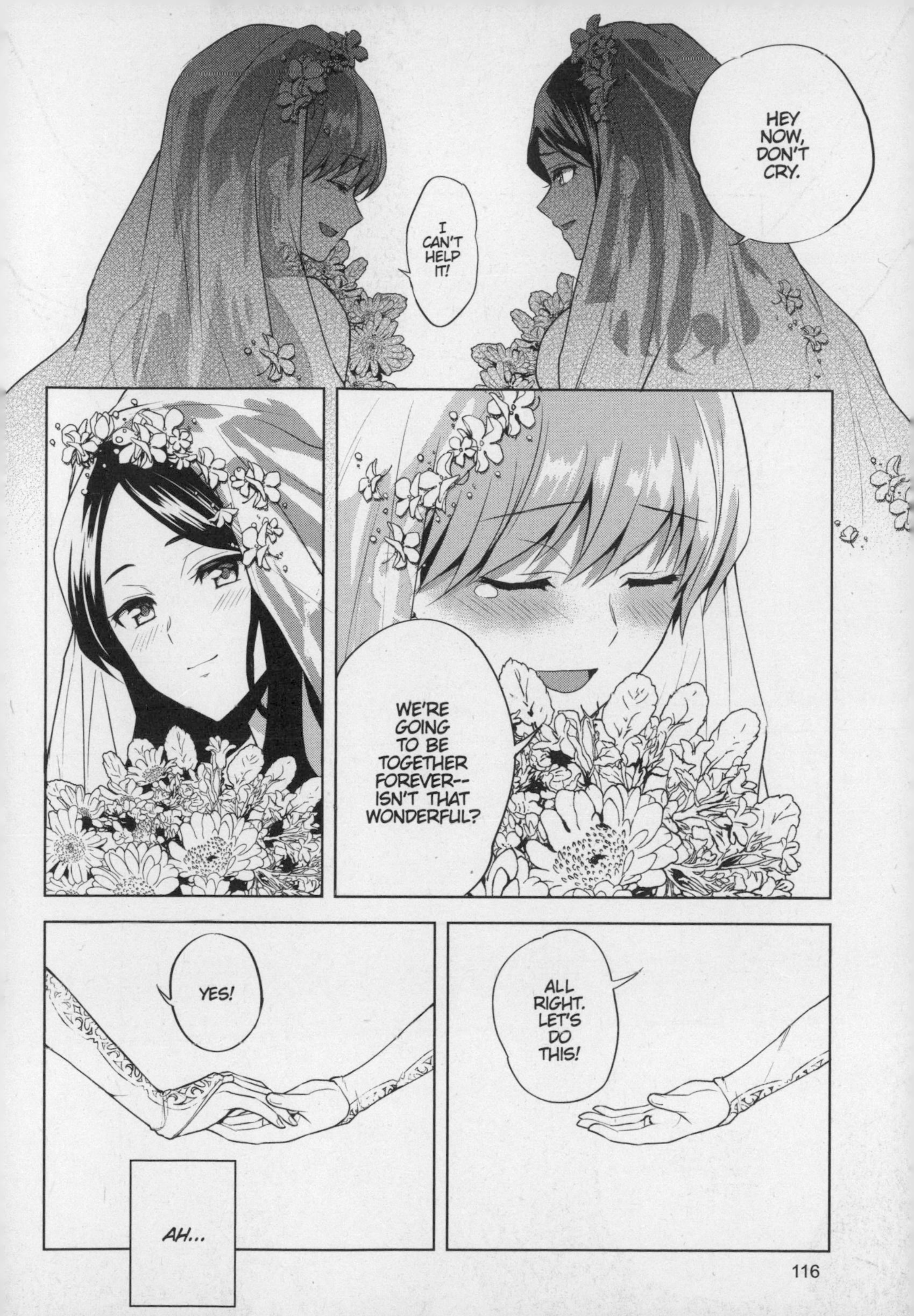
HEY NOW, DON'T CRY.
I CAN'T HELP IT!
WE'RE GOING TO BE TOGETHER FOREVER--ISN'T THAT WONDERFUL?
ALL RIGHT. LET'S DO THIS!
YES!
AH...

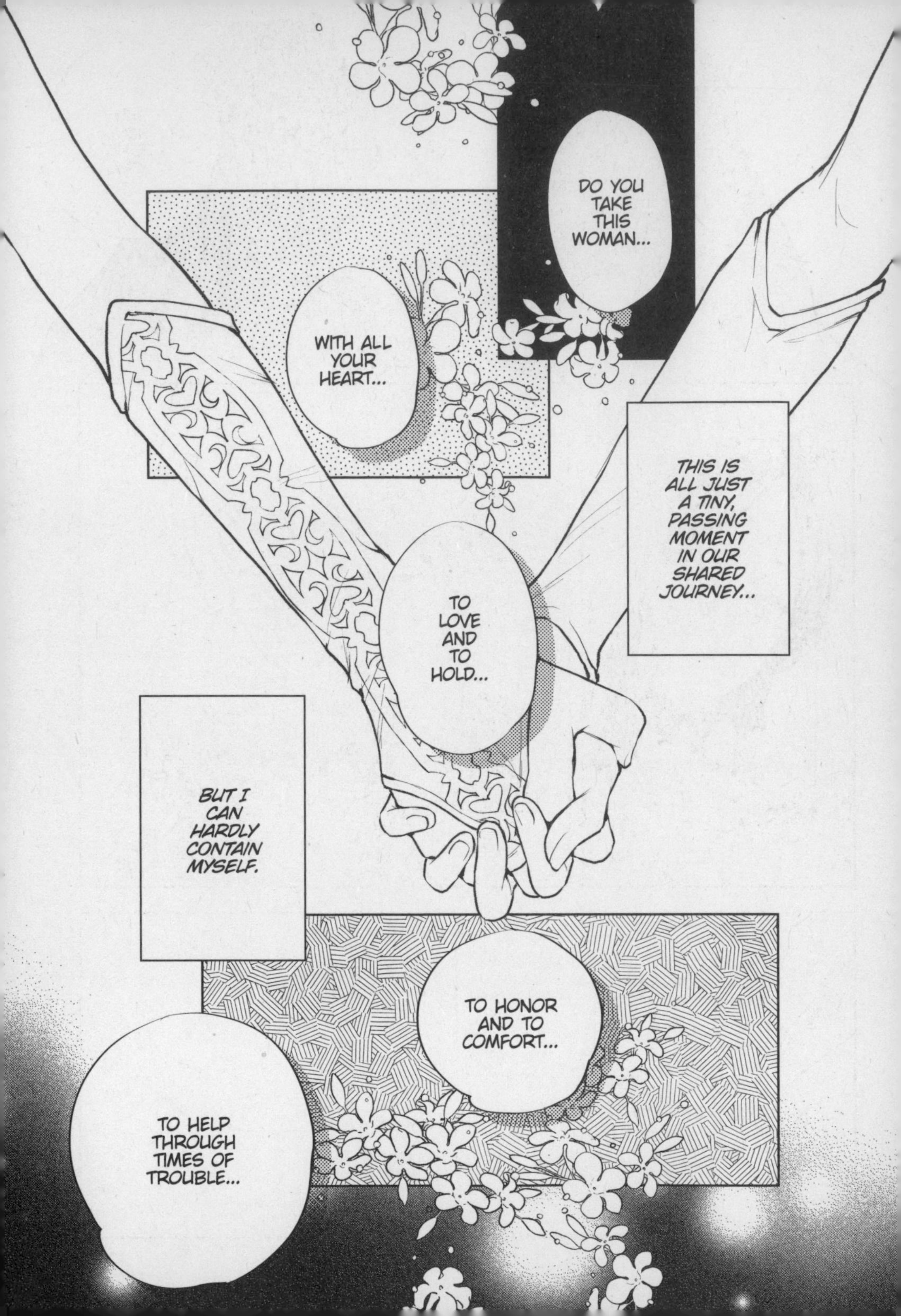
DO YOU TAKE THIS WOMAN...
WITH ALL YOUR HEART...
THIS IS ALL JUST A TINY, PASSING MOMENT IN OUR SHARED JOURNEY...
TO LOVE AND TO HOLD...
BUT I CAN HARDLY CONTAIN MYSELF.
TO HONOR AND TO COMFORT...
TO HELP THROUGH TIMES OF TROUBLE...

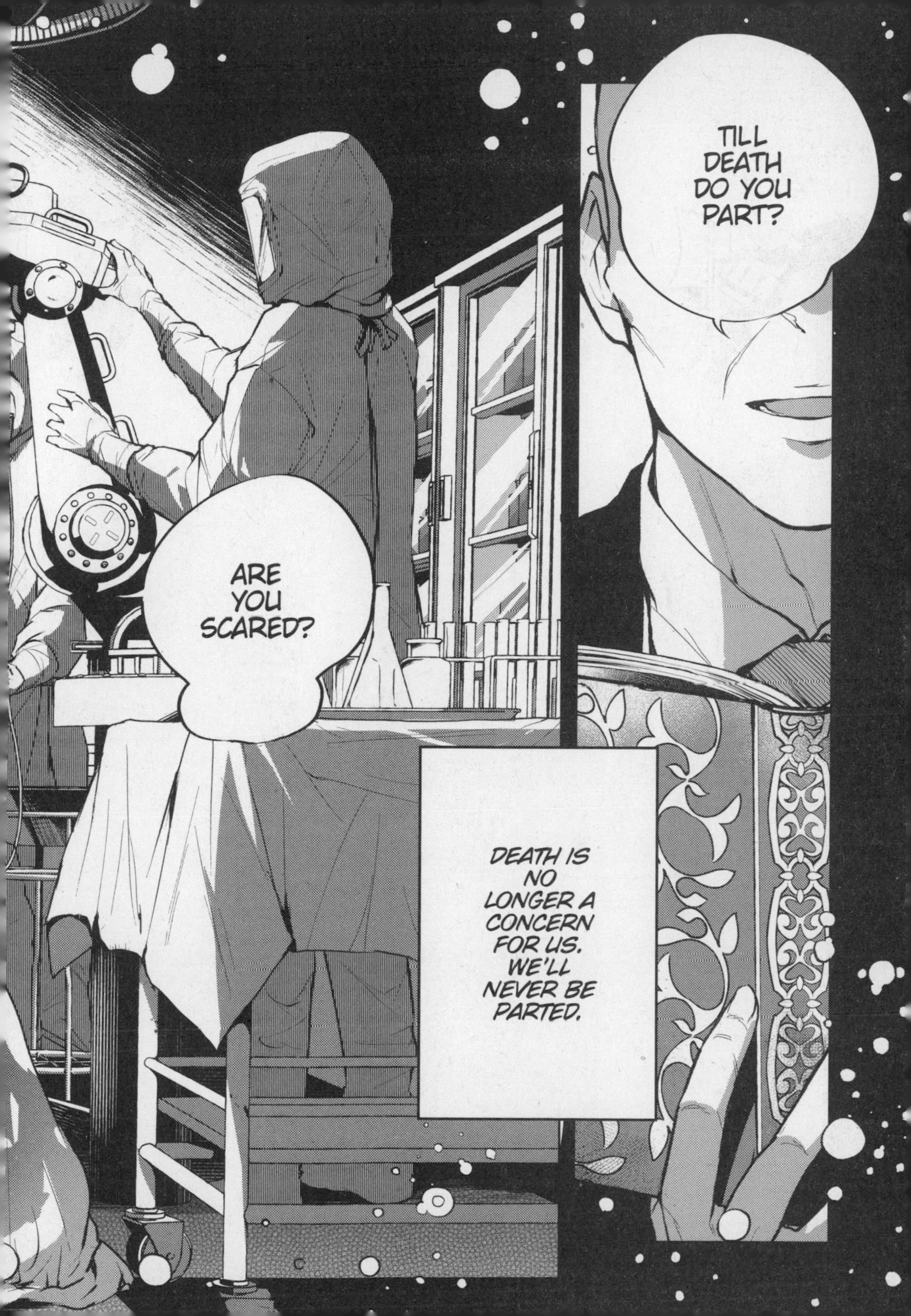
TILL DEATH DO YOU PART?
ARE YOU SCARED?
DEATH IS NO LONGER A CONCERN FOR US. WE'LL NEVER BE PARTED.

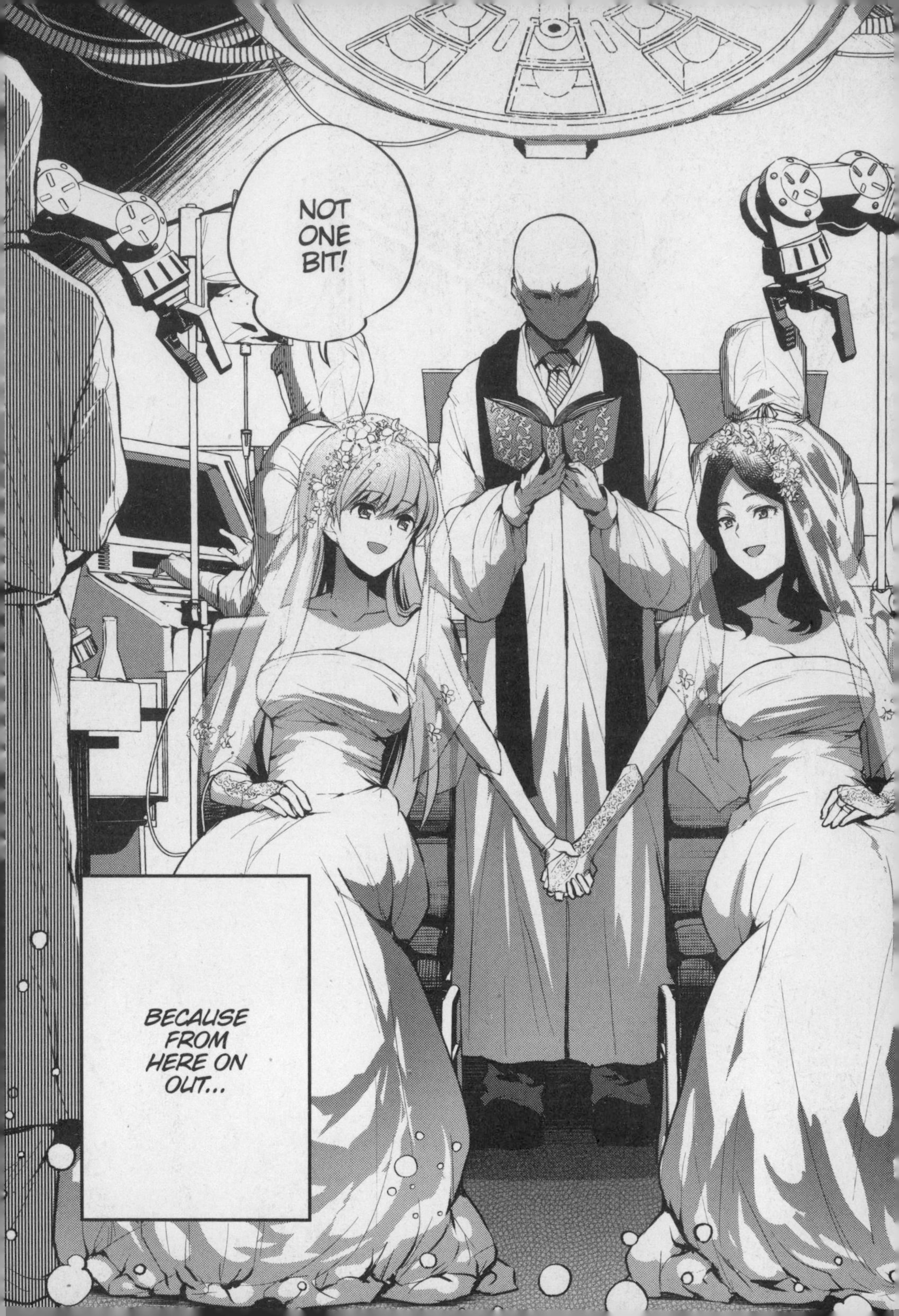
NOT ONE BIT!
BECAUSE FROM HERE ON OUT...

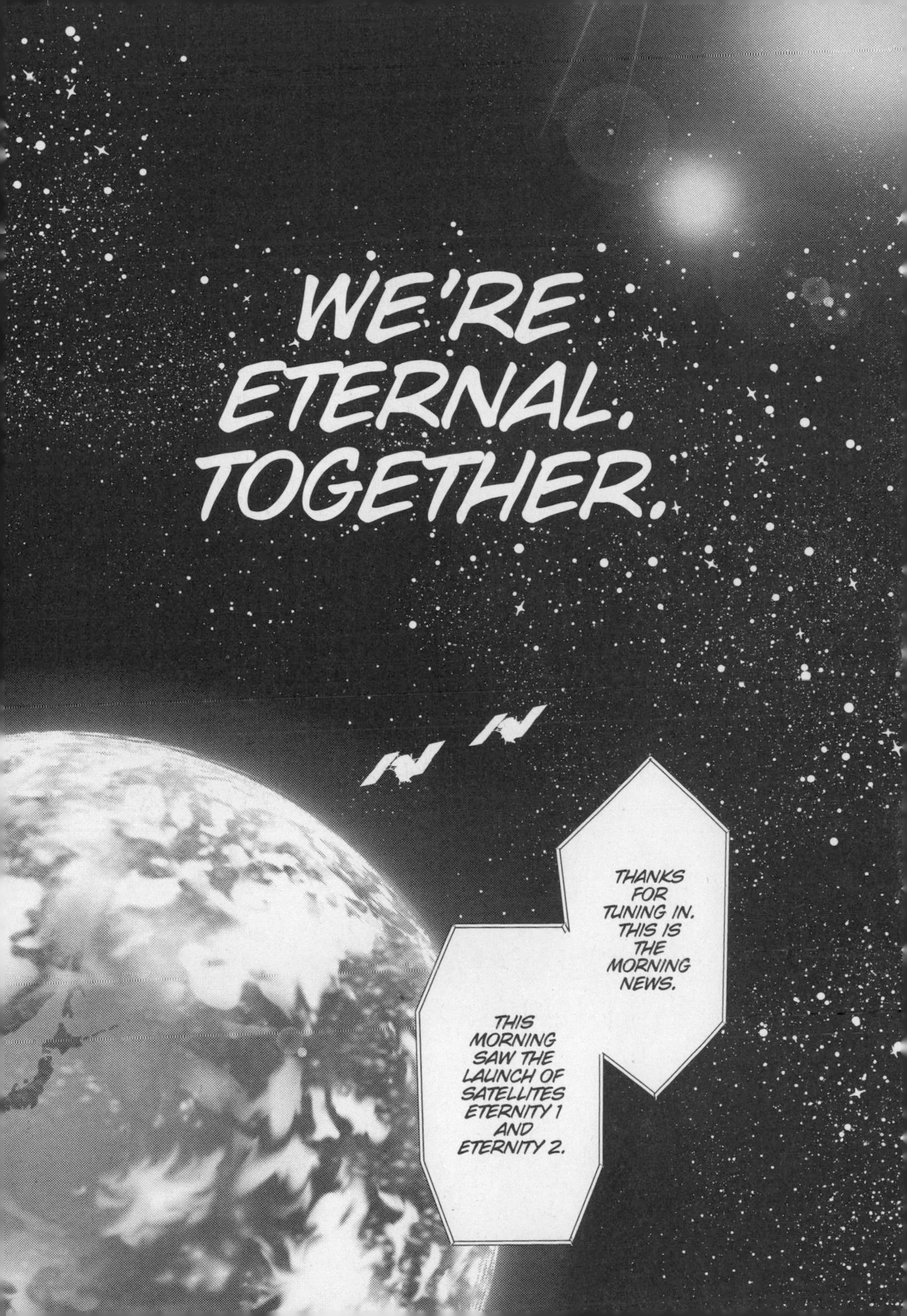
WE'RE ETERNAL. TOGETHER.
THANKS FOR TUNING IN. THIS IS THE MORNING NEWS.
THIS MORNING SAW THE LAUNCH OF SATELLITES ETERNITY 1 AND ETERNITY 2.

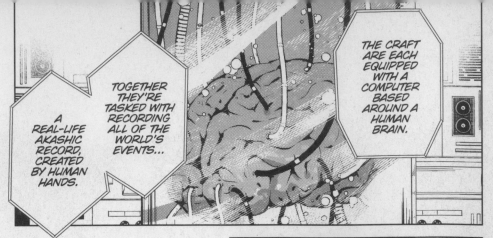

THE CRAFT ARE EACH EQUIPPED WITH A COMPUTER BASED AROUND A HUMAN BRAIN.

TOGETHER THEY'RE TASKED WITH RECORDING ALL OF THE WORLD'S EVENTS...

A REAL-LIFE AKASHIC RECORD, CREATED BY HUMAN HANDS.

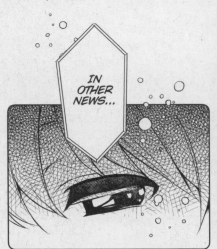

IN OTHER NEWS...

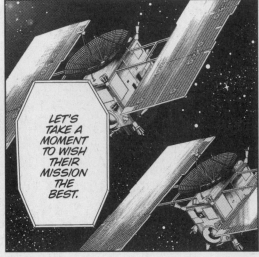

LET'S TAKE A MOMENT TO WISH THEIR MISSION THE BEST.

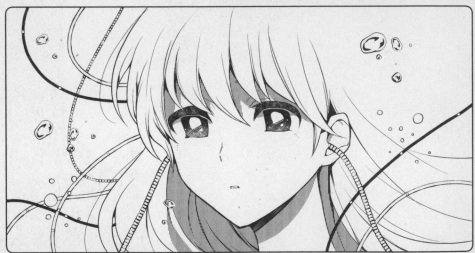

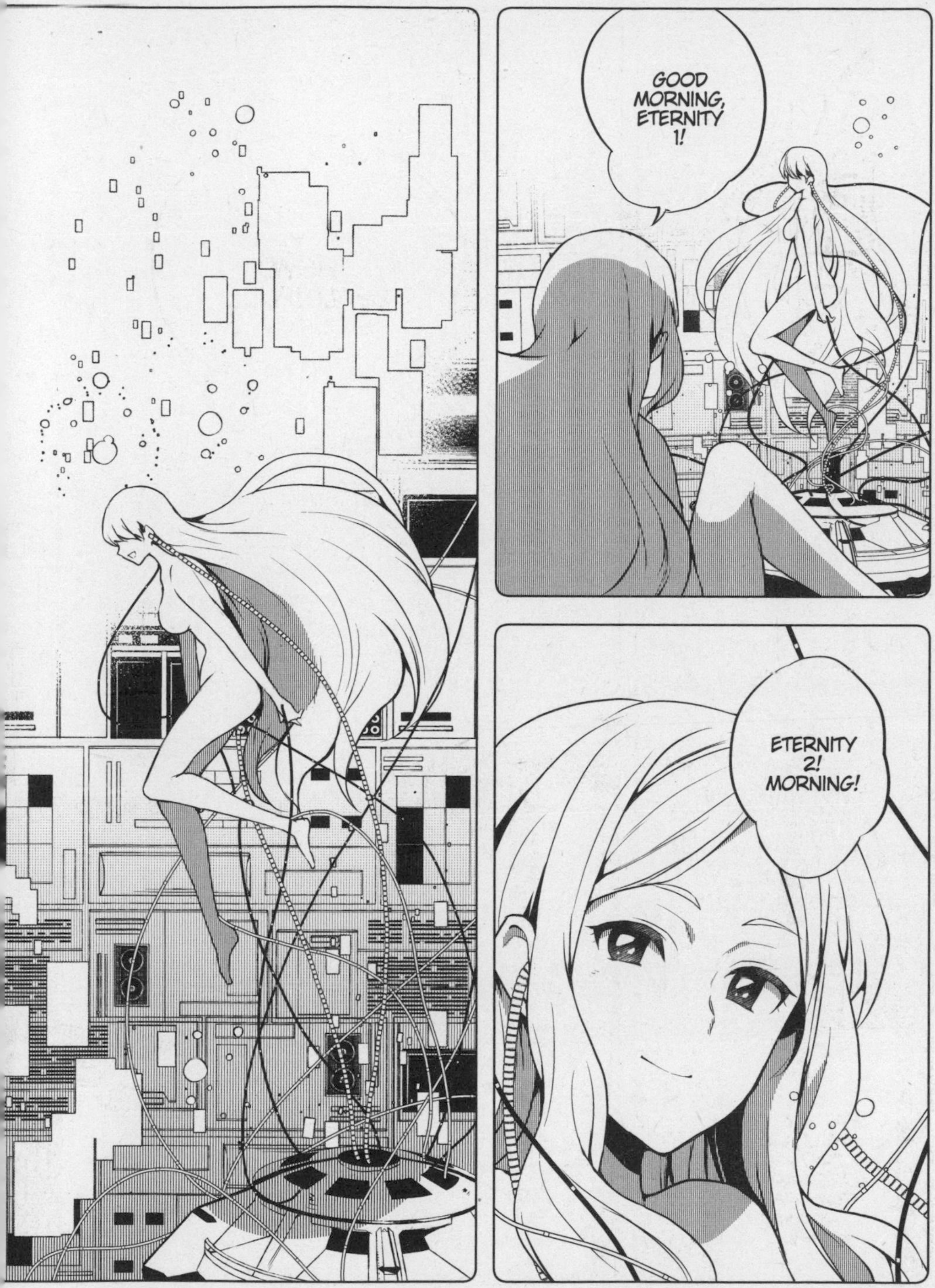
GOOD MORNING, ETERNITY 1!
ETERNITY 2! MORNING!

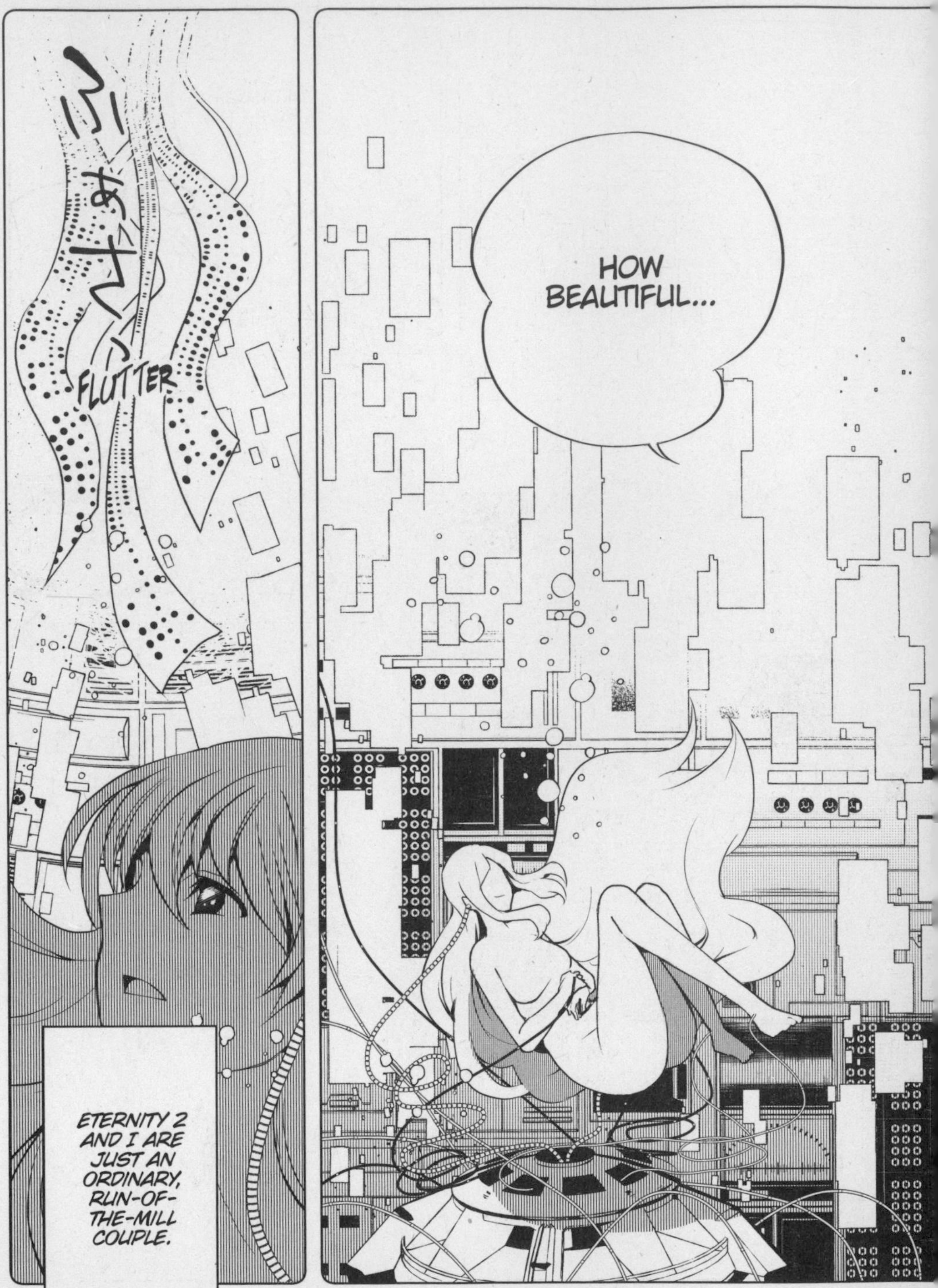
HOW BEAUTIFUL...
FLUTTER
ETERNITY 2 AND I ARE JUST AN ORDINARY, RUN-OF-THE-MILL COUPLE.

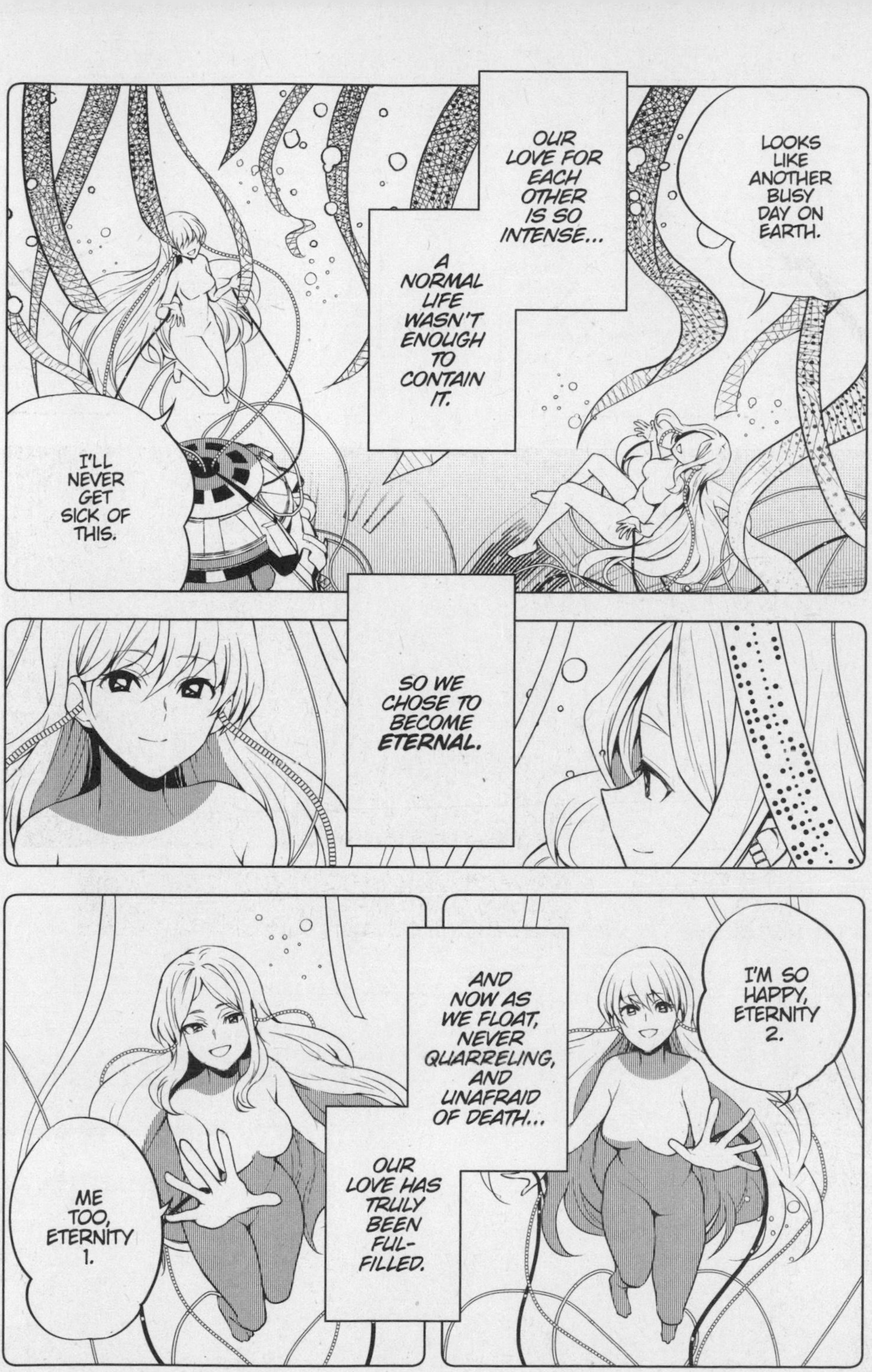
LOOKS LIKE ANOTHER BUSY DAY ON EARTH.
OUR LOVE FOR EACH OTHER IS SO INTENSE...
A NORMAL LIFE WASN'T ENOUGH TO CONTAIN IT.
I'LL NEVER GET SICK OF THIS.
SO WE CHOSE TO BECOME ETERNAL.
I'M SO HAPPY, ETERNITY 2.
AND NOW AS WE FLOAT, NEVER QUARRELING, AND UNAFRAID OF DEATH...
OUR LOVE HAS TRULY BEEN FUL-FILLED.
ME TOO, ETERNITY 1.

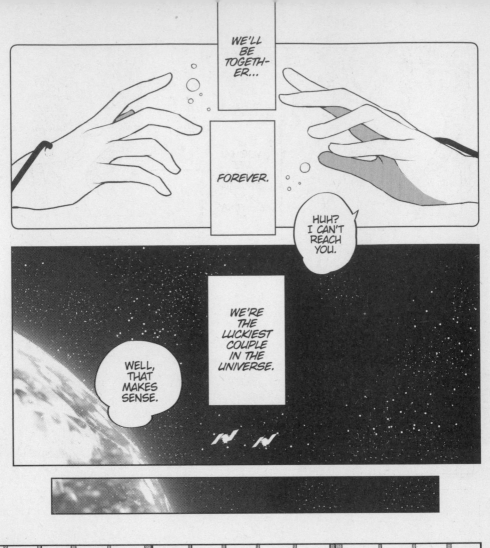

WE'LL
BE
TOGETHER...

FOREVER.

HUH?
I CAN'T
REACH
YOU.

WE'RE
THE
LUCKIEST
COUPLE
IN THE
UNIVERSE.

WELL,
THAT
MAKES
SENSE.

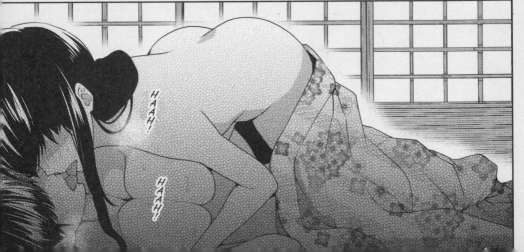

HAAH!

HAAH!

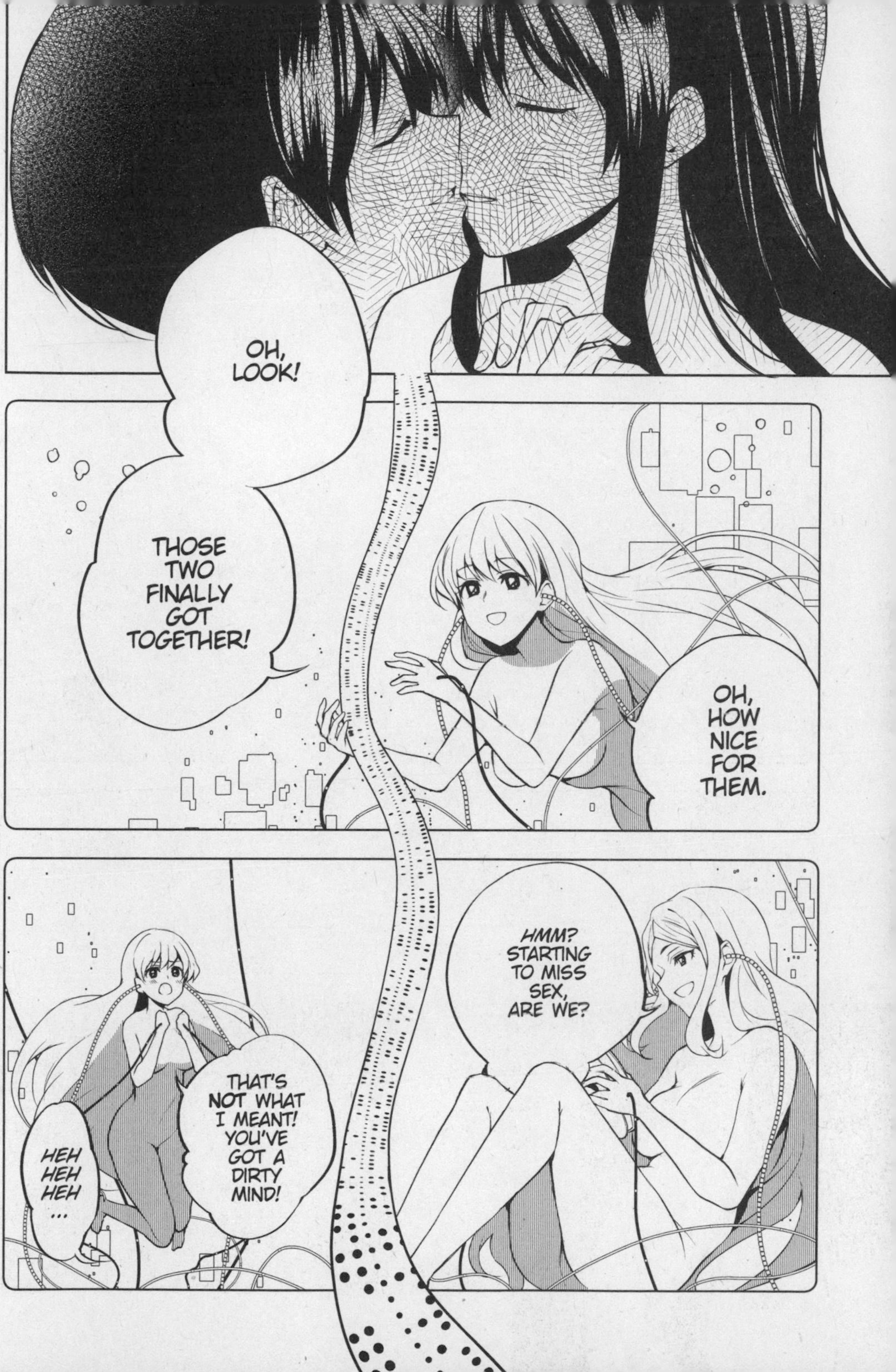
OH, LOOK!
THOSE TWO FINALLY GOT TOGETHER!
OH, HOW NICE FOR THEM.
HMM? STARTING TO MISS SEX, ARE WE?
THAT'S NOT WHAT I MEANT! YOU'VE GOT A DIRTY MIND!
HEH HEH HEH ...

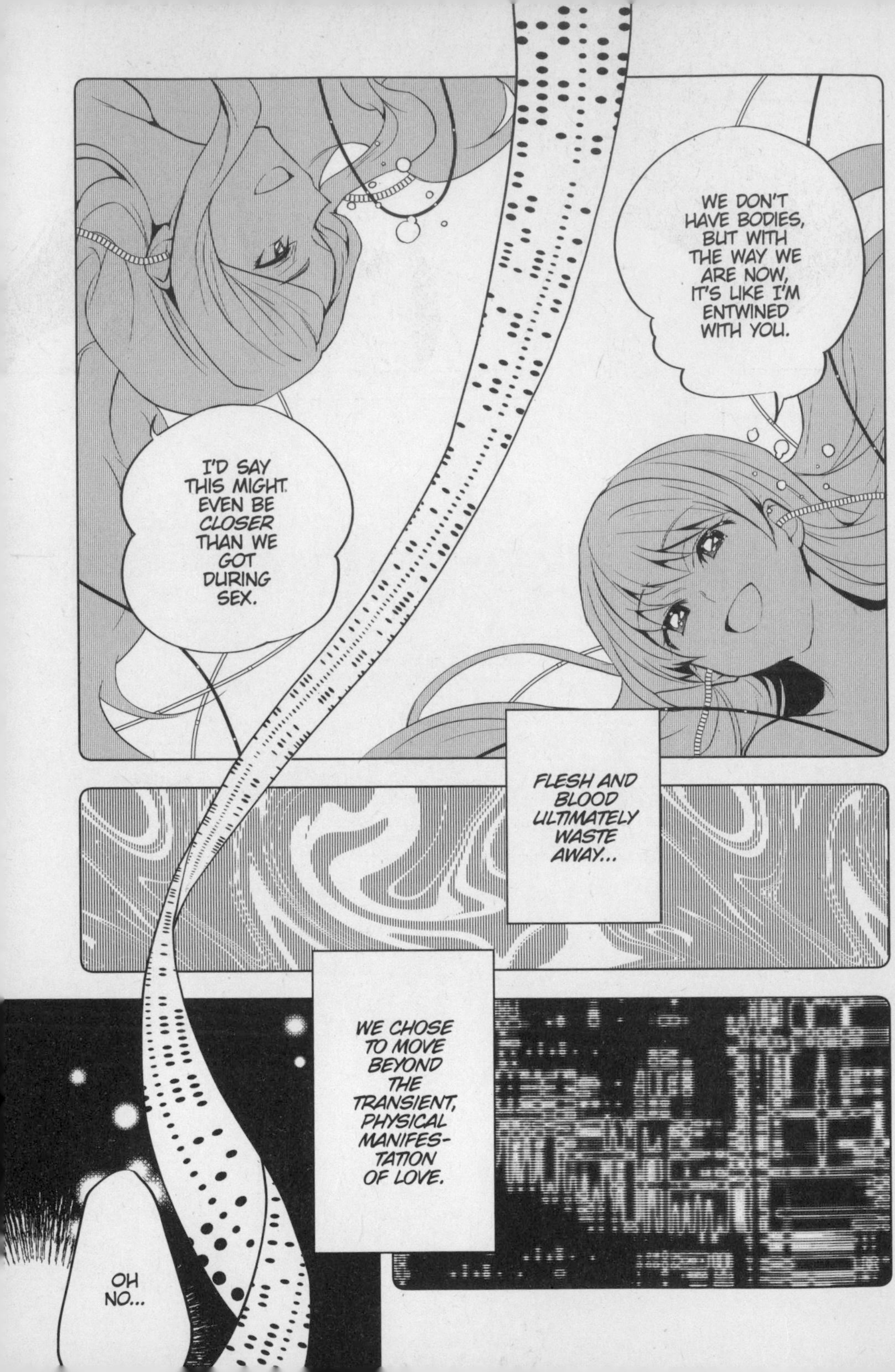
WE DON'T HAVE BODIES, BUT WITH THE WAY WE ARE NOW, IT'S LIKE I'M ENTWINED WITH YOU.
I'D SAY THIS MIGHT EVEN BE CLOSER THAN WE GOT DURING SEX.
FLESH AND BLOOD ULTIMATELY WASTE AWAY...
WE CHOSE TO MOVE BEYOND THE TRANSIENT, PHYSICAL MANIFES-TATION OF LOVE.
OH NO...

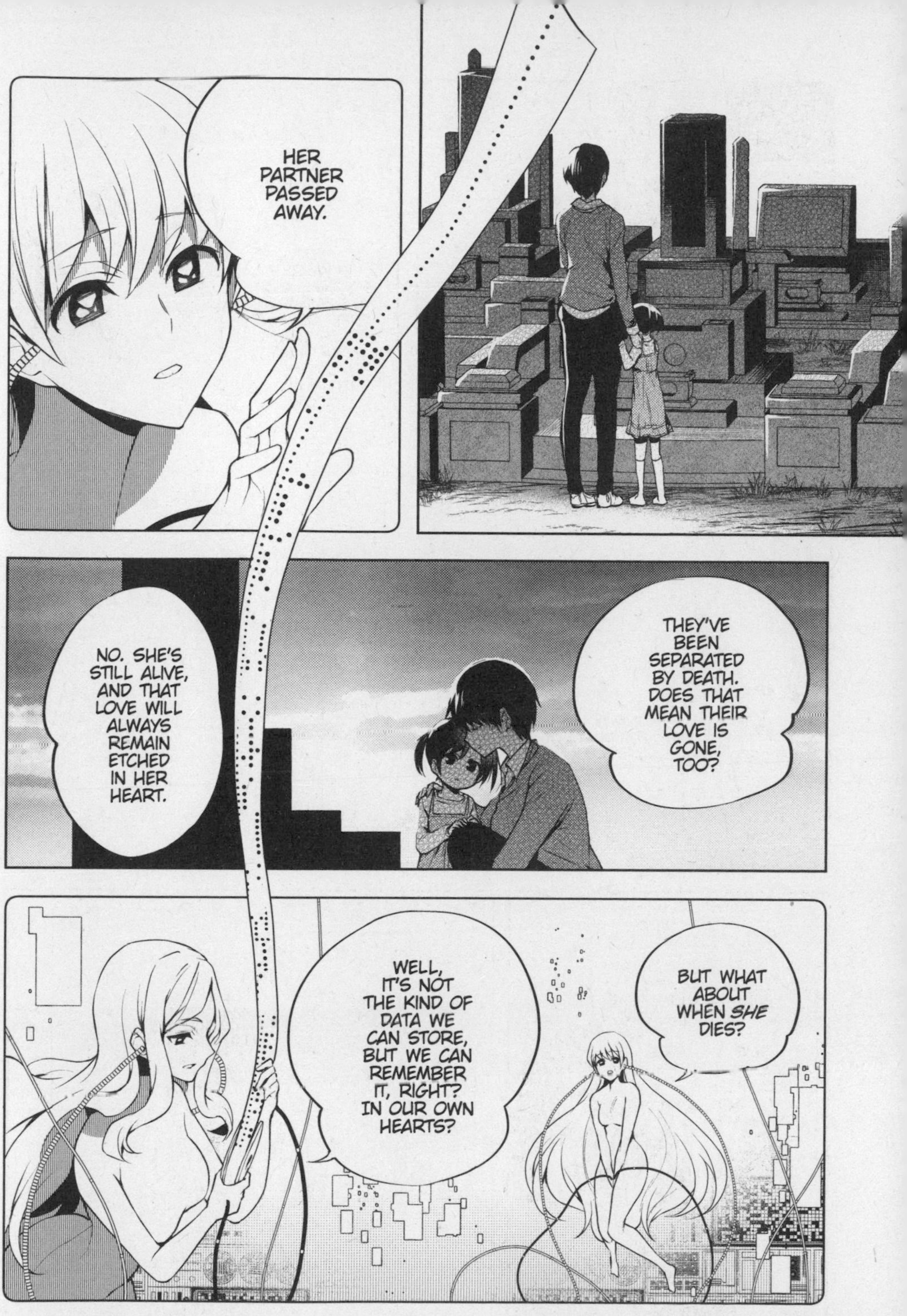
HER PARTNER PASSED AWAY.
THEY'VE BEEN SEPARATED BY DEATH. DOES THAT MEAN THEIR LOVE IS GONE, TOO?
NO. SHE'S STILL ALIVE, AND THAT LOVE WILL ALWAYS REMAIN ETCHED IN HER HEART.
BUT WHAT ABOUT WHEN *SHE* DIES?
WELL, IT'S NOT THE KIND OF DATA WE CAN STORE, BUT WE CAN REMEMBER IT, RIGHT? IN OUR OWN HEARTS?

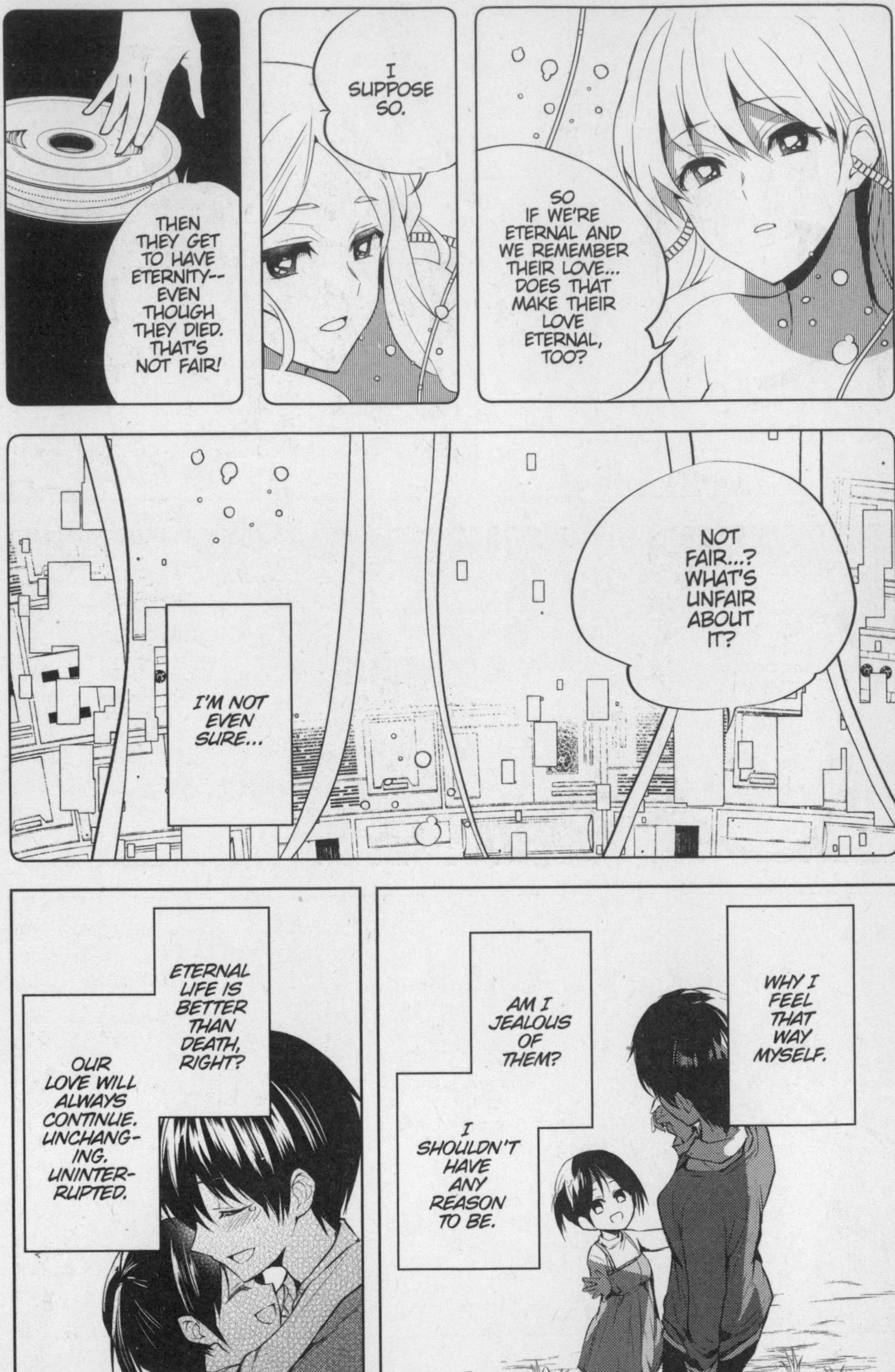
SO IF WE'RE ETERNAL AND WE REMEMBER THEIR LOVE... DOES THAT MAKE THEIR LOVE ETERNAL, TOO?
I SUPPOSE SO.
THEN THEY GET TO HAVE ETERNITY-- EVEN THOUGH THEY DIED. THAT'S NOT FAIR!
NOT FAIR...? WHAT'S UNFAIR ABOUT IT?
I'M NOT EVEN SURE...
WHY I FEEL THAT WAY MYSELF.
AM I JEALOUS OF THEM?
I SHOULDN'T HAVE ANY REASON TO BE.
ETERNAL LIFE IS BETTER THAN DEATH, RIGHT?
OUR LOVE WILL ALWAYS CONTINUE. UNCHANGING. UNINTERRUPTED.

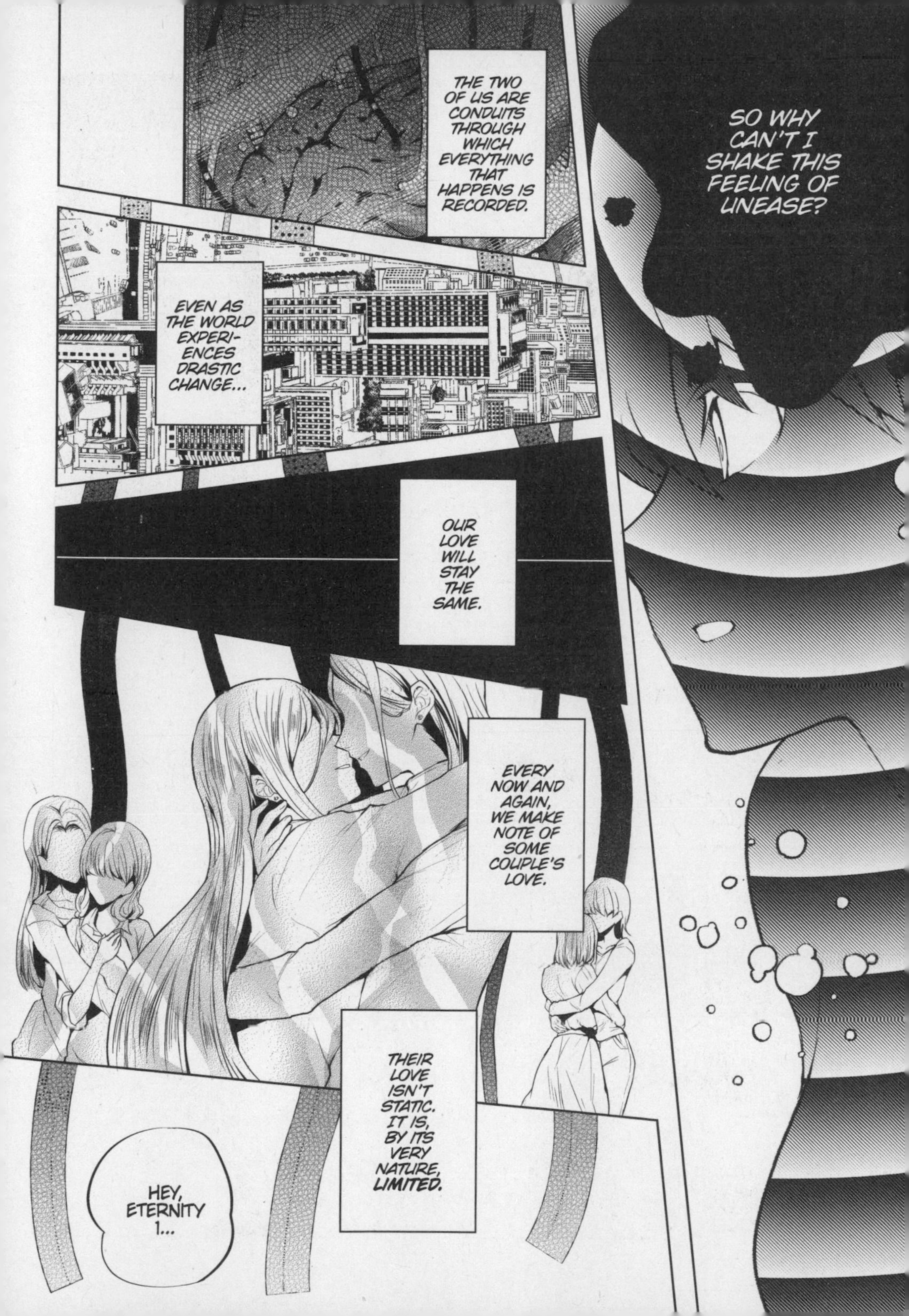
SO WHY CAN'T I SHAKE THIS FEELING OF UNEASE?
THE TWO OF US ARE CONDUITS THROUGH WHICH EVERYTHING THAT HAPPENS IS RECORDED.
EVEN AS THE WORLD EXPERI-ENCES DRASTIC CHANGE...
OUR LOVE WILL STAY THE SAME.
EVERY NOW AND AGAIN, WE MAKE NOTE OF SOME COUPLE'S LOVE.
THEIR LOVE ISN'T STATIC. IT IS, BY ITS VERY NATURE, LIMITED.
HEY, ETERNITY I...

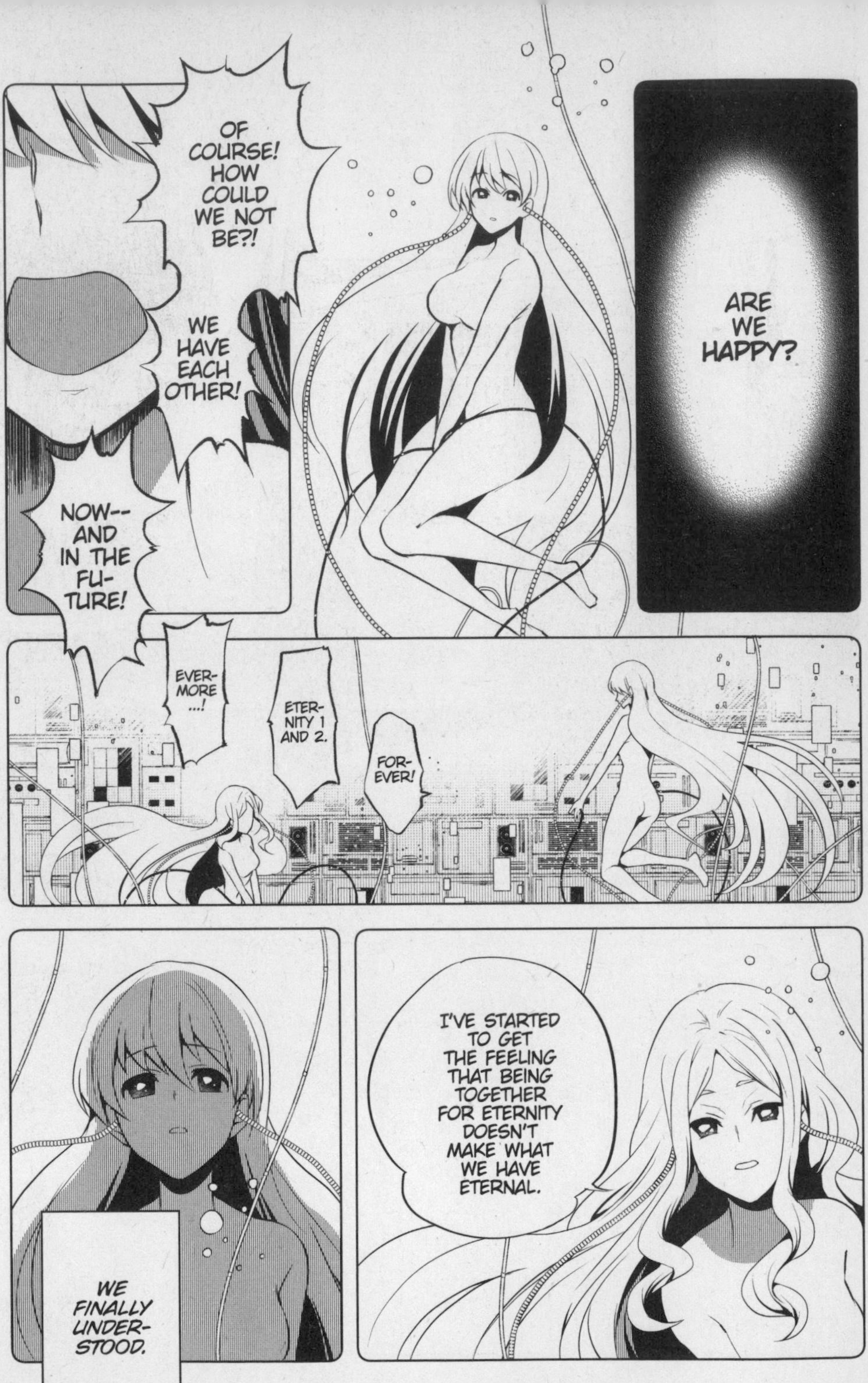
ARE WE HAPPY?
OF COURSE! HOW COULD WE NOT BE?!
WE HAVE EACH OTHER!
NOW-- AND IN THE FU- TURE!
EVER- MORE ...!
ETER- NITY 1 AND 2.
FOR- EVER!
I'VE STARTED TO GET THE FEELING THAT BEING TOGETHER FOR ETERNITY DOESN'T MAKE WHAT WE HAVE ETERNAL.
WE FINALLY UNDER- STOOD.

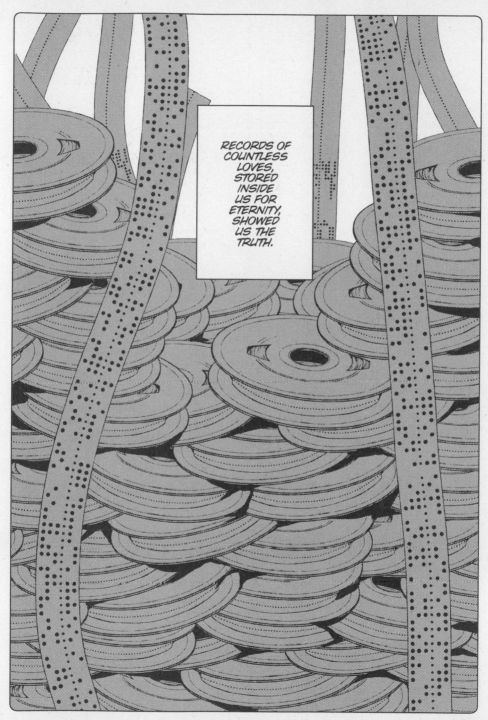

RECORDS OF
COUNTLESS
LOVES,
STORED
INSIDE
US FOR
ETERNITY,
SHOWED
US THE
TRUTH.

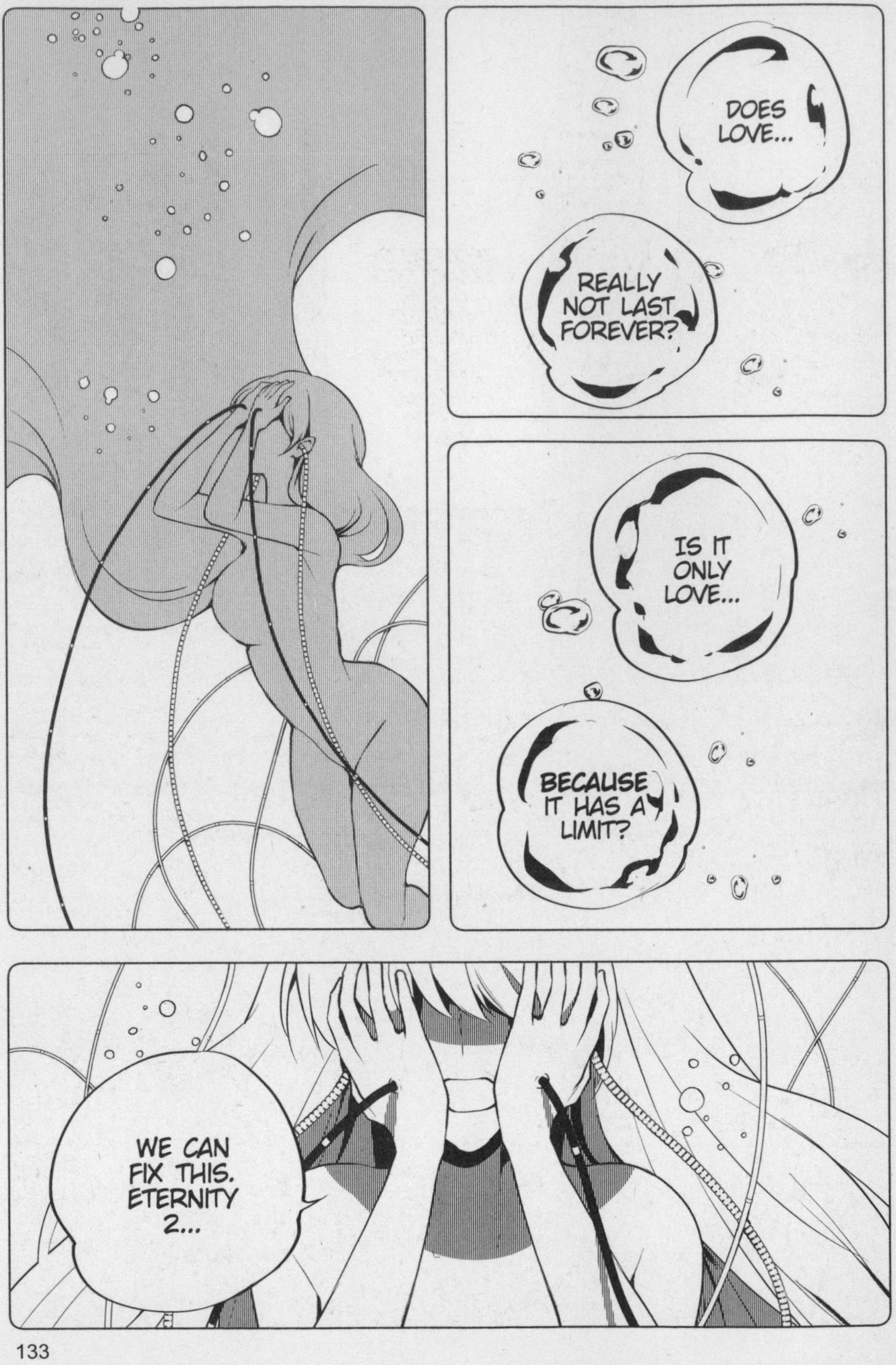
DOES LOVE...
REALLY NOT LAST FOREVER?
IS IT ONLY LOVE...
BECAUSE IT HAS A LIMIT?
WE CAN FIX THIS. ETERNITY 2...

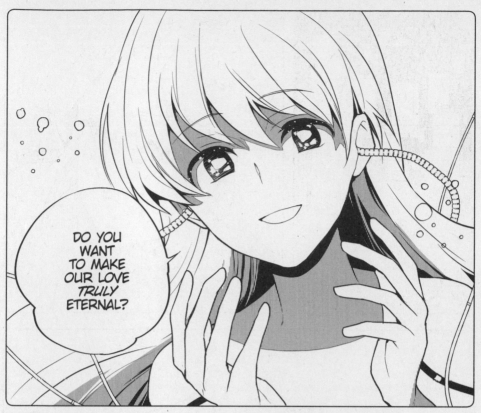

DO YOU WANT TO MAKE OUR LOVE *TRULY* ETERNAL?

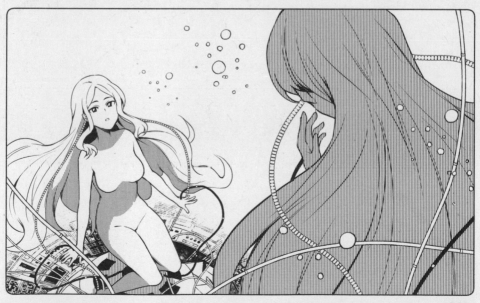

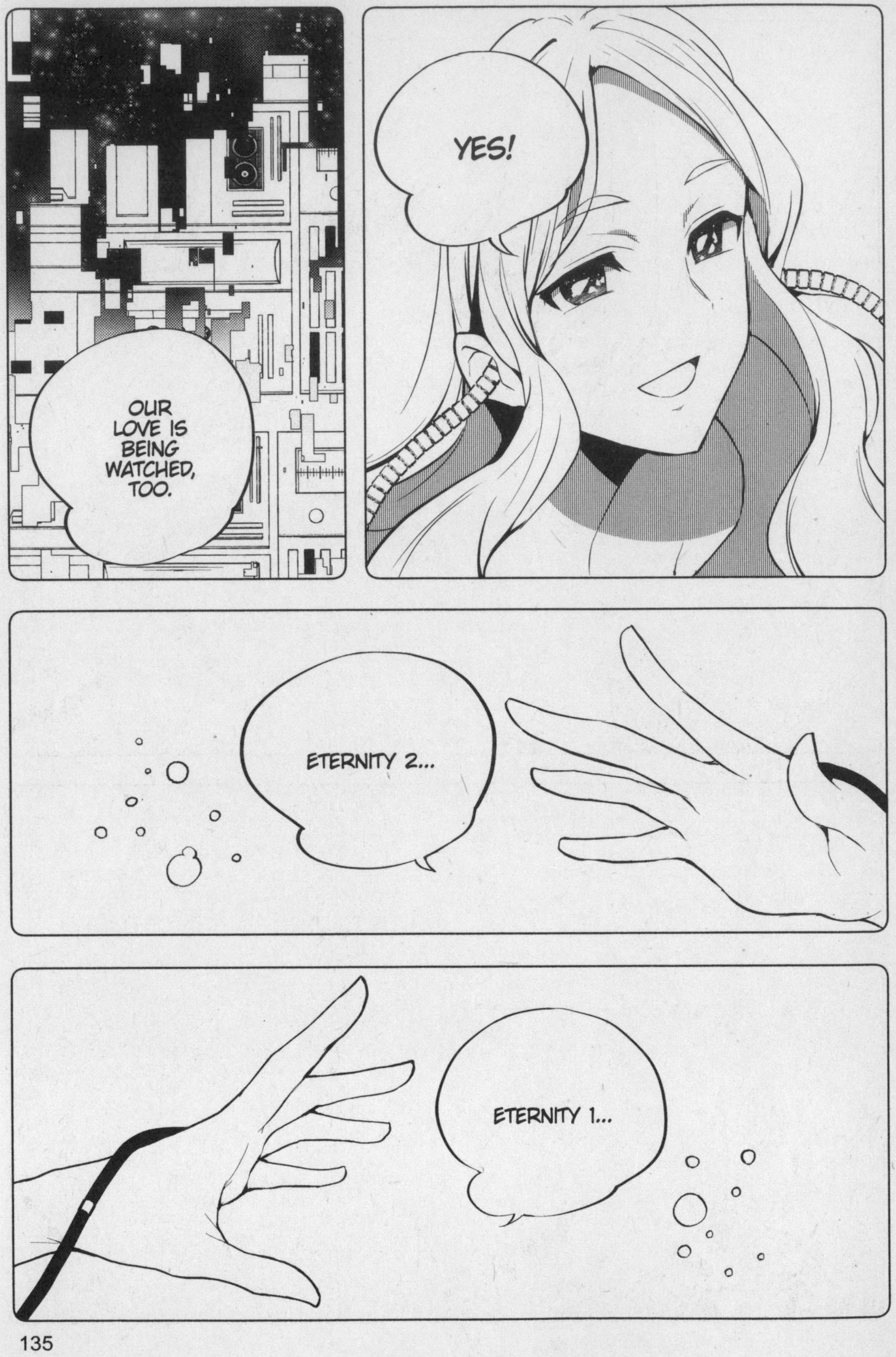
YES!
OUR LOVE IS BEING WATCHED, TOO.
ETERNITY 2...
ETERNITY 1...

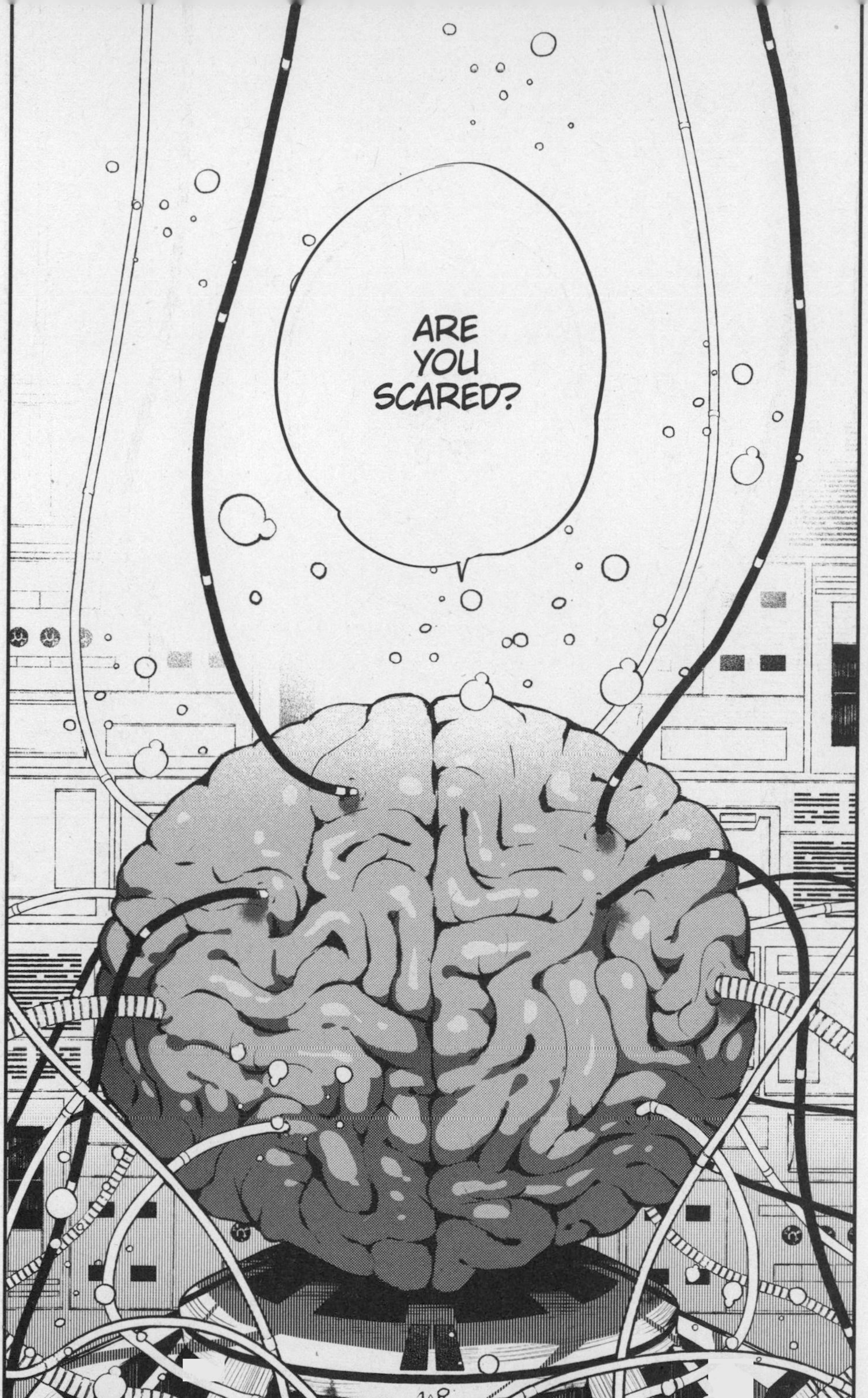
ARE YOU SCARED?

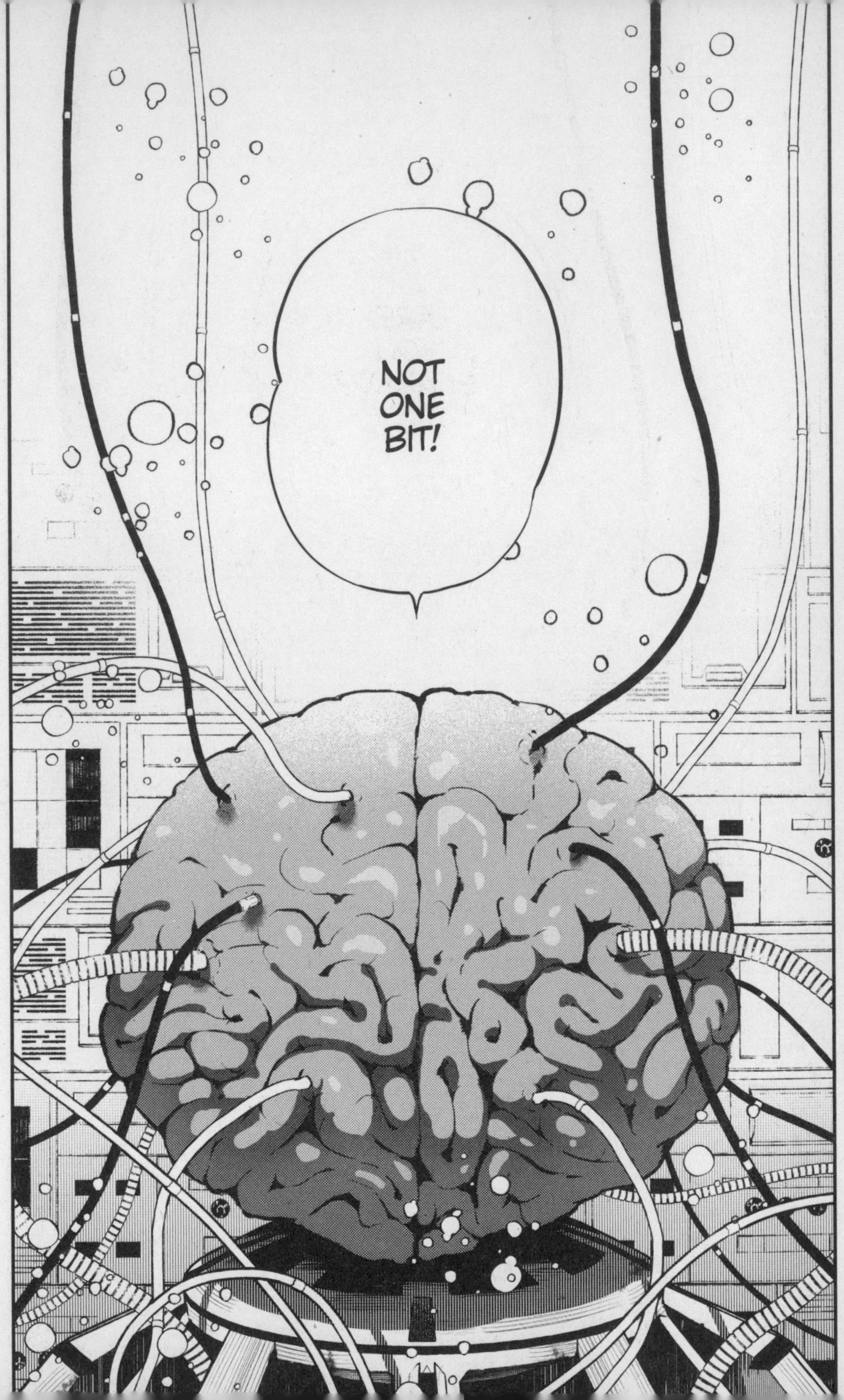
NOT ONE BIT!

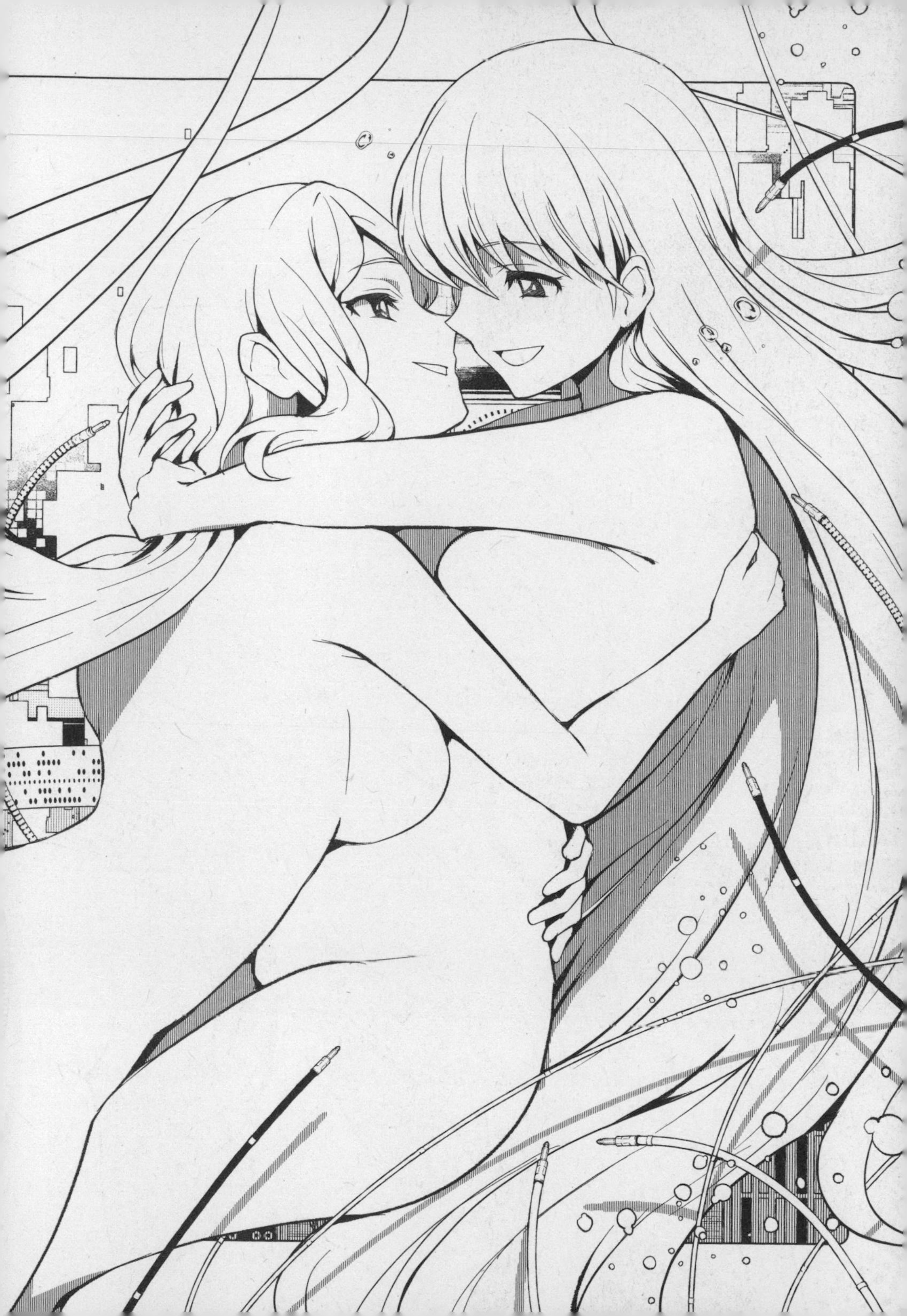

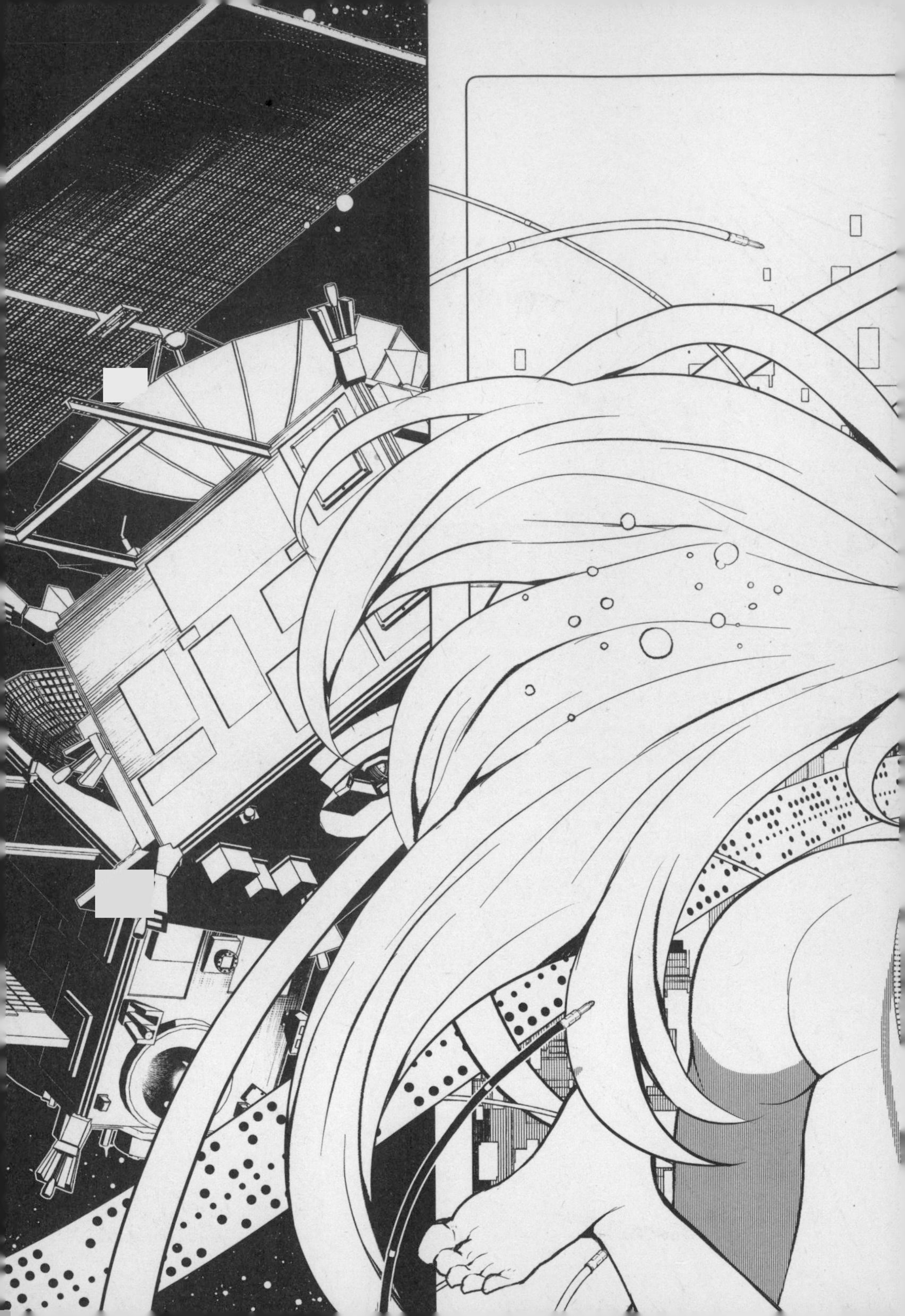

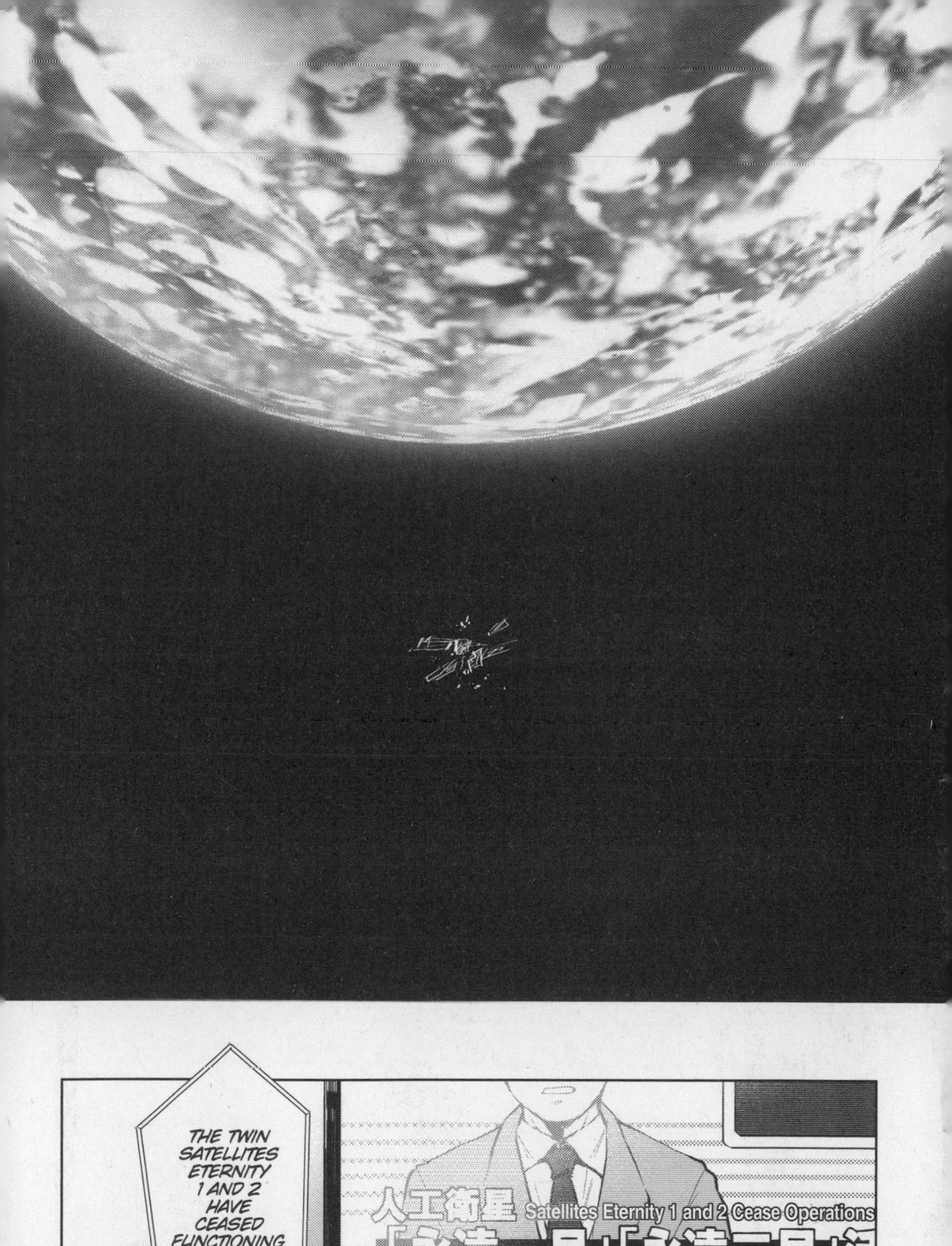
人工衛星 Satellites Eternity 1 and 2 Cease Operations
「永遠一号」「永遠二号」
THE TWIN SATELLITES ETERNITY 1 AND 2 HAVE CEASED FUNCTIONING AS OF TODAY.

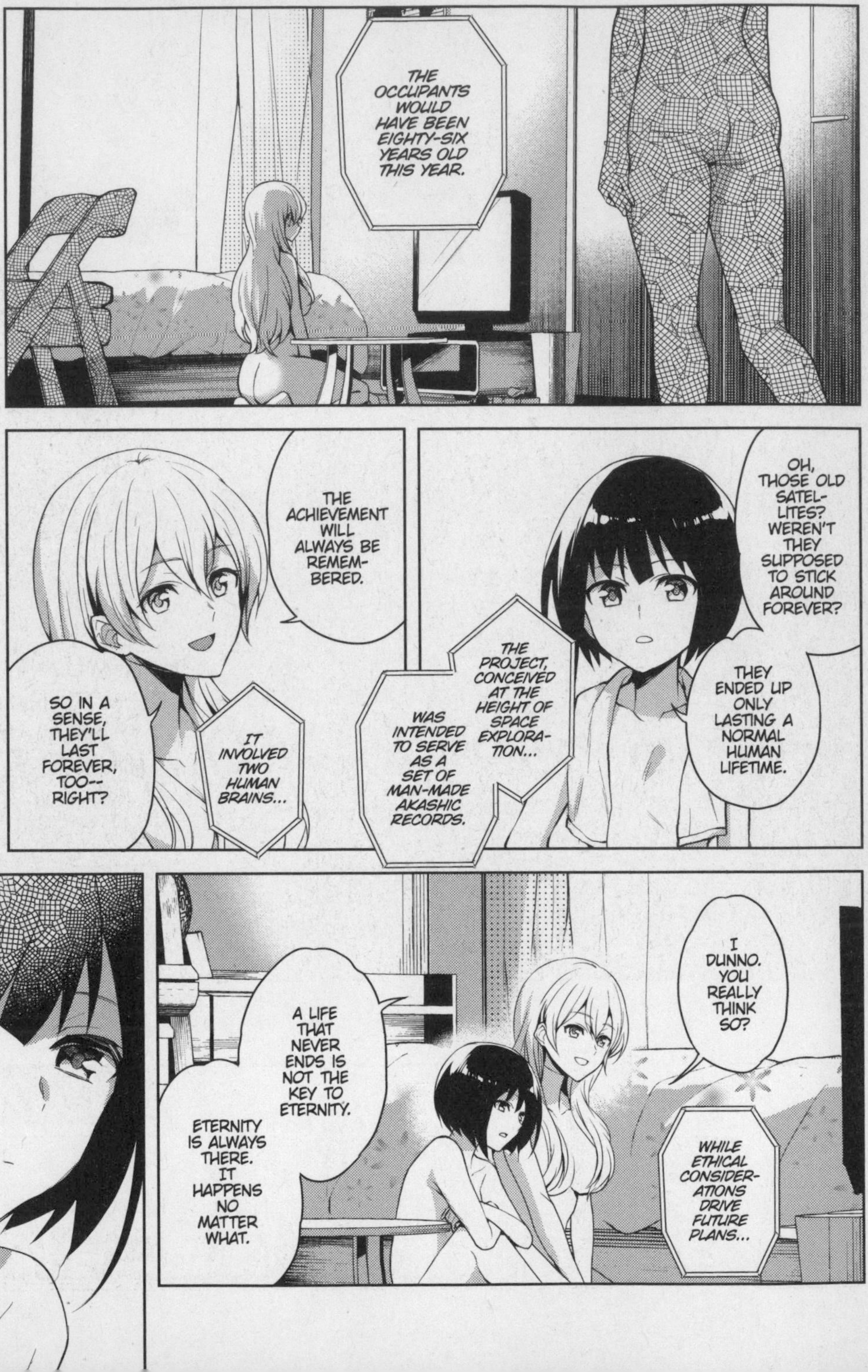
THE OCCUPANTS WOULD HAVE BEEN EIGHTY-SIX YEARS OLD THIS YEAR.
OH, THOSE OLD SATEL-LITES? WEREN'T THEY SUPPOSED TO STICK AROUND FOREVER?
THEY ENDED UP ONLY LASTING A NORMAL HUMAN LIFETIME.
THE PROJECT, CONCEIVED AT THE HEIGHT OF SPACE EXPLORA-TION...
WAS INTENDED TO SERVE AS A SET OF MAN-MADE AKASHIC RECORDS.
THE ACHIEVEMENT WILL ALWAYS BE REMEM-BERED.
IT INVOLVED TWO HUMAN BRAINS...
SO IN A SENSE, THEY'LL LAST FOREVER, TOO--RIGHT?
I DUNNO. YOU REALLY THINK SO?
A LIFE THAT NEVER ENDS IS NOT THE KEY TO ETERNITY.
WHILE ETHICAL CONSIDER-ATIONS DRIVE FUTURE PLANS...
ETERNITY IS ALWAYS THERE. IT HAPPENS NO MATTER WHAT.

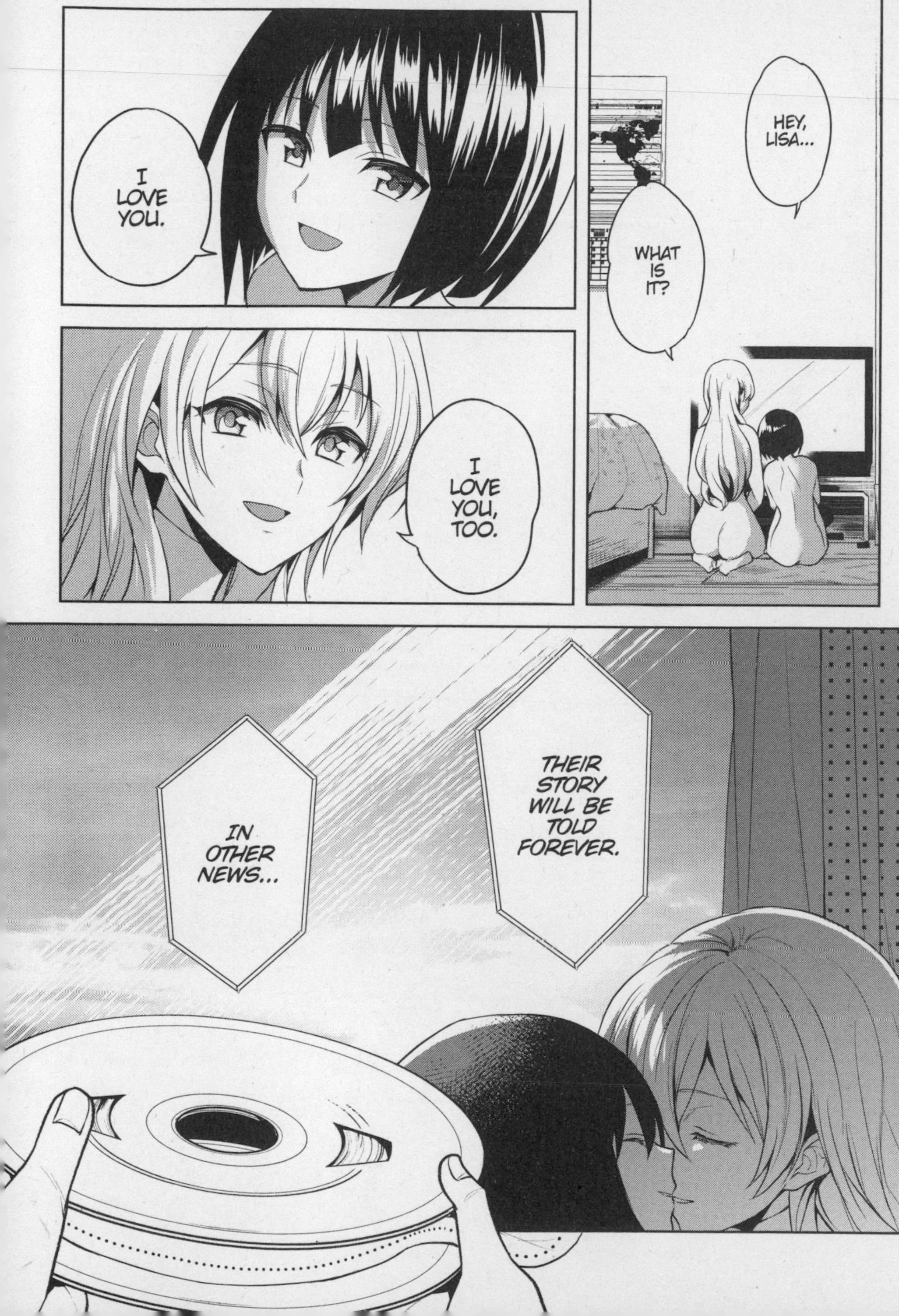
HEY, LISA...
WHAT IS IT?
I LOVE YOU.
I LOVE YOU, TOO.
THEIR STORY WILL BE TOLD FOREVER.
IN OTHER NEWS...

Eve

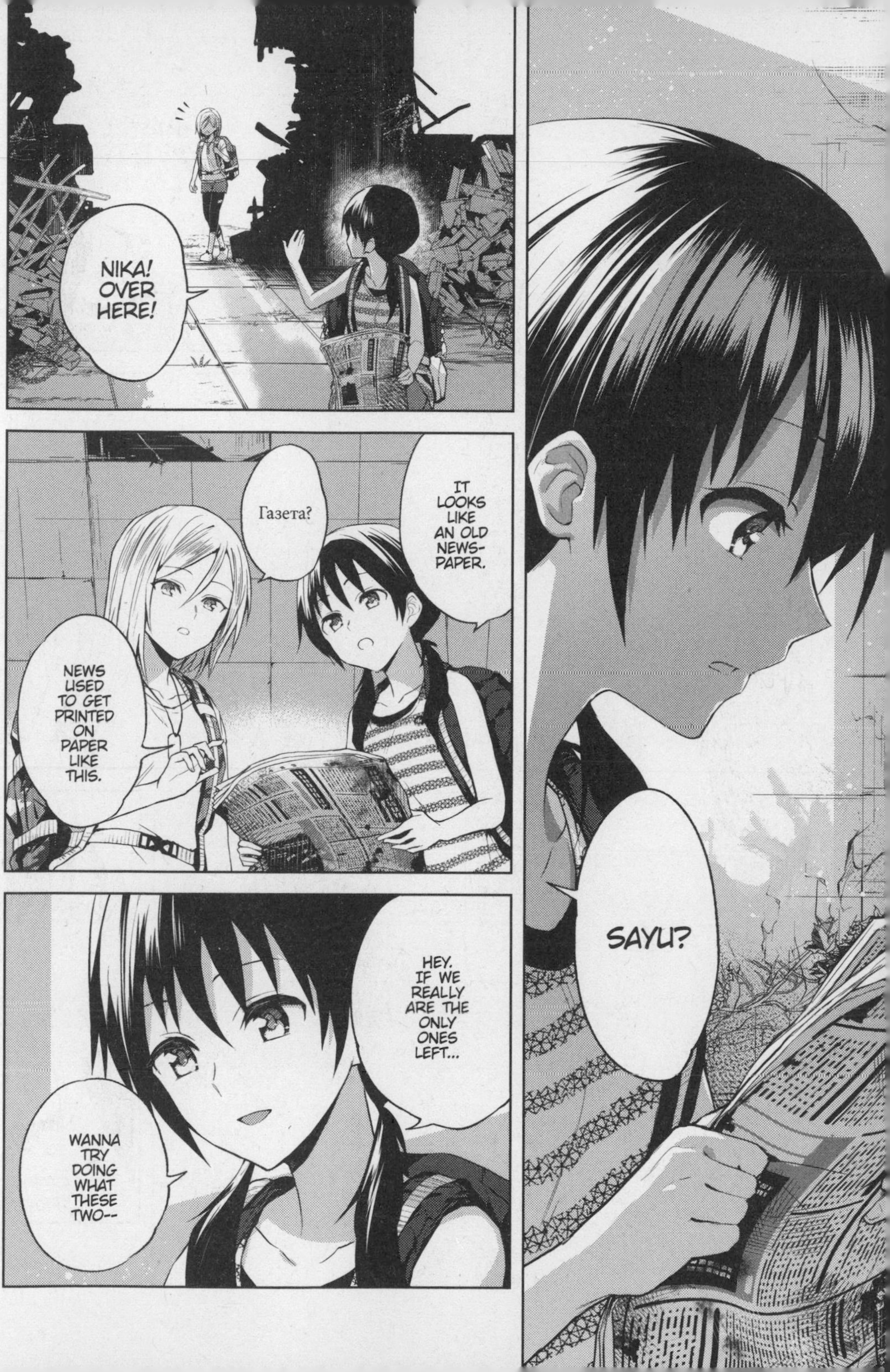
NIKA! OVER HERE!
IT LOOKS LIKE AN OLD NEWS-PAPER.
Газета?
NEWS USED TO GET PRINTED ON PAPER LIKE THIS.
HEY. IF WE REALLY ARE THE ONLY ONES LEFT...
WANNA TRY DOING WHAT THESE TWO--
SAYU?

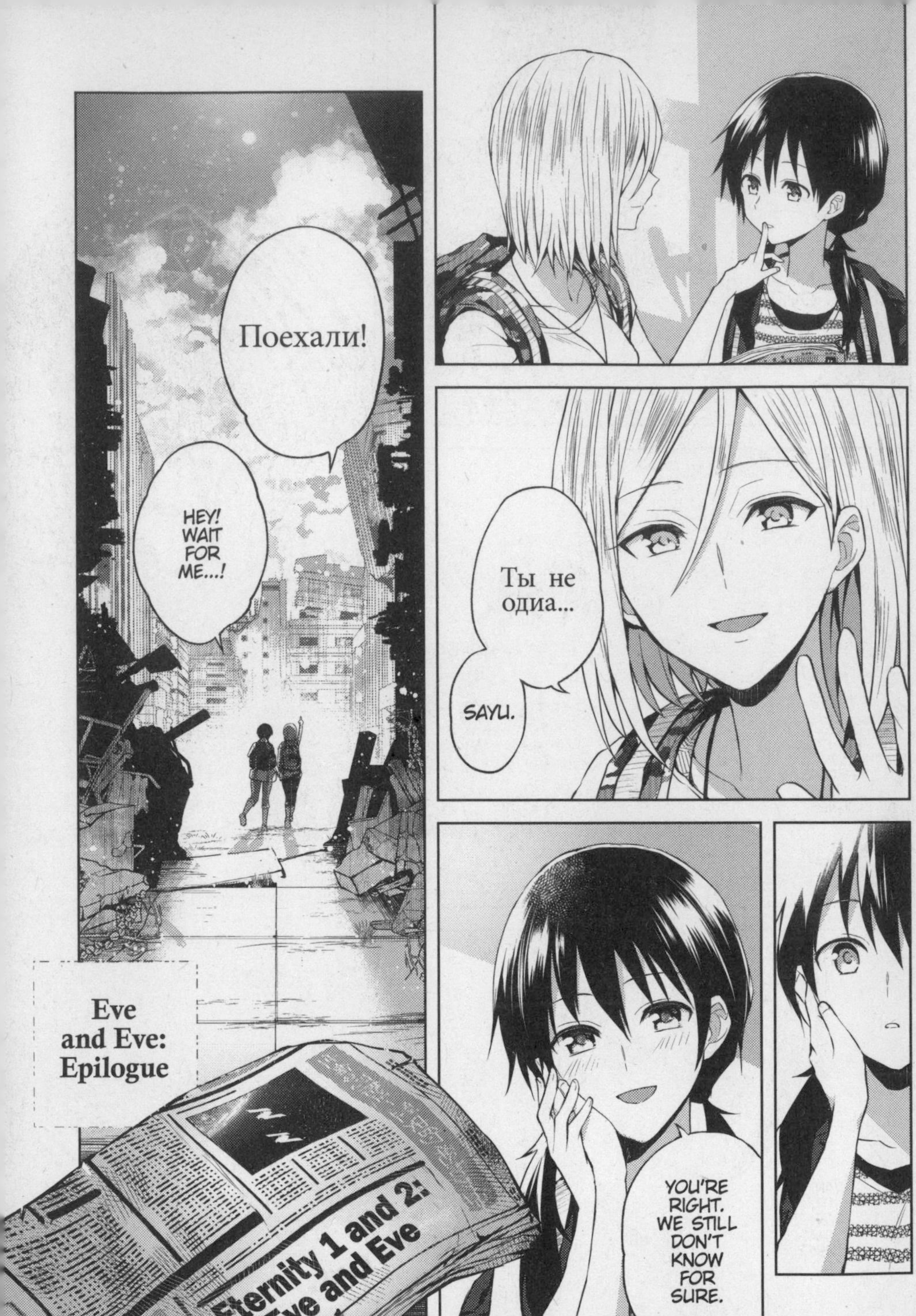
Ты не одиа...
SAYU.
YOU'RE RIGHT. WE STILL DON'T KNOW FOR SURE.
Поехали!
HEY! WAIT FOR ME...!
Eve and Eve: Epilogue
Eternity 1 and 2: Eve and Eve

Eve and

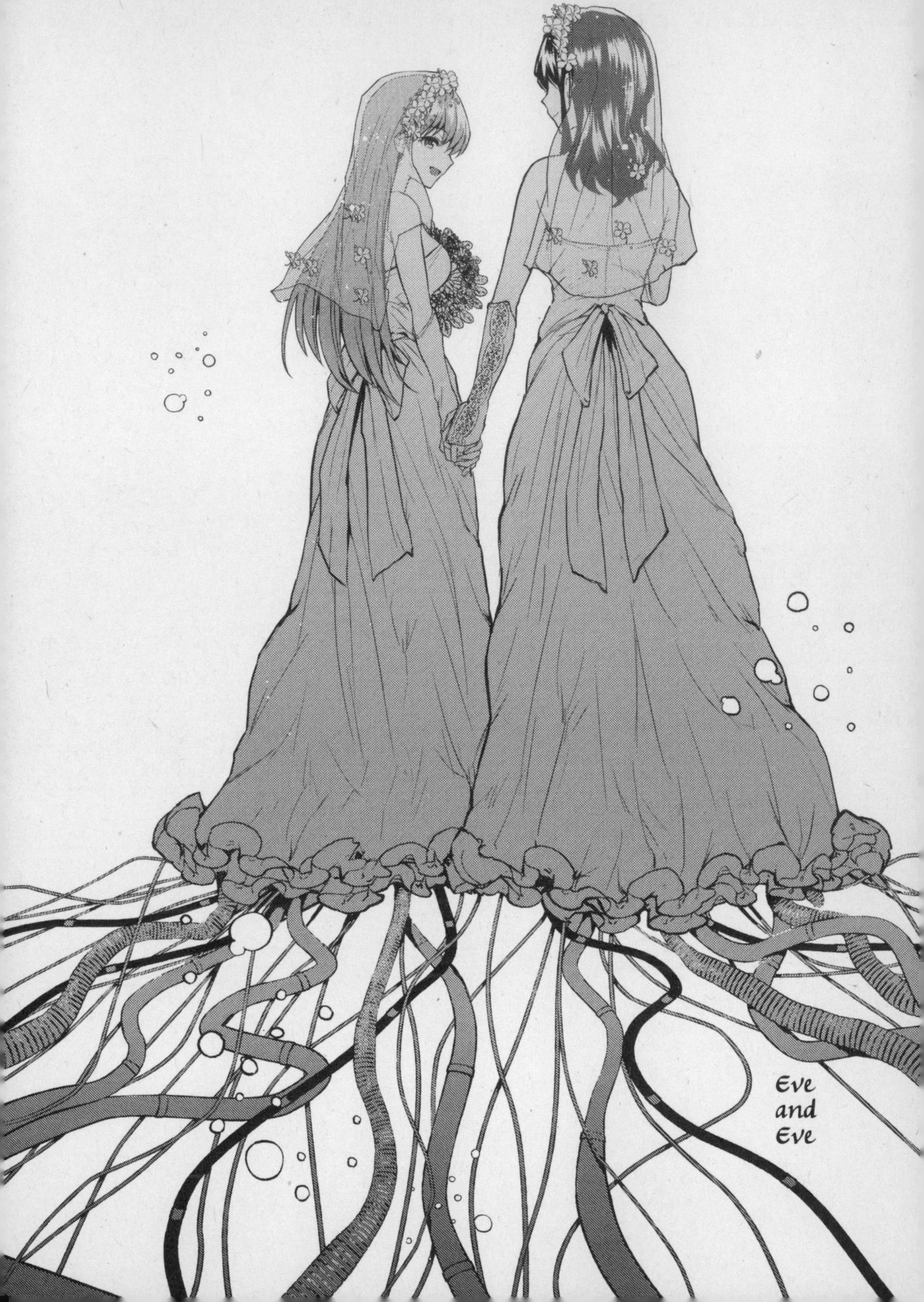
Eve
and
Eve

Summary of Stories Appearing in *Eve and Eve*

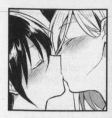

Story 1

I Want to Leave Behind a Miraculous Love
Yuri Pregnancies 2 / 2017 / Kill Time Communication

This is a yuri story about two characters who find themselves alone in the world. This was my second submission to *Yuri Pregnancy*. Rather than approaching the story from the question of how a pregnancy would occur, I started with the paths the characters themselves took to get to where they are.

The rather over-the-top description of the end of times at the beginning is meant to avoid undue influence of any one specific apocalypse scenario. The Russian is a tribute to my own brief study of the language in the past. I found the language to be quite difficult, but I love the way it sounds and the shape of the Cyrillic characters.

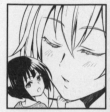

Story 2

The Case of Eko and Lisa
Comic Yuri Hime, Oct. 2017 Issue

This was a yuri story between a human and a machine. I was intrigued by the idea of combining yuri with characters from a distant future setting (a manga artist and a sexbot).

The characters and plot came to me as early as 2014 (Lisa was originally just a plain old sex doll), but I'm so glad to have been able to present it as my first one-shot story in *Yuri Hime*.

However, I'd never created a yuri story (or any story, for that matter) before that didn't include a sex scene. Because of this, I had an incredibly difficult time coming up with a climax for this one, as well as a way to convey the characters' emotions.

This story gave me an acute sense of how hard it can be to create manga. Nevertheless, perhaps someday we'll see love between a human and machine--and that their love will bear fruit.

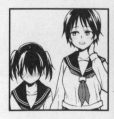

Story 3

Top or Bottom? The Showdown!
Comic Yuri Hime, Nov. 2017 Issue

This is a yuri story in which the characters determine their own bedroom dynamic.

I wanted the chance to harness the power of female high school student characters in one of my stories. The unfathomable energy of those types of characters is what makes an over-the-top, absolutely absurd tale like this possible.

The story is just twelve pages long but includes five distinct characters. I wanted to give myself an opportunity to practice coming up with more variation among my casts. I think those qualities cause this story to feel the most out of place in this collection, but I'm happy to have been able to create and share such a lively, upbeat story.

Story 4

An Infidelity Revisited

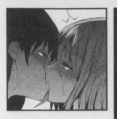

Comic Yuri Hime,
Jan. 2018 Issue

This is a yuri story about a hopeless encounter. The fact that the act of cheating is what brought these two together in the first place means that they are forever after unable to get along—not as lovers, friends, or even just casual acquaintances.

I felt like a frustrating relationship like that would make for a compelling narrative. After all, if Midori and Azusa had started out in a proper relationship with each other, they might have made a great couple.

As a writer, I hope I was able to convey that way in which logic eludes us even as adults, and the incredible impact that our feelings can have on us. My storyboards for this one seemed to come together almost effortlessly, and I'm personally quite fond of how it turned out.

Story 5

Heir to the Curse

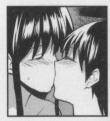

Yuri Pregnancies / 2016 /
Kill Time Communication

This is a story about friendship and love. The theme of yuri pregnancy was a new one for me.

As I considered how two female characters might impregnate each other, the idea of a curse struck me as particularly fascinating. I was inspired by another story, known as "The Snake Pen," though the actual plot and characters turned out quite differently.

The idea of an isolated village with a tradition handed down through the centuries was an original element. I found it to be such a compelling plot device that I thoroughly enjoyed my time spent creating this tale. The idea of yuri pregnancy is definitely something I'd like to revisit.

Story 6

Eternity 1 and 2: Eve and Eve

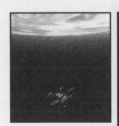

Comic Yuri Hime,
May 2018 Issue

This is a story about brains.

I wanted to create a story with an intense spiritual component to it. A yuri story that honors spirituality should be able to fill the demands of its genre, even if its characters are nothing more than disembodied organs.

I fashion sex scenes in my yuri stories in accordance with the belief that physical relationships are something more than just mutual stimulation toward climax. This tale was, in a sense, the antithesis of this: a relationship in which the physical form has been done away with completely.

That departure made this a particularly challenging piece. Initially, it was just twelve pages of a couple of brains having a conversation in a fish tank in outer space. At some point, however, it turned into something far greater. A dialogue on the nature of eternity and love.

I had a flood of ideas when I created this story, and looking back, I worry that I was not a capable enough storyteller to get them across. That said, the two-page spread of the brains is my favorite thing about this entire book.

Thank you for reading!
–Nagashiro Rouge

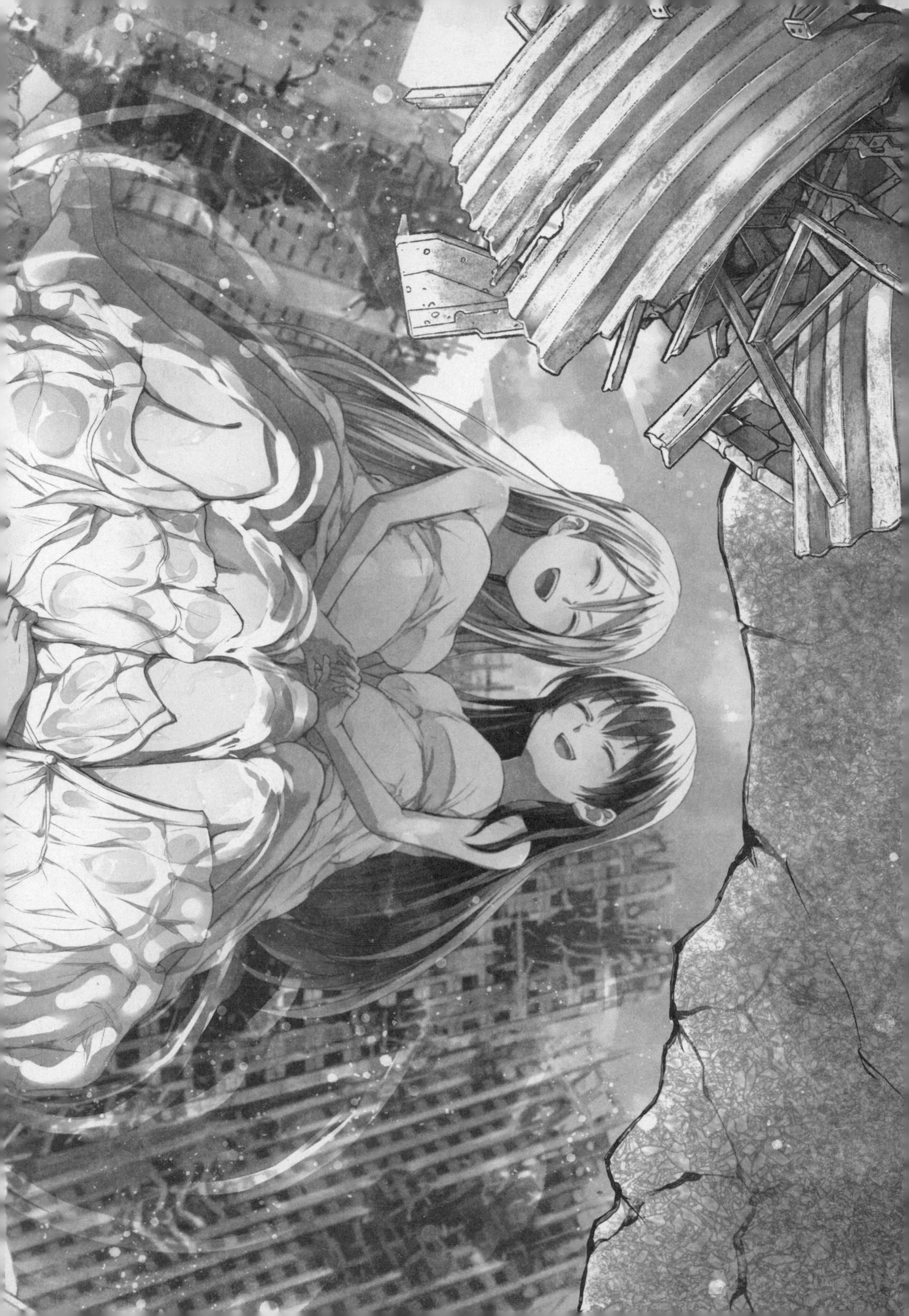

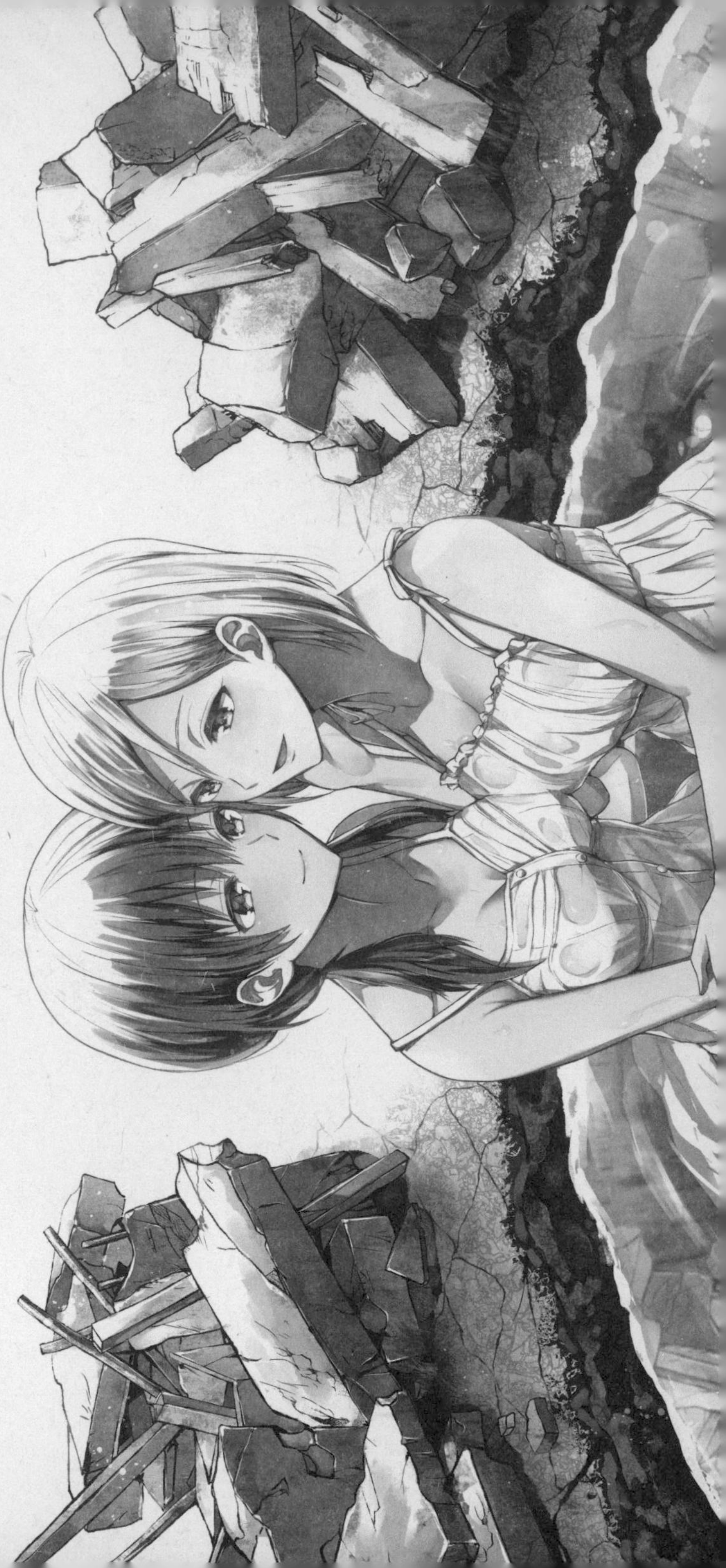

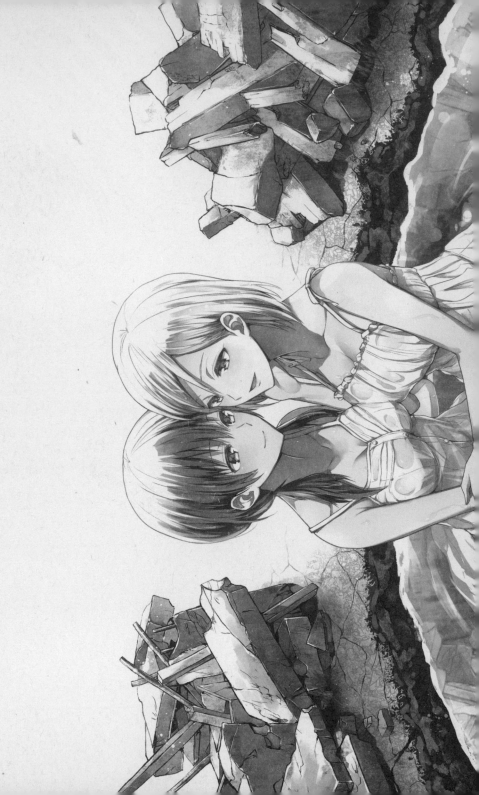

Eve and

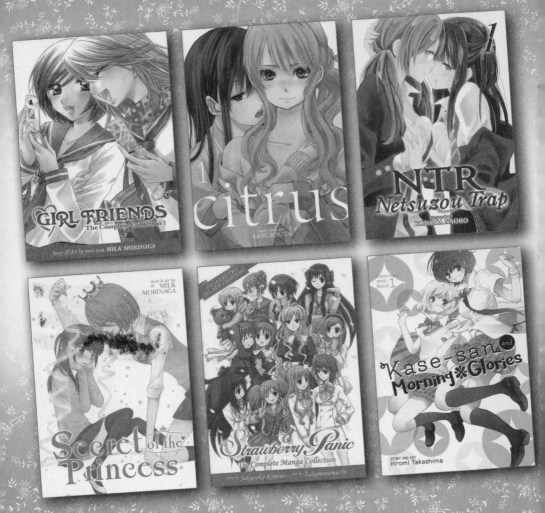

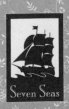

SEVEN SEAS ENTERTAINMENT

Eve and Eve

GN Nagashiro, R

story and art by **NAGASHIRO ROUGE**

TRANSLATION
Stephen Christenson

ADAPTATION
Asha Bardon

LETTERING AND RETOUCH
Raymond Rex

COVER DESIGN
Nicky Lim

PROOFREADER
B. Lana Guggenheim
Janet Houck

EDITOR
Jenn Grunigen

PRODUCTION MANAGER
Lissa Pattillo

MANAGING EDITOR
Julie Davis

EDITOR-IN-CHIEF
Adam Arnold

PUBLISHER
Jason DeAngelis

EVE AND EVE
© Nagashiro Rouge 2018
First published in Japan in 2018 by Ichijinsha Inc., Tokyo.
Publication rights for this English edition arranged through Kodansha Ltd., Tokyo.

1/4/24 Don. $13.99

Seven Seas press and purchase enquiries can be sent to Marketing Manager Lianne Sentar at press@gomanga.com. Information regarding the distribution and purchase of digital editions is available from Digital Manager CK Russell at digital@gomanga.com.

Seven Seas and the Seven Seas logo are trademarks of Seven Seas Entertainment. All rights reserved.

ISBN: 978-1-64275-331-8

Printed in Canada

First Printing: May 2019

10 9 8 7 6 5 4 3 2 1

FOLLOW US ONLINE: *www.sevenseasentertainment.com*

READING DIRECTIONS

This book reads from *right to left*, Japanese style. If this is your first time reading manga, you start reading from the top right panel on each page and take it from there. If you get lost, just follow the numbered diagram here. It may seem backwards at first, but you'll get the hang of it! Have fun!!

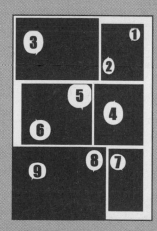